Snow
CRAZY

ARNIE WILSON

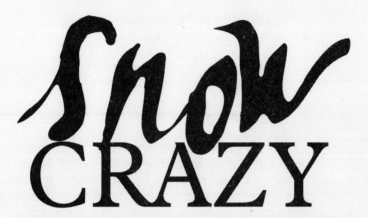

Snow CRAZY

**A HUNDRED YEARS OF STORIES OF DERRING-DO
FROM THE SKI CLUB OF GREAT BRITAIN**

metro

Published by Metro Publishing Ltd,
3, Bramber Court, 2 Bramber Road,
London W14 9PB, England

First published in hardback in 2003

ISBN 1 84358 067 5

British Library Cataloguing-in-Publication Data:

A catalogue record for this book is available from the British Library.

Design by ENVY

Printed in Great Britain by CPD (Wales)

1 3 5 7 9 10 8 6 4 2

Papers used by Metro Publishing are natural, recyclable products
made from wood grown in sustainable forests. The manufacturing processes
conform to the environmental regulations of the country of origin.

For Vivianne, my wife,
and my daughters Samantha,
Lara, Amber and Melissa.
Skiers every one.

Acknowledgements

Trawling through scores of weighty tomes dating back 100 years is a daunting and almost endless task which would keep a single researcher busy for the best part of a lifetime. I would like to thank my cheerful team of helpers who made it possible

ELISABETH HUSSEY
'The best way of stopping an avalanche is to throw your hat at it; for which reason it is dangerous to go about bareheaded.'

NICK DAVIES
'We have tried the sample of ski wax you kindly sent us, and find it as beneficial for greasing boots as it is as a hair restorer.'

KATE HEFFER
'We think you were quite right to make your will before going on the mountain with him. He is a dangerous fellow.'

CHRISTABEL CAIRNS
'As he eats only cheese, you would be quite safe in placing your lunch in his rucksack'

ROBERT HUCKIN
'A broken binding that doesn't hold the foot adds a sense of glorious uncertainty to the run'

CHARLOTTE RAYNER-BROWN
'Had you made a Christiania swing you would have avoided the bush. The only way to get out was to shout for help'

ARLETTE SCHIELE
'I was not at all troubled with snow blindness, and greatly prefer this arrangement to any smoked spectacles.'

NICK HUTCHINGS
'A jodel carries further than anything but we (fortunately?) cannot jodel. I have tried a powerful "Rouser" whistle warranted to kill a taxi at 200 yards'

CONTENTS

PREFACE

'Man is perverse', wrote Arnold Lunn in 1920.

> He leaves the green valleys with delight, and
> wanders among the glaciers with joy, only to
> discover that he is haunted among the snows by the
> beauty that he has deserted, only to long for the
> welcome of meadows and streams and flowers and
> trees scented with the promise of May. A few days
> later, and he will be looking from those same
> meadows at the peaks of old adventure, and if three
> or four days of tantalising fair weather follow, he
> will scarcely find strength to resist their upward call.

Plagiarism, so the joke goes, is appropriating another author's
work – but if you steal the works of more than one author it's
called research. In which case, I have done an awful lot of
research – mainly, as it happens, into one author's work: Sir
Arnold Lunn. But there have been many others, so fortunately
I can glory in the title of researcher rather than robber.

For the past year, aided occasionally by young helpers — for whom the skiing annals of yesteryear must seem even more surreal than they do to me — I have been breathlessly tiptoeing through a remarkable treasure trove of the skiing world, engrossing myself in the priceless records of the Ski Club of Great Britain, which celebrated its centenary in May 2003. These records comprise for the most part the *British Ski Year Book* and *Ski Notes and Queries* — the club's two principal publications, which eventually made way for a ski magazine, *Ski survey,* now *Ski and Board*, which I am fortunate enough to edit.

The anecdotes I have 'rediscovered' have been a revelation. Partly because of the times in which they were written — during the 'golden age' of skiing before the First World War, the 'silver age' between the First and Second World Wars, and a 'gothic age' thrown in for good measure. Don't ask me to recite the dates of these ages. They are somewhat arbitrary and loosely defined, but Arnold Lunn gave them substance, at least in his mind and writings. These anecdotes are poignant, charming, quaint and often hilarious (but not always deliberately so). They also provide, *en passant*, a fascinating window on the world as it was before, during and after those savage wars, which so preoccupied and devastated the lives of previous generations during the 20th century

As I pored over these accounts, not only burning the midnight oil but sometimes finding myself still spellbound as the first hints of grey dawn streaked across the horizon, I felt a keen sense that all the wonderful real-life but now, sadly, mostly long-gone characters were standing and looking over my shoulder, making sure I selected the *crème de la crème* of their writings.

If I failed them, heaven forbid, they would surely be turning in their graves. Come to think of it, though, they might welcome the opportunity of making a few more turns! After all, Arnold Lunn mentioned in the 1920 *British Ski Year Book* a letter from one of his great ski-touring friends, Ralph Evans, who said, 'Perhaps the four of us will get together for another May run when we have gone over to the "other side" ... We shall never get all the conditions right again in *this* life.'

They are all here: Arnold Lunn, whose noble musings, perhaps more than any other, sum up the unique ambience and mysticism of skiing's golden age; the dry wit of his great friend Hugh Dowding, who was to steer the RAF to their greatest victory during the Battle of Britain; Lunn's staunch Swiss ally Walter Amstutz, master skier and inventor of the 'flying kilometre' on ski; E.C. Richardson, the feisty and amusingly quarrelsome 'father' of British skiing, and the principal impetus for the formation of the Ski Club of Great Britain; the pedantic but sincere Vivian Caulfeild, (born in 1874 but 'should, personally, have preferred a later date'), who could argue till the cows came home – and frequently did – about the finer points of ski technique; the *joie de vivre* of Alan d'Egville, whose colourful and amusing drawings and paintings – a joyful reflection of his own high jinks – captured the spirit of the age; the eloquent Gerald Seligman and his lifelong fascination with the composition of the humble snowflake, who said of skiing, 'very few other sports do quite so completely cater for both the athlete and the artist'; his brother Richard Seligman, a founder member of the Ski Club of Great Britain, who rounds off this book so poignantly; and the delightful Jimmy Riddell, elegant of ski and eloquent of pen, and many more.

One or two, mercifully, are still with us, most notably Arnold Lunn's son, Peter, captain of the British team at the 1936 Winter Olympics when downhill skiing made its debut. Peter Lunn has since been skiing just about every winter's day (and water-skiing during the summer months), although he is now at an age when most 'mature' skiers would be happy just to settle into an armchair to watch *Ski Sunday*.

In 1961, then a young man of 47, Peter, who describes himself as a 'skiing glutton', told how he had been ticked off by his doctor for skiing with a swollen knee. At his happiest while enjoying his passion, Peter wrote,

I do not ski to make money ... I do not ski to satisfy

ambition ... I do not ski because the exercise is good for me, because I am quite prepared to ski against medical advice. I cannot even claim that I ski because it enables me to return refreshed to my work ... I ski only because I love skiing, even when it hurts me. My skiing is harmless ... it does not help make the world a better place; it profits nobody but myself.

Another Peter – my old Fleet Street friend and colleague Peter Hardy – also still very much alive I am glad to say, has been another figure looking over my shoulder, so to speak. I have shared more skiing adventures with Peter than most and I like to think we share the same sense of humour too, especially when it comes to 'gripping yarns' from the slopes of yesteryear. So, as I trawled through the venerable tomes in the Ski Club of Great Britain's 'Sir Arnold Lunn' Library in Wimbledon, I imagined Peter watching over me too and, whenever I found anything which made me chuckle helplessly or filled me with astonishment or delight, I mentally sought confirmation from him as well that it should be rediscovered.

He, I knew, would share the hilarity of a letter received by the Ski Club from the Swiss resort of Lenzerheide in 1921, describing the antics of two skiers. One was an Englishman who

> should have broken his neck years ago – who was so keen on skiing that he often got some practice in England by skiing on hoar frost in his garden. He said it was quite exciting and the ski ran fast; but the last time he tried it they ran away with him, and in the end he was deposited in a heap of manure – the only advantage being that the fall was softer than he was expecting. When particularly bored he used to try skiing down his front stairs and doing Christianias in the hall.

The other was a German from the Black Forest who

was not particularly keen on skiing through trees,
but there are so many in the Black Forest that
sometimes it had to be done.

So on these occasions he used to fasten a thick
piece of rubber round his head to save his brains
from being spilled in any argument with a tree; in so
far as I know, they are still 'reposing in peace in his
skull'. But then he *was* odd. He was always
supposed to wrap up each toe separately in brown
paper to guard against frostbite, and had his skiing
coat lined with dried figs in case he got lost in a fog,
of which they get a fair number in that district.

Marvellously eccentric detail from the 1920s.

I make no excuses for lingering over the early years. It seems
to me that the further back in history one goes, the more
interesting it becomes, whereas the most recent events are less
interesting because we are more familiar with them. It has been
the most extraordinary and unexpected privilege to be able to
sift through the thoughts and minds of these dedicated ski-
runners (as the early skiers dubbed themselves).

I have been helped immeasurably by the redoubtable
Elisabeth Hussey, who worked for Arnold Lunn for many years
and then edited *Ski survey* for a remarkable 18 more. I have also
occasionally borrowed from her excellent but unpublished
biography of Lunn, *Arnold Lunn – Ski Pioneer*.

To add laziness to larceny, I have rather ungallantly left
Elisabeth to bridge the gap between the years of the *British Ski
Year Books* and *Ski Notes and Queries*, and the *Ski survey* years
leading up to the new millennium. If she will forgive me, I see
her, and indeed Peter Lunn, as bridges between 'Now' and
'Then', enabling Arnold and his colleagues to communicate
with us today. Peter has been a truly invaluable help in
proofreading my efforts, which produced this wonderful aside:
'So conscientious am I about checking your facts whenever

possible that I looked in the mirror to make certain that my eyes in fact are blue.'

My old friend Nigel Lloyd, one of the original ski writers of the modern age, with whom, like Peter Hardy, I have also skied for 25 years, has been inspirational too, as has Caroline Stuart-Taylor, the Ski Club's chief executive, whose unwavering support and sense of humour have kept me going on the long trail through the archives. Another close friend (former TV colleague and long-time skiing companion Chris Tizzard) and I have also produced a video, *When Men and Mountains Meet*, using substantial archive footage, to help celebrate the Ski Club's centenary.

The result of our labours in the library – reviewing the rich past both on celluloid and in the printed word – is, I hope, a spirited attempt to condense into a single book some of the great ski writing of the past and some of the happiest, *funniest* and most evocative tales of British ski pioneers relishing their role as they explored the mountains they felt so passionate about.

If Arnold Lunn, who started skiing before the Boer War and kept going for most of his long life, seems to dominate this collection, it is because his writings were both prolific and wonderfully descriptive. And, since for so many of its 52 volumes he had to shoulder the responsibility of writing much of the contents of the *British Ski Year Book*, his thoughts run like a rich seam through every volume. Sometimes I have tried to resist including him on various topics, but usually I have surrendered to his tellingly descriptive, if sometimes slightly purple, prose. Here and there, I have taken the liberty of rearranging extracts of his essays to enable them to be spread more easily through the chapters.

Is that all right, Sir Arnold?

Then here goes.

Arnold Lunn, Esqr.,
Palace Hotel des Alpes,
Mürren

12/1/26

Sir,

I am written to you by auspices of the Railway Direktion to
ask you to do me so good pleasures as to bring to notice of all
sports-persons of your control by publishment in the *Skis
Year Buck* or *Ski Notices & Questions* the enclosed rules for
usages of railway.

If these are with rigour observed, I feel there would be
saved much confusings of persons, and that winter-sports in
the High Alps will go with a swim as not before without the
observance of sames.

Trusting that these are meeting with your approval by
publication I am now to close.

Begging to remain by yours faithfully,
THE DIREKTION
Lindenalp–Bahn

It is brought to notice of all sportspersons as follows
   by the Railway Direktion.

That peoples should dismount from ski before entering sports-
trains, and remove same ones from trains before alighting to
sport.

All ski should be tied by twos to point of depart to avoid
   danger of heads and other limbs.

It is expressly forbidden to be run over by the sports-trains.

Ski-runners must not use the railway.

It is forbidden to leave feet on the seats of the cars on
   pain of cleaning sames.

SNOW CRAZY

It is forbidden to hold the overhead whilst standing on the underhead rails, on pain of death.

It is forbidden to sit more than twelve persons on each seat, unless there is more room in other trains.

Any person keeping his eye on a seat for a friend shall have no claim on the Direktion if another sportsman sits on it.

Passengers wishing to open the windows of the cars can only do so with the consent of all other passengers, and in the event of a dispute, the decision of the conductor shall be final, and the window shut.

Sports passengers must not cross the lines whilst the train is in motion.

It is forbidden to play at the snowalls with the drivers of the sports-trains.

It is not permitted to take tickets without payment.

No descension of the railway is permitted without ski.

It is forbidden to arrest the train at no station.

All snow must be left at the station of depart: sports passengers must not melt in the cars.

Lugers must keep same sides of their luges as trains and sports-peoples at stations and otherwise unless in the cars where their luges must not be.

It is specially notified that all sports-trains will leave at time of depart prompt.

The breaking of the above rules is by penalty of fine or imprisonment or both without options of either. By order of the Direktion.

Lindenalp,
Januar 1926

XVIII

Chapter 1

IN THE BEGINNING

They travel over the very highest mountains
by the swiftest speed, and faster than thought ...
and the winds whiz about their ears, and
their hair stands on end.

It started with a snowflake. And then several more. One crystal, of course, doesn't make a winter, and it is also a touch difficult to ski on a solitary *flocon de neige*. But a few billion and we're getting somewhere. Or at least we are if we happen to have a pair of ski. (In the early days, the plural of ski was, indeed ... ski.) But if we could travel back in time a millennium or two, we'd find that snow – beautiful as its freshly glinting crystals have always been as they bring a magical hush to the countryside – was usually considered a tiresome nuisance. The ski was invented, albeit in a very rudimentary form, to get from A to B.

There has been skiing of a sort in China – or at least in Mongolia – for thousands of years. Primitive skis helped Mongolian peasants to fish, hunt, farm and even fight each other. But it was, of course, nothing like the 'Alpine' (downhill) version we enjoy today.

According to Mark Heller's *Skier's Encyclopaedia*, the Pahsimi, who lived in the hills south-east of the Kirghiz steppes, strapped on footwear called *mu-ma* (wooden horses) when they were out hunting. In a translation from the *Kuang Chi*, an encyclopaedia of the Sung dynasty, we learn that 'When the hunter has bound these boards under his feet ... and goes over the snow on the flat, he prods the earth with a stick, and glides like a ship ... and overtakes the fleeing deer.'

In 1942, the *British Ski Year Book*, published by the Ski Club of Great Britain, printed a letter from W.K. Pyke-Lees concerning a contemporary description of the use of skis by a 13th-century Siberian tribe known as the Urianguts, whose most famous leader was Genghis Khan. The passage is translated from a 'Great Collection of Histories' (*Jami At-Tavarikh*) written in around 1300 AD by Rashid ad-Din, a Persian physician.

It begins,

> They believe that there is no happier life than their own. Their country being very cold, they hunt much over the snow. They bind to their feet long lengths of wood that they call *chana*, using a staff in their hands to push them along the snow, like the pole of a boat. They shoot down the mountainsides so swiftly that they catch up with animals. Anyone who is not accustomed to these wooden skates is apt to hurt his feet, especially in descending. But those who are accustomed to them can travel great distances speedily. This is something you must see, in order to believe it.

The following is an account of the 'Laplanders of Finnmark, their Language, Manners and Religion' by Knud Leems, Professor of Laplandic at Copenhagen, 1767:

> They travel over the very highest mountains by the swiftest speed, and faster than thought. By a certain wooden machine, of an oblong figure, fastened to their feet, commonly called wooden scandals, they are carried with such rapidity over the highest mountains, through the steepest hills, making no use of a staff,

which, in the midst of their course, they hang carelessly
and negligently from their shoulder, and the winds
whiz about their ears, and their hair stands on end.

Early skis were designed for travel and communication. They
were never intended for sport. And, even when the
Scandinavians, particularly the Norwegians, started using 'ski' for
jumping and cross-country, they were rarely used for downhill
racing, and certainly the practice did not involve skiing through
modern slalom gates. It was the British who helped make such a
concept popular.

In his 1944 book *Ski Track on the Battlefield*, V.A. Firsoff traces
the military history of ski from the earliest days (6000 BC or
thereabouts – through the time of King Harold Haardraade of 1066
fame, who allegedly said, 'on ski can I stride') and mentions, *en
passant*, something called *l'arrête Briançon* – a French technique
designed to check dangerous speed, in which practitioners were
invited to 'sit down into the snow a little sideways and the desired
effect is almost simultaneous'. The book also discusses the 'Holy
War against the Big Stick' – a reference to the determined efforts to
stop ski-runners using a gigantic pole or, later, two sticks held
together to 'ride', balance or turn. Vivian Caulfeild, for whom 'stick
riding' was anathema and taboo, spent years trying to stamp out
the practice.

Before Arnold Lunn and co. helped revolutionise the whole
concept of skiing, the Norwegians held that 'Langlauf' (cross-
country) and jumping were sacrosanct. And they should have
known – after all, weren't they the pioneers and most brilliant
exponents of the ancient sport? For them, said Lunn, 'Downhill
racers were pariahs, despised as weaklings who lacked the strength
to compete in the Langlauf or the courage to jump.'

Lunn even tells the story of a young Norwegian who, at a dinner
party, was overheard saying, 'Do you know who is the man in all
the world who has done most harm to skiing? I will tell you – it is
Mr Arnold Lunn.'

No wonder that Lunn, when told that Norwegians are 'born
with ski on their feet', was tempted to reply, 'This must make
things very difficult for Norwegian midwives.'

There were occasional flashes of Norwegian encouragement,

however. 'Our first Norwegian ally,' said Lunn, 'was Captain Christian Krefting, a former winner of the Norwegian Military Ski Championship.'

After a visit to Mürren, the Captain had written,

> It was an alluring thought to come to Switzerland as a Norwegian and show these newcomers to our sport what skiing really was ... We laugh at English skiing and say that the English only take trains uphill and come down the nursery slopes behind the hotels and practise a lot of peculiar twists and turns, and we think they understand nothing of what skiing really is. This was how I looked at things.

But what he witnessed astonished him.

> I stood at the different points where the races started and felt quite giddy looking down. To watch these plucky young Englishmen coming down these steep hills with an incredible speed ... kindled in me an ambition to be able to master these hills as well as these men did. I have long ago given up the idea of being able to impress by my Norwegian knowledge of skiing.

Later, Colonel Ivar Holmquist, the Swedish president of the International Ski Federation (FIS), wrote to Lunn, saying, 'We Scandinavians are very grateful to you for the unprecedented development of Downhill skiing technique for which we have to thank you.' It must have been a similar feeling when, in more recent times, the French finally had to acknowledge that the Australians could teach them a thing or two about wine making.

Back in the 1860s, Californian miners, heavily influenced by Scandinavian immigrants who had joined their ranks, were trying to avert winter inactivity and more than a dash of cabin fever. These early ski racers, with names like 'Cornish Bob' Oliver, Napoleon 'Little Corporal' Norman, 'French Pete' Riendeau, 'Quicksilver' Handel and 'Gray Flash' Pollard, introduced reckless but exhilarating races to the High Sierras. Careering down the slopes at speeds of up to 80 mph, they battled for cash prizes and the champion's title.

But which was the world's first ski club? There are two contenders, one of which is surprising. Tradition has it that it was founded at Kiandra – in Australia's Snowy Mountains, of all places – by Norwegian, Australian and Chinese gold miners.

However, there is some doubt. According to L.J. Clarke, writing in the 1968 *British Ski Year Book*, Tom Mitchell, at the time Australia's prime ski historian, told him his version of the world's first 'inter-racial (not to mention international) ski contest', which was apparently held near Kiandra.

'The races were somewhat informal,' Clarke reported, 'as the contestants were at liberty to crack each other over the skull with their heavy, pointed ski sticks as they sped downhill on flat boards.' But races on skis they were (though hardly as dignified as those that would later be held between the British and the Swiss).

'What is odd, though,' continued Clarke, 'is that, after this promising beginning, very little happened for half a century.' (Much the same hiatus seems to have occurred in California after the miners' races during the 1860s.) The Fairfax *Walkabout Australian Travel Guide* suggests,

> Over the years Kiandra has developed a remarkable skiing mythology. Certainly it is known that the residents of Kiandra were skiing in 1861 after some Norwegian miners had shown other miners how to convert a fence post into a workable ski, and certainly by the 1870s there were competitions and a ski club had been established in the area. But whether these competitions and the club were the first in the world is anyone's guess ... One thing is certain – Kiandra, being the highest town in Australia until the establishment of Cabramurra, was the first Australian town where skiing was commonplace in wintertime.

The other contender – also in 1861 – is the Trysil Ski og Skytterklubb (Skiing and Shooting Club) in Norway. Assuming Kiandra is a genuine contender, it would all rather depend, one supposes, on which was first – the northern or southern hemisphere's winter!

Twenty years later, a pioneering Englishman got skiing started in the Swiss mountain village of Grindelwald. According to one version of events from the local tourist office, 'The first skier, an Englishman named Gerald Fox, appeared in 1881. He fastened his skis all ready in the hotel room. He put his long stick in the snow and glided away. In squatting vauld he glided down the slope, the wooden stick like a folding boat balancing.'

Apart from the Ski Club of Great Britain, the two ski clubs which have had the most profound effect on British skiing and racing are the Kandahar, formed by Arnold Lunn in Mürren on January 30, 1924, and the Downhill Only, which started a year later across the Lauterbrunnen Valley in Wengen. (Lunn's son Peter, then aged just nine, was sworn in as a founder member of the Kandahar while he was asleep in bed.)

In Telluride, Colorado, miners came hurtling down the slopes in search of something else: women. Sheltering beneath the towering San Juan mountains at the end of a beautiful but remote box canyon, not so far from the New Mexico border, Telluride has such a wild and hellraising history that even Hollywood would be hard pressed to do it justice.

It was the Swedish miners' skill on skis, making a fast descent from the mines at Tomboy down to Telluride, that enabled them to be first in the queue for the services of the so-called 'soiled doves'. The story goes that there was only one bathtub in town, which was owned by an intriguing character called L.L. Nunn who was credited with supplying Telluride with the first alternating current in the world. Since it was understood that before liaising with local prostitutes a miner would need a bath and, for some reason, a suit, the Swedes were also first in the queue for Nunn's tub. That was the story, anyway.

This was skiing wild-west style, and hardly the sort of company the Ski Club of Great Britain's original members would have sought out. It was a mix of genteel aristocrats, gentlemen and, not long afterwards, a good number of army and naval officers that, soon after the turn of the century, started what was arguably the most influential ski club in the world.

A well-known Jerusalem photographer friend of mine – Werner Braun, who had been the official photographer at the trial of the German war criminal Adolf Eichmann in 1961 – once told me, with a slightly cynical grin, that there are several 'exact spots' in

Bethlehem where Christ was supposed to have been born. In a similar way, there are many skiing 'cradles' and 'fathers'. Is there really a father of skiing? Was it Sondre Auversen Norheim, the Norwegian skier and ski maker, who in 1866 gave the first-known demonstration of the Telemark and Christiania turn? The Austrian army officer Matthias Zdarsky who gave us linked 'stem-christiania' turns? His pupil Hannes Schneider, who switched from Telemark to the classic Austrian style (incorporating the famous 'Arlberg Crouch')? Or Sir Arnold Lunn, who gave us the 'modern slalom'? Lunn (awarded the title of 'foster father, prophet, nurse and tutor' of skiing by Lord Schuster) even gave us his own candidate: E.C. Richardson, a founder member of the Ski Club of Great Britain who seemed to be involved in just about every controversy surrounding the early days of organised skiing in Great Britain.

Indeed, the material that forms the main structure of this book – gleaned from dozens of volumes of the *British Ski Year Book* and *Ski Notes and Queries*, its quarterly companion – is sometimes almost savage in its frankness. No doubt it was largely good natured, but some of the attacks carried out on one another by senior figures in the Ski Club make almost hair-raising reading. All this was put into perspective in the preface to Arnold Lunn's *The Story of Skiing*, published in 1952 to commemorate the Ski Club of Great Britain's Golden Jubilee in the following year. In the book, Lunn quotes Ken Foster, editor of the Downhill Only club's *DHO Journal,* after 'pained reaction abroad' to one of the journal's cartoons.

Foster wrote to Lunn,

> DHO members as a class are a conservative race, and they like their Hon. Editor to keep to the accepted formula, which is to start by taking a crack at the Labour Government and then look around for someone else to be rude to. (*You* as a rule.)
>
> Possibly people overseas do not realise that irreverence has been a leading feature of British skiing from the earliest days ... the earliest writers on skiing, led by Lunn, faithfully reproduced this atmosphere of debunking, writing down and healthy ridicule. Others

since (myself included) have followed in your footsteps, and in fact the last thing I wrote about you was so rude that the editor of *Ski Notes and Queries* refused to publish it. We understand all this among ourselves but probably it does seem odd to a foreigner.

The DHO was formed a year after the Kandahar Ski Club and was its biggest rival. 'There were a lot of very fierce ladies in charge of junior training both for the DHO and the Kandahar,' says Elisabeth Hussey, 'and they fought to get the best young skiers to take part in their training. But now the clubs are on very good terms and work very well together.' As an unintentionally lapsed member, I have my own story about the DHO and wish now that I could remember the name of the cheerful club official who gave me what I'm sure was a tongue-in-cheek answer to my question when I put it to him in Wengen, 'How does one join?'

I have told the story of his response many times. 'Simple,' he said. 'First of all you have to be the right sort of chap.' This could be tricky, I thought at the time. 'Then you go to the top of the mountain with one of our members,' he continued. 'I light my cigar and if it's still alight when you get down … you're in!'

Jimmy Palmer-Tomkinson, one of Britain's greatest pre-war racers (tragically killed while practising for the British Championships in 1952), who was in the 1936 British Winter Olympics team and later captained two Olympic teams, wrote amusingly about ski racers,

> In the Grand National, a man who can't ride, or a horse that can't jump, is a menace; both are now refused entry. At bridge or poker, the man who plays out of his class is a fool and probably ends up in the bankruptcy court. At Wimbledon, a certain standard is insisted upon and, even then, several qualifying rounds are necessary; the same applies to golf and many other sports.
>
> But in skiing, for some unaccountable reason, you have only to hurl yourself down the hill minutes after everyone else to be considered extremely sporting. This is of course nonsense, because there is no obvious

merit in being sporting about losing when you know from the start that you have no chance of winning. Conversely there is nothing unsporting in recognising that the competition is above your class and refraining from entering.

One of the great ski film maker Warren Miller's jokes concerns the three things you can do with skis: 'Turn left, turn right – or sell 'em!' But in the beginning, it seems, actually making a turn on ski was considered rare – even impossible.

According to A. Manwaring Robertson, writing in the *Year Book* about 'Early Days in Grindelwald', 'In 1904, turns were practically unheard of, at any rate, among the English at Grindelwald.' So what was the slalom technique *du jour*, one wonders. Simple. 'We "ran" varying distances and fell heavily, picked ourselves up and re-climbed the practice slope.' (The word 'slalom' means 'downhill track in the snow' in the Morgedal dialect of Telemark, the Norwegian county where Sondre Norheim did his bit of ski pioneering.)

In many ways the early history of the Ski Club of Great Britain is almost the history of Alpine skiing itself. It is littered with acts of great derring-do, often eccentric, sometimes hilarious, all recorded in the quaint and colourful language of the 'golden age' of skiing in the pages of the club's own *Year Book*.

Those early pioneers declared,

> We intend at all times to give the widest publicity in our power to skiing in the British Isles, and look hopefully forward to the day when the ash boards and their owners will be a comparatively familiar sight on our mountains, and will not be greeted with open-mouthed wonder by the country yokel as at present.

Skiing was not just confined to the wilds of the countryside, however. In those days of snowier winters, even London, it seems, had its attractions. In one of the earliest articles in the Ski Club of Great Britain's *Year Book*, 'Silk Purses From Sows' Ears', William Richardson reported,

I think a few days every year might be spent on ski near London, if only people would make experimental trips to localities they know, and publish results in this book for the benefit of others. We do not expect silk purses out of sows' ears, but why not some quite nice purses?

It might be worthwhile for a Londoner, on a clear, frosty day, with snow of six inches or so, to take ski down to Haslemere by the 11 a.m. train from Waterloo, leaving a greatcoat at Witley Station *en route*, ski up to Hindhead, play about in the Punch Bowl, and lunch at one of the inns or hotels. *Dry socks are well worth taking, as an English train is cold about the feet in winter.*

For those who travelled further afield, finding suitable accommodation was sometimes hit and miss. Lunn was fond of quoting the poet Thomas Love Peacock on this: 'On his travels, he always asked to see two things in an inn: the mustard pot and the lavatory. If both were clean, he booked.'

In the early, liftless days, of course, there were no pistes as such either. As one early Ski Club member, Andrew Walser, put it, 'There were none of those frightening icy pistes, and the skier more or less rolled down through soft snow. In fact the whole thing was more like a good foam bath than anything else.'

Arnold Lunn's son Peter loved a good foam bath as much as any. But for many a year there has been one unanswered question in his mind: 'The Austrians have a saying that in life there are two supreme sensations.' He smiles, with the brightest of twinkles in those blue eyes of his. 'One of them is skiing in powder snow. I hope that one day somebody will tell me what the other one is.'

Chapter 2

A Club is Born

*It was universally agreed that undressing should be
reduced to a minimum. There was a tacit under-
standing that only the most perfunctory attempt at
toilet would be considered desirable ...*

In 1903, Henry Ford was about to introduce his first mass-
production motor car, Pepsi-Cola was registering its trade mark,
Sweet Adeline was top of the pops and Norway was firmly
resisting attempts to give women the vote.

It was not an auspicious year in which to start a ski club. More
than 130 mountaineers – many of them, inevitably, British –
would be lost that summer making assaults on unscaled Alpine
peaks and attempting to pluck rare plants from inaccessible
ledges and crags. But that was the British way. Just as the British
had dominated climbing in the previous century, they would now
– for a few crucial decades at least – pioneer downhill skiing and
racing. It was the beginning of the 'golden age' of skiing.

On May 6, in London, a dozen or so young men, anxious to
share Norway's Nordic skiing prowess and develop the sport's
downhill potential, sat down to dinner at the Café Royal in

London's Regent Street and drew up plans for a daring and almost unheard-of project: to start a ski club.

It was resolved that the club, to be called the Ski Club of Great Britain, should be formed 'to assist members in such matters as where to go, what sort of ski to purchase, from whom initial instruction could be had, what the general condition of the snow was in such and such a place at such and such a time of year ...'

At the Annual General Meeting two years later, they would decide that 'the annual subscription ... shall be 5s [25p] for gentlemen, and 2s 6d [12½p] for ladies, payable in advance.' Women, who tended to ski in long skirts and were perceived as lightweights, were of peripheral interest.

But what of the men? Were there actually 12 of them at the inaugural dinner? Curiously, no one seems absolutely sure – and perhaps it doesn't matter. Every account of this momentous event – both contemporary and decades later – varies when it comes to the numbers involved that night at the Café Royal table, from 10 to 14. The issue is confused further by the entry a year or two later in the club's first series of publications, the *Ski Club of Great Britain Year Book*, which apologises for missing out one founder member's name in the original account of the dinner. In *Miscellaneous Notices, &c*, we find the following entry: 'In the article on the formation of the club in the first number of the *Year Book*, the name of Mr George P. Pollitt was omitted from the list of those mentioned as being present at the inaugural dinner.' Curiouser and curiouser. But then perhaps he didn't actually join the club.

John Collard, a particularly diligent researcher and Ski Club member, who spends much of his spare time in the Ski Club's library, has one theory, although recently he's had his doubts:

> At one stage I thought the key to the whole thing might be that one, or possibly two of the men who sat down for dinner that night did not actually join the club – and that, to complicate matters, there were one or two men who were not at dinner who did join. This would have explained the confusion. But now I'm not so sure.
>
> Two of those present – Boulter and Pollitt – signed the menu under the heading of 'The Members of the Ski

Club', but perhaps left before the 'unanimous decision' was taken to start a ski club. Both became members, but could not be classed as founders. As for the fourteenth person hinted at, he too might have left early or been unable to come after all. (The dinner had been arranged at short notice, and was held on a Wednesday.) To speculate, the most obvious name missing from the list of founders is that of JB Wroughton, brother of EH Wroughton who was present.

Whatever the numbers, from such small beginnings, the Ski Club of Great Britain would become one of the most celebrated, influential and powerful in the world. Predictably, although Mrs Pankhurst was already on the warpath, there were no women at the table – and they would not be involved in any meaningful way for many years. Indeed, the club expressly kept them from high office. The Committee, it was decided, 'shall have power to invite ladies to become members of the club; they, however, may not be elected to the Committee.'

Women were, however, a much-discussed subject. In *A Lady's Tour*, N. Eardley-Wilmot wrote,

> The accommodation was limited; and, as you never know your luck in these kind of places, it was universally agreed that undressing should be reduced to a minimum. There was a tacit understanding that only the most perfunctory attempt at toilet would be considered desirable ... The most suitable dress for a lady on such occasions is a flannel shirt, knickerbockers, and a very short skirt. Gaiters are excellent ... to keep out the snow, but can be discarded by the expert.

By way of contrast, here was a toe-curlingly patronising male view of women on skis:

> Unlike men, ladies have no liking for somersaults and other violent disarrangements of their persons. [However,] I should like to mention an entirely unfounded notion which prevails among the

uninitiated ... that ski-running requires a strength of physique not possessed by women as a rule. In my opinion, there is no more risk for women in ski-running than in any other of their sports. Great physical strength is of minor importance. A woman who is sound in wind and limb, and who has sufficient personal courage to sail her own boat, drive her own motor ... is amply qualified to become a first-class ski-runner.

I believe it has been privately asserted by men, very privately, of course, and only when emboldened by the absence of their wives, that women are a doubtful blessing on tour ... *No one will deny that women are much more obedient on tour than men* ... Of course, women should endeavour to give a minimum amount of trouble, and all offers of assistance should be graciously but firmly declined, unless absolutely necessary. My last remark is for ladies only. It should be remembered that no mere man can ever venture to become surly as long as the ladies of the party remain good tempered under adverse circumstances.

Strangely, in a fascinating 17th-century account by M. Regnard of 'A Journey to Lapland', women are dealt with rather more chivalrously: '.... descending the steepest precipices ... mounting the most craggy mountains ... the women are no less adroit in the use of these planks than the men. They go to visit their relations and travel in this manner the longest and most difficult journeys.' Having reached Stockholm, he continues, 'Here at length terminated our hazardous journey, of which I would not have been deprived for a great deal of money and which I would not begin again for much more.'

That all-male dinner in the cellars at the Café Royal in May 1903 had been arranged by E.C. Richardson, then 33 and educated at Harrow and Cambridge, who would later be generously described by Sir Arnold Lunn as 'the father of British skiing'. (In fact, Lunn himself, who popularised downhill racing and pioneered the modern slalom concept – and once observed that it was 'as strange for a Briton to have so much influence on skiing as it would be for an Eskimo to revolutionise cricket' – is now widely regarded as being its most influential figure.)

Also present at that inaugural dinner on May 6 was Richardson's brother, C.W. Richardson. They had learned to ski in Norway, but had recently visited Davos, the 'cradle of British skiing', where they had been told that 'the snow was, except quite late in the year, entirely unsuited' to the sport.

They persevered, however, and 'were amazed to find some ski tracks other than our own'. The tracks belonged to F.T. Leaming and F.G. Fedden. Once their ski tracks had crossed, it became clear that a small, hard core of 'ski runners' was out there, and that the formation of some sort of ski club might have certain attractions.

Only a few weeks after the Richardsons had founded the Davos English Ski Club, the four men formed the nucleus of the Ski Club of Great Britain's inaugural dinner. Also present, as far as we can ascertain from the variety of conflicting reports, were H.M. Elder, E.H. Wroughton, W.R. Rickmers, G.H. Fowler, H.R. Yglesias, R. Seligman, Edgar Sayers (who was elected the club's first president) and, as we now know, the mysterious George P. Pollitt. There were possibly others. We may never know the complete list.

Like encountering British cars on the continent after the last war, seeing other people's ski tracks in the snow, as the Richardson brothers had in Davos, was still a novelty. During a fortnight in the Cairngorms with the newly formed club, E.H. Wroughton observed,

> Unfortunately a thaw had set in, and the snow was too wet. The day would have been absolutely barren of interest if we had not, to our great surprise, seen fresh ski marks near Loch Moraig. The sight of a man's footprint in the sand could not have astonished Robinson Crusoe more.

We found them to have been made by Dr Wagner of Dundee. He was on his way from the Pass of Killiecrankie via Deeside to Aviemore. He had slept the previous night in a crofter's or shepherd's lodge, and, being laden with a sleeping sack, cooking apparatus and provisions for three days, was fully prepared to spend other nights on or in the snow.

15

Meanwhile, readers of the *Year Book* were informed that Colonel Malcolm, DSO had telegraphed from Grantown-on-Spey, saying,

> I have today visited all the districts between Dalwhinnie, Grantown and Tomatin. The snow lies thick and unbroken 500 to 1,000 feet above the river Spey, and is in fine condition for skiing. Below that level the snow lies in deep drifts, but patchy, with firm surface. The deepest snow is between Dalwhinnie and Aviemore, also above Carrbridge and Tomatin. Good frosts every night lately.

With no ski lifts or proper ski resorts, ski-runners could wander far and wide with their 'ski' – wherever there was snow – in search of terrain where they could indulge their passion for a craze that was still some years away from arousing the curiosity of the world of winter sports, let alone dominating it. But in those days there was a price to pay for every run: a steep price. Before there were even mountain railways running in winter to give ski-runners a 'lift' to the slopes, you had to earn your turns by walking up. Typically, two long runs from the upper slopes down to the village would be a good day. One run would satisfy many. Three would be near-Herculean.

In the early days, the use of sealskins attached to the base of the skis to help ski-runners get a grip on the snow as they traipsed up the slopes was frowned upon as 'hated' and 'despised'. Members were told, 'For the club's Third-Class tests, the use of seal's skin or other artificial aid to climbing is prohibited.'

The object, in the early days, was more to explore the possibilities of skiing in Britain than the Continent, but soon Norway, whose ski-runners and jumpers were lionised by their British followers, and Switzerland would become the focus. Arnold Lunn said,

> We may fairly claim that we inspired the Swiss not only to climb their own mountains, but also to race down them on ski.
>
> In Norway, skiing is a religion. Indeed skiing performs many of the functions once performed by the church. The discipline of langlauf (cross-country) has

replaced the discipline of the medieval fasts. *Ondurris*, goddess of langlauf, calls us to forsake worldly pleasures and to persevere in the straight and narrow path of the ascetic.

Lunn enjoyed such religious parallels. In 1931 he observed,

> That God is best worshipped in the fields and woods rather than in a stuffy church is a favourite sentiment with those who spend their Sundays looking for God in one of a procession of cars that bear these nature worshippers along the asphalt roads of old England. The rapid increase in week-end accidents suggests that some of them may, no doubt, find God rather more rapidly than they had expected.

In his book *Mountain Jubilee*, Lunn makes an important distinction about Swiss skiing 'cradles': 'Davos was the birthplace of British skiing,' he wrote, 'and Mürren of modern ski racing. For it was at Mürren that the Kandahar was founded and the slalom evolved.' He also recalled that 'the oldest international downhill racing meeting', between the Anglo-Swiss Universities, was organised at Mürren.

The historic Roberts of Kandahar race, which began the so-called 'Kandahar Revolution', was held for the first time in 1911, not in Mürren, where it would settle the following year, but in another Swiss resort: Montana. And so began the curious link between skiing and the Afghan town at the centre of the recent war against the Taliban.

Lord Roberts, a veteran of India who went on to become Commander-in-Chief of the British Army, had been decorated for gallantry in an Afghan campaign in 1880, when he gloriously relieved the town of Kandahar. He was persuaded by Henry Lunn to donate a cup for the ski race, even though he had never skied in his life — or even been to the Alps in winter. The name Kandahar would become synonymous with ski racing at the very highest level and inspire the inauguration of one of the world's most prestigious ski clubs.

The Kandahar club has perhaps the most exclusive ski badge in the world: the Diamond A-K, awarded (extremely rarely, if ever!) to any skier winning the silver A-K badge four or more times.

Elsewhere in Switzerland, St Moritz had been a summer health resort and spa for centuries, but Davos was a complete newcomer to holidaymakers. As a winter-sports resort, St Moritz, like Davos, began as a health resort for recovering tuberculosis sufferers, otherwise known as 'consumptives'. According to W.G. and Margaret Lockett's 1942 *Year Book* article, 'The Development of Winter Sports in the Engadine', 'Alpine winter sports were introduced to the world by invalids and their companions.' The article explains that

> most of these were consumptives ... at one time very ill indeed.
>
> The people who lived in the Engadine and in the Davos Valley knew, centuries back, that theirs was an extremely healthy climate. When the doctors ... succeeded in persuading invalids to visit the Alps in winter, they very soon saw ... the possibilities and delights of sport in the wonderful sunshine of the snowy mountains. To them we owe the Alps as a winter-sport playground ...
>
> Down to 70 years ago the Alpine resorts that now resound with the joys of sport were almost inaccessible snow deserts, the inhabitants of which spent their long winter in dreary dullness and loneliness. *Such horrible killing cold regions were dreaded and shunned.* The world knew nothing of the glory of Alpine winter sunshine or the splendour of the snows.

When one doctor, Alexander Spengler, suggested that invalids should try wintering in the Alps, the idea was dismissed as 'absurd – nay, worse than absurd ... it was wicked! Surely everybody knew that cold was the greatest enemy of the consumptive!'

And the Alpine winter was 'Arctic' – even 'Siberian'!

'It would have been bad enough,' said the authors, 'to persuade *healthy* people to visit the frozen mountains ... but to tempt invalids to go there was murderous.' They would soon change their tune, of course, as the Locketts concluded,

The true pioneers of winter sports, our plucky forefathers, when stricken by disease, undertook the adventure, as it then was, of the journey to and residence in these uncomfortable Alpine villages without so much – without almost anything – that makes these resorts such a pleasure to us nowadays. Our inventive, discovering forebears did not, literally, take their cure lying down ... but demanded skating rinks, built toboggan runs, invented racing 'machines' for snow and ice, and prepared the way for this age of skiing.

Even by 1922, skating was still high on the list of British winter sports enthusiasts. This was made clear in the *Year Book* of the time, in which Lieutenant-Colonel H. de Watteville, in 'A Winter in Tirol', wrote, 'There was no skating at Kitzbühel except on the little lake; no curling at all; no ice hockey, and no tobogganing of any kind.' In the same year, Arnold Lunn wrote, 'It is worth noticing that English skating, which has been killed many times by the prophets, seems a peculiarly lively corpse.'

There was another bizarre problem about British skaters: they took up far too much space, as Lunn explained many years later in the 1943 *British Ski Year Book*, in an essay on 'The English in Switzerland':

> The English skater keeps his unemployed leg rigidly to his side, and sweeps over the ice in long, sweeping curves. Not individual display but combined skating is the ideal of the English school ... It is a pity that four Englishmen skating a 'combined' need more space than 50 foreigners waltzing in the degenerate Continental style.

This they did for some years but, as 'Kipling's England slowly passed away', trouble was brewing. Said Lunn,

> The 'lesser breeds without the law' began to murmur against the English hegemony of the ice rink, and hotel proprietors began to think in terms of square metres per skater, with the result that the English

skaters suddenly discovered that they were no longer wanted. English skating vanished from the ice rinks of the Alps.

Luckily, they had a new sport to pursue: skiing.

But as Arnold Lunn's son Peter points out in his book, the *Guinness Book of Skiing*, 'in those early days, skiing was the despised winter sport. Skaters were greatly admired and tobogganing was widely practised and taken very seriously. Skiers, on the other hand, were regarded as figures of fun; spectators, especially small boys, delighted to mock them as they fell around.'

As British skiers gradually turned their attention to the Alps – in those days a journey of 24 hours or more – recently constructed mountain railways provided the exciting possibility of speeding up the hike back to the mountain tops. But it would be a few years yet before this concept would be fulfilled.

It was reported at the time,

> It is probable that, if a sufficient number of runners were keen enough on such a tour, the Jungfrau Railway might be induced to facilitate matters by running a train from Scheidegg to Eismeer Station ... it would then become possible to ski to the Eiger Glacier, train to Eismeer Station, and so reach the Bergli in an easy day ... whereas at present the climb by the glacier and Viescherwand is decidedly tiresome.

In those early days, although wealthier Britons could visit winter-sports resorts in the Alps – particularly in Switzerland – to enjoy skating, horse-drawn sleigh rides, tobogganing and perhaps a little excursion 'on ski' there was no need to travel abroad. Indeed, there are still some members of the club who concentrate their endeavours on Scotland to this day. However, this letter to the editor of the *Ski Club Year Book* from Donald T. Mackintosh of Kingussie is as true today (even allowing for better communications) as it was in 1906: 'The skier who thinks of coming here in quest of his favourite sport would do well to inquire by telegram as to the state of the snow.'

On a good day, however, the great snow expert, Gerald Seligman, compares Scotland almost favourably with the Alps. In a wartime book review, he wrote,

> More than once I have returned from the Alps to spend a few days in the Highlands, always expecting, but never experiencing, anti-climax. The Scottish landscape may lack the excitement of gleaming glaciers, and the brilliant contrasts of summer snow, but cliffs and crags are cliffs and crags wherever they may be, and the grandeur of the Scottish scene is unassailable by whatever standards it be judged.
>
> Moreover, Scotland possesses something which few other countries have – the combination of russets and gentle blues and purples and vivid greens; these provide the most lovely effects that I have ever known in any part of the world.

Meanwhile, the *Ski Club Year Book* was not slow to plead for articles. 'Will English ski-runners in all part of the world make notes of their experiences this winter,' it urged, 'and send them, with any interesting photos and drawings, to the Editor of the *S.C.G.B Year Book*, 15, Cedar House, Cheniston Gardens, London. If this were done, the utility of this publication would be greatly enhanced.'

Tales of derring-do would soon be arriving. The British on skis have always been fearless, if not always equally effective. This is summed up, perhaps, in this classic quote from the very first *Ski Club Year Book*: 'It is impossible to be lost – as one is bound to come out *somewhere* ...'

Letters continued to find their way to the club. Many asked for advice and other tips. Here is a very early selection of some of the most intriguing replies. Frustratingly, we seem to have no record of the actual questions!

Answers to correspondents

C.W.R. – *We have tried the sample of ski wax you kindly sent us, and find it as beneficial for greasing boots as it is as a hair restorer.*

C.R.W. – *You are too self-conscious. The ski-running-cum-yachting jersey would be quite* de rigeur *[sic] at dinner.*

G.J.G. – *The best way of stopping an avalanche is to throw your hat at it; for which reason it is dangerous to go about bareheaded.*

E.C. – *The hills round Klosters are very slippery; it was most unfair to bar sealskin.*

M.J.B. – *In future members are to be roped on all Club tours. A qualified surgeon will form one of the party.*

Chic, high-profile ski resorts like Val d'Isère and Courchevel had yet to be invented. Zermatt was a climbing village famous for the Matterhorn – conquered for the first time less than 40 years previously – but not for its skiing. (When compared with the Puntiagudo (2,493m), a Chilean volcano, a patriotic Swiss once said, 'The Matterhorn is like a sound tooth, Puntiagudo like a decaying tooth.')

Arnold Lunn, who visited Zermatt as early as 1908, and went on to climb Europe's most famous peak, described how the local people lived on goats' milk and cheese – and skis were unknown.

In 1870s St Moritz, there were complaints about the food. 'The great drawback of spending the winter at St Moritz is the want of good food,' wrote one correspondent. 'The milk and bread and butter are good,' he continued, 'but the meat is bad, and the soup invariably requires a certain amount of *Liebig's Extract* to make it worth eating.' (This was a recently invented way of preserving the flavour of meat. In the 1860s, Baron von Leibig was invited to be a shareholder in a firm producing and transporting the 'skinless and boneless extract' to Europe by the ton!)

In January 1890, the *St Moritz Post* and *Davos News* published a letter from Mr Walter M. Moore from Canterbury, New Zealand, which said,

I believe I may lay claim to the honour of being the first English traveller who ever spent a winter in the Engadine. I have no doubt that some of the residents

in Pontresina, Samaden and St Moritz may remember
the English lad who spent a winter there 22 years ago.

Unfortunately, owing to a misprint, Mr Moore was referred to as
'the English *cad*'.

The Ski Club of Great Britain – born in Caxton Street, in
London's Westminster – progressed via nearby Hobart Place to
the prestigious environs of Eaton Square, where it was based for
most of its history. But in 1996, as the new millennium
approached, it was rehoused in the now familiar White House
building in leafy Wimbledon. Today the club is still perhaps best
known for its 'Reps': those resourceful, skilful and above all
helpful enthusiasts dedicated to escorting Ski Club members
around the most interesting slopes. The club sent out its first
volunteer representatives to the Alps to look after its members in
1928. But, in a sense, the first embryonic reps were known as
'snow agents' and in the early days were all based in Britain.

In November 1906, a number of 'snow agents' were appointed
to report snowfalls in their districts ... There were 'agents at
Buxton, Sheffield and Shrewsbury; in Yorkshire at Litton (above
Skipton) and Sedbergh; in the Lake District at Troutbeck, near
Windermere; and in Scotland at Glasgow, Tomintoul, Dalwhinnie
and Kingussie.'

'No agent has yet been obtained in Wales,' the record books
tells us, 'and the nearest was Mr Wingfield, at Shrewsbury. The
information obtained ... from the agents was distributed by
telegram to such members as had expressed their wish to receive
it; but they were only ten in number.'

Ski racing in those days was still in its infancy. The Ski Club's
first *Continental Reports for Season 1905–1906* focused on the Ski
Club Schwarzwald's championships in the Black Forest, in which
Maier (peasant) had won what appeared to be the first
championships in 1900. Dr H. Hoek then dominated the
proceedings for the next three years. The full table of victors
appeared like this:

1900 Maier (Peasant)
1901 Hoek
1902 Hoek

1903 Hoek/Biehler (Student)
1904 Biehler
1905 Kaiser (Peasant)
1906 W. Muller (Student)

Soon H. Archer Thomson, an early editor of the original *Year Book*, would be reporting on the Ski Club of Great Britain's very first competition:

> The first competition in the annals of the Club was brought off on 17th February, 1908, at Kitzbühel, in the Tyrol. Some ski-runners consider competitions not only unnecessary but also, as in mountaineering, wholly alien to the true spirit of the sport. This seems an extreme view ... In mountaineering, to hold races up or down rock peaks or over crevassed glaciers – apart from the feeling of desecration that the very idea conjures up in the heart of the cragsman – would be putting a premium on foolhardiness, and would inevitably lead to the loss of human life. In the kindred sport of skiing, however ... competitions are open to no such suggestions.

In a 'Combined Curving and Speed Race' (Downhill), members noted that 'Smythe Hughes put in the remarkable number of thirty curves. Rickmers, who, taking a careful course with three or four curves in it, got down in the excellent time of 38 seconds.'

It is perhaps important at this stage to introduce a key figure in the history of not only the Ski Club of Great Britain, but of skiing in general – according to his son Arnold, 'the first tourist agent to discover the possibilities of the winter Alps'. And yet, paradoxically, this man never climbed or put on a pair of skis in his life. His name was Henry Lunn. Arnold described his father thus: 'The only pioneer of skiing who never skied.'

Chapter 3

THE 'PM OF MÜRREN' – AND THE SNOOTY MUPPLES

My father was a queer mixture of merchant adventurer and mystic. He loved making money, but was uneasy on the rare occasions when he had a substantial balance in the bank, for he could not resist a sneaking suspicion that Jesus Christ meant what he said in his warnings about wealth.

Who was Henry Lunn? Who better to tell us than his son Arnold, who, through his father's early enterprises, rose to fame as Britain's most famous ski pioneer. In the 1943 *British Ski Year Book*, Arnold Lunn paints a picture of this man in a way that only a son can. It illuminates not only Lunn 'Senior' himself (and to some extent Arnold Lunn too), but the times in which he lived, and the snobbish social mores and attitudes of the day. The account is an amalgam of earlier descriptions in two of Sir Arnold's books, *Come What May* and *Mountain Jubilee*.

One crucial description explains why, strangely, Henry Lunn never skied. 'My father had no taste for and certainly no talent for games,' says Lunn 'junior'. I make no excuse for reproducing here the bulk of Arnold Lunn's *Year Book* account of his father's role in the development of winter holidays in Switzerland, because it throws a uniquely authoritative spotlight on the immediate pre-history of the British on the slopes.

Lunn wrote,

> My father, who was born on July 30, 1859, was the son of a Lincolnshire tradesman. In his early youth he discovered that he could exchange mice at a profit, through the columns of the *Exchange and Mart*. From mice he passed on to poultry, the Brahmapootra and the game bantam, and thence to the implements necessary for a game which was then known as Sphairistike, and which is now known as lawn tennis. He patented an invention for attaching scoring dials to tennis rackets ... which was warmly welcomed by people who had some difficulty in remembering the sequence 15, 30, 40, Deuce, Vantage, Game. The Prince of Wales bought one of these dials and my father promptly informed the world that the business was under royal patronage.
>
> My father was a queer mixture of merchant adventurer and mystic. He loved making money, but was uneasy on the rare occasions when he had a substantial balance in the bank, for he could not resist a sneaking suspicion that Jesus Christ meant what he said in his warnings about wealth.

It was this which caused him to sell his share in the business which he had created for a thousand pounds, and to spend his capital in training himself for the career of a medical missionary in India, where Arnold was born. (According to a later article by Lunn, in 1967, his father had set out to be a missionary after a dream in which he was approaching a very large house with a friend. 'This is my home,' he said in his dream, 'and those are my children playing tennis. I have had a great success, but there is not a spark of religion in the place.')

But his health broke down in India. Arnold Lunn wrote,

> On his return, he founded *The Review of the Churches*

to promote Christian reunion, and it was in the columns of this paper that the tourist agency which still bears his name was born.

He suggested that a group of divines representing different churches should meet at Vossevangen in Norway, and 'should spend the days in winter sports and the evenings in conference.' The ship by which they were to sail was wrecked after they had booked their passage, and a second ship to which the pilgrims were transferred promptly sank to the bottom of the sea. My father accepted the omens, and booked rooms in the Bear Hotel at Grindelwald.

Had either of these ships remained afloat, my father might have developed an agency for Norway, and I might have wasted many years trying to convert British skiers to the joys of langlauf (cross-country) and ski-jumping. In that case, of course, my old sparring partner, Alec Keiller (a prominent cross-country and ski-jumping pioneer) would have felt constrained to invent the slalom.

Twenty-six Reunionists arrived in Grindelwald on January 7, 1892. The party included representatives of the Church of England, the Methodists, the Baptists and other communions. I cannot believe that they received a very warm welcome from the old habitués of the winter Bear, for the pioneers of winter sports were from much the same social strata as the Alpine Club, that is from members of the learned professions and, in general, from members of that upper middle class, for whom my brother Hugh had coined the useful portmanteau word 'mupples'.

The Bear habitués spent their days between tobogganing parties to 'The Happy Valley' and the chaste austerities of English skating. They never skied. Sometimes they went further afield, for the Bear's habitués included members of the Alpine Club, and the Wetterhorn or Jungfrau was usually climbed once or twice in the course of a winter. The old Bear, like Monte Rosa at Zermatt, or Couttet's at Chamonix, was one of the shrines of the Alpine elect. It was not exactly a club, but those who were not accepted by the habitués felt slightly chilled as they crossed the sacred threshold. In the early 90s there was one point on which all 'mupples' were agreed, the social stigma involved in allowing oneself to be 'personally conducted' to Switzerland.

The Bear Hotel, therefore, lost caste when the Lunn pilgrims arrived, and the mupples had not even the satisfaction of making their displeasure felt, for the pilgrims were satisfied with their own society, and it is impossible to freeze out those who are not trying to climb in.

Encouraged by the success of this first experiment, my father resolved to summon a formal conference to discuss reunion at Grindelwald. He invited the Prime Minister, the entire bench of bishops, and the leading Free Churchmen to attend a conference at Grindelwald, as his guests. He was 32 years of age, and unknown outside of Methodism, and his conviction that he was the proper person to convene a conference to consider reunion argues a certain confidence in not only his mission, but in himself.

Mr Gladstone replied in a courteous letter regretting that 'the pressure of political duties', etc. One bishop accepted the invitation, as did most of the leading Free Churchmen. My father hoped that the galaxy of divines, all of whom must be supposed to have retained their amateur status ... would attract a sufficient number of paying tourists to save him from bankruptcy.

But Arnold Lunn said his father was 'quick to realise that it was not enough to proclaim the glories of the Alpine sun in mid-winter, or to advertise the joys of winter sports'. He wrote,

The kind of clientele which he hoped to attract had an ingrained prejudice against anything which savoured of the personally conducted tour. The stigma attached to the Lunn tripper had to be exorcised before he could hope to entice the aristocracy from the Riviera and the 'mupples' from England. It is, of course, appearances which count, not facts – *the problem was to devise some means whereby people could travel Lunn without appearing to travel Lunn.*

My father therefore enlisted the co-operation of a Harrow master, Mr John Stogdon, and offered him a capitation fee if he would sign a letter to Etonians and Harrovians announcing the good news that Doctor Henry S. Lunn had discovered a valley called Adelboden, which was ideal for winter sports. The response was immediate.

The proprietor of the Grand Hotel at Adelboden had opened his hotel with immense misgivings, but the Grand and another hotel were filled to overflowing at Christmas, and the numbers booked for the year exceeded 440. Before many years had passed, Dr Lunn's firm had sent more than 5,000 clients to the Alps every winter, and had contracts with over 30 hotels.

The success of the 'Etonian and Harrovian parties' led to the foundation of the Public Schools Alpine Sports Club (PSASC). The principal object was to reserve the *exclusive* use of certain hotels for members of the Club ... The principal qualification for the Club was a public school or university education.

Certain other clearly defined qualifications were accepted. The rules were strictly adhered to, and many would-be clients were unable to book rooms during the Club season. Clients were booked by *Alpine Sports Ltd*, which my father founded mainly in order to spare his select winter clientele the ignominy of 'Lunn's Tours' labels on their luggage (*which would have been considered very 'non-U' – non-upper class*). The problem of travelling Lunn without appearing to travel Lunn had been solved.

The success of the Club was immediate and its influence in popularising winter sports was immense. Many of the most famous of Alpine centres were first opened in winter under the auspices of the Club. The complete list of centres which were either first opened by the Club, or in some cases popularised by the Club after an unsuccessful attempt to open on their own, were Adelboden, Ballaigues, Beatenberg, Campfer, Celerina, Kandersteg, Klosters, Lenzerheide, Maloja, Montana, Morgins, Mürren, Sils-Maria, Pontresina and Wengen ...

It was under the auspices of the Club that the world's senior challenge cups for downhill and slalom racing were inaugurated ... The PSASC gave formal expression to a principle which, in the 90s, had made of hotels such as the Monte Rosa at Zermatt a closed preserve for those who visited Switzerland to climb Swiss mountains by day, and to dine with congenial Englishmen at night. The uncongenial were quietly frozen out.

Indeed, Sir Martin Conway, a former President of the Alpine Club, made this point at a dinner of the PSASC: 'In the olden days,' he said, 'they only went to the Alps in the summer, and one of the great charms was the character of the people by whom they were surrounded and the companionships which they made year by year. But a great change came. The old comradeship of the hotels was rendered impossible, the old habitués were swamped and drowned in the multitude ...'

The Club acted on the principle that nobody had any grievance if they were kept awake before midnight. But members had a just grievance if they were woken up in the early hours by the noisily inebriate. In England, social extinction was, and perhaps still is, expressed in the statement 'he had to resign his clubs' and unruly members of the PSASC never failed to respond to the threat of expulsion.

Although Arnold Lunn's son Peter – a great racer in his day – described his grandfather's club as 'blatantly snobbish', he understood that it played a 'more important role in the early development of downhill and slalom racing than any other'.

But times were changing and, increasingly, Henry Lunn found himself being left behind in a rapidly disappearing age. As the novelist L.P. Hartley famously put it in his novel *The Go Between*, 'The past is a foreign country. They do things differently there.'

Arnold Lunn put it like this:

> The flight from form had begun, and the England of the 20s was very different from the England in which the PSASC had been founded. The very name, with its emphasis on the public schools, thought an asset in the early days ... was a liability when our rivals began to assert that adults were disciplined like public schoolboys at Club hotels ... The Club, which might have survived these changes in fashion, was killed by the financial crisis of 1931. The Chancellor of the Exchequer urged Englishmen to stay at home in order to save the pound. The consequent collapse of the winter sport traffic between Great Britain and Switzerland not only killed the Club (having survived the short period when I was chairman of the company), but also resulted in the transference of my father's firm to other proprietors.

Later, he would add, 'I was so firmly imbued with the belief that Lunn was a dirty four-letter word that my father's name does not occur in my book *A History of Ski-ing*, and my name is discreetly omitted from the long chapter on the Kandahar Ski Club.'

Henry Lunn was eventually knighted by the King and decorated by the Kaiser for promoting Anglo-German relations, an irony not lost on his son. 'The Club which he founded,' said Arnold Lunn,

> owed its success to the implicit guarantee that its members would be protected against the risk of meeting Germans in Swiss hotels. In the preliminary advertisement of Mürren, just before it was opened in winter, he wrote: 'Mürren has always been a favourite with English visitors, and has never been invaded by our Teutonic cousins in summer.'

'My father,' said Lunn, pointedly,

> worked for Anglo-German friendship not because he
> liked Germans but because he disliked war. Anglo-
> German tension rose sharply in the years before the
> First World War, and I remember a furious telegram
> from the Club Committee at Lenzerheide provoked by
> the fact that the proprietor of the hotel had actually
> dared let two bedrooms to Germans during the Club
> season. My father was forced to make a special journey
> to Lenzerheide to placate the indignant members.

Arnold Lunn describes an intriguing incident involving his father
(a fanatical Liberal) and the wife of Herbert Asquith, the British
Prime Minister of the day. 'She was a frequent visitor to Mürren,'
he wrote, 'and I remember once intruding into a room where my
father and Mrs Asquith seemed to be engaged in a vivacious
argument.' (Both father and son enjoyed a fight, observes Elisabeth
Hussey, Arnold Lunn's assistant editor for many years.)

> At that time Mrs Asquith was very interested in
> classical dancing, and had offered to perform a *pas
> seul* in the Palace ballroom. My father insisted that this
> was quite inconsistent with the dignity of her position
> as the wife of the Premier. He warned her that a *pas
> seul* in the best classical manner would be represented
> as a cabaret turn by her enemies and might have
> disastrous effect on the fortunes of the Liberal Party.

'Mrs Asquith was very nettled,' Lunn's father told him. 'She told
me that she had successfully defied convention all her life, and
that nobody had ever prevented her doing what she had set her
heart on doing.'

Sir Henry, apparently, had responded by saying, 'Perhaps not in
England – but I'm Prime Minister of Mürren!'

Chapter 4

British Winters Were Whiter Then

You adjust your body for a rapid slide, but your
ski stick motionless, and over you go upon your face.
Then you stop upon the level, and have just time to
say 'what a lovely view this is' when you find
yourself standing on your two shoulder blades with
your ski tied tightly round your neck.

Although the Ski Club of Great Britain was officially launched in May 1903, it already, in a sense, had some history. Those 'founding fathers' hadn't just taken up the sport overnight, as it were. Some had been at it for a while. And so, even though the first records of the club were not published until 1905, in the very first *Ski Club of Great Britain Year Book* there were already accounts of earlier adventures available to record on its pages. In those days, the fashion was not to use Christian names, but initials – a practice that gave us the likes of W.H. Auden, W.B. Yeats and G.K. Chesterton.

Arnold Lunn made an early attempt to join the club – as early as 1905, when he was a lad of 17 – but was turned down. 'It was not on social grounds, however,' says his son Peter.

My father was at Harrow and I do not think they knew about my grandfather's very humble origins. They feared my father would use his membership to promote the family travel business. He was perhaps unduly proud of being the only person who had ever been blackballed by the Ski Club of Great Britain.

Lunn decided to form his own club – the Alpine Ski Club – in 1908, the year he climbed the Matterhorn, while he was still at Oxford. W.R. Rickmers, a founder member of the Ski Club of Great Britain, became an honorary member, saying the new club was 'a necessity to form a counterweight to those rather conceited Ski Club of Great Britain people'. Those 'conceited' people finally allowed Lunn to join in 1910 – the year his father Henry was knighted for 'services to Anglo-German relations'.

Lunn had also been blackballed from the Alpine Club. 'I can recall the terrible shock the news was to him when it came,' says Peter Lunn. He would not be allowed to enter the Alpine Club's doors until 1937. Once elected, he congratulated the club on 'opening the stable door once the horse was in'.

Even before the turn of the century, skiing was beginning to grip the imagination of those of independent means. One of the first Englishmen to attempt a major excursion 'on ski' was Sir Arthur Conan Doyle, who had escorted his wife to a Swiss sanatorium in the hope that the Swiss climate would help her recover from tuberculosis. In March 1894, he joined a group which struggled over the Mayenfelder Furka pass from Davos to Arosa, the subject of an amusing feature in *Strand* magazine. He wrote,

> Ski are the most capricious things on earth. You adjust your body for a rapid slide, but your ski stick motionless, and over you go upon your face. Then you stop upon the level, and have just time to say 'what a lovely view this is' when you find yourself standing on your two shoulder blades with your ski tied tightly round your neck.

Intriguingly, it seems it was Henry Lunn who provided the

inspiration and location for the 'death' of Conan Doyle's world-famous detective, Sherlock Holmes. Arnold Lunn tells the story in the 1968 *Year Book*:

> Conan Doyle was far from content with having created in Sherlock Holmes a detective whose relation to all other detectives of fiction is comparable to the relation of Toscanini to all other conductors. He was ambitious to be taken seriously as a great novelist, but his novels in which Holmes did not figure were competent but no more, and received rather lukewarm reviews.
>
> In the course of a mountain walk at Grindelwald with my father, he remarked that until he ceased writing detective stories, nobody would take him seriously as a novelist, and that he therefore proposed to kill Holmes, but he had not yet made up his mind where to kill him. My father, who wanted to do a good turn to the Oberland, immediately suggested the Reichenbach Falls, a suggestion which Conan Doyle adopted with enthusiasm.

Had Holmes rather than Conan Doyle been the skier, one cannot help thinking he might have produced something quite macabre in the way of anecdotes, rather like the redoubtable Olive Hockin's account of her 'Day's Expedition from London'. She wrote,

> I gradually made my way along the length of the ridge, the highest point of which, where the old gallows still stands, is just over 1,000 feet – a wild and lonely part, with no living creature in sight. I left the high land somewhere above Pilot Hill ... and the seven or eight mile tramp along the frozen road, as the sun went down in a blaze of gold, was not the least enjoyable part of the day.

One of the earliest accounts of a ski tour in Great Britain was a description of an excursion to Durham and Northumberland (1901–1902) by G.F. Lucas, who encountered an early version of bumps – though not formed, of course, in the now time-honoured way by the passage of hundreds of skiers digging and carving the snow while turning. (These are better known as moguls, a word probably derived from the Swiss and Vorarlberg dialect for molehill: *Mögeli.*) Lucas writes,

> It was reported to us that ski were generally used by the shepherds in that part of the country some 50 years ago, but we were unable to verify that statement. The smooth descent was pleasantly varied by large bumps, which brought some of us to grief, until the proper method of negotiating them was discovered.

In *Possibilities Of North Wales*, H.W. Chubb and C.R. Wingfield are in exuberant mood:

> When your innkeeper tells you on a warm summer day that snow lies for four winter months around his house, and that snow-ploughs are no good to clear the road because it is filled up level with the high stone walls on each side, *then jumps the heart of the ski-runner!*
>
> The summer aspect of North Wales is known to humanity at large, but its winter dress only to residents and to those climbers who rejoice in ice-coated rockwork, chimnies [sic] and arêtes. These ... do not attract the man on ski.
>
> On the north side of Lyn Ogwen ... is a mountain named Carnedd Llewelyn, second only in height to the loftiest point of Snowdon. Ski, perhaps, might be of service for some parts of the ascent ... but no beginner should leave the true route to explore on the right-hand side; if he does so, a precipice ... doubtless overhung with a snow cornice in winter, will end his days.

Intriguingly, the word *line* – meaning a good ski route down a mountain – was, apparently, already in use. 'Speaking broadly,' say Messrs Chubb and Wingfield, 'Capel Curig is not good for ski, and nothing beyond a few isolated lines can be looked for.'

This is by no means the first time that one begins to realise that some of the skiing parlance and concepts we tend to regard as 'modern' have, in fact, been around for a century or more.

Describing a visit to Derbyshire in November, 1904, E. Wroughton wrote,

> The heavy snowstorms that swept over the north of England during the later end of November ... gave the Ski Club of Great Britain its first opportunity of arranging a tour at home ... It was unfortunate that Mr Wingfield and myself were the only two members able to attend ... The sullen roar of some blasting operations in the vicinity reminded us vividly of the sound of an avalanche, and for a moment we thought it possible that the noise was to be accounted for by such an occurrence.

Young Arnold Lunn, who would dramatically refine the concept of slalom skiing and dominate British ski racing for years to come, was still a teenager, but he would surely have been intrigued with Wroughton's description of some typical Derbyshire terrain, involving not slalom gates, but those you might find in a farmyard.

Wroughton recalled,

> We covered between 17 and 18 miles each day. Trying to shoot through a half-opened gate when going at good speed not only tested nerves and skill, but introduced a spirit of friendly rivalry, which added to the excitement of the run. On Eldon Hill, we kept a good look-out for disused mining shafts.
>
> Two or three miles along the road from Smalldale, mostly up hill, brought us to the village of Peak Forest, where we enjoyed light lunch, and submitted to a searching cross-examination from the villagers. *Everywhere we went, we created a sensation.* Our boots, rucksacks and ski, particularly the latter, obtained a full share of the most flattering attention.

Even skiers' present-day delight in 'face-shots' (when powder snow billows into your face) was familiar to early club members, including E. Wroughton, who wrote, 'The fog had lifted in the valley, and on two occasions we were able to let ourselves go, and enjoyed *the satisfaction of feeling the snow spurting around us and sprinkling our faces.'*

Meanwhile, in 'An Expedition To Buxton', readers of the *Year Book* were fascinated to read the following:

> Bitter experience as golfers had led us to the impression that there were many precipitous gradients on the links, and so we went that way, causing no small stir in the streets ... Soon the golf links were reached, and to our disgust, the mountains had turned into mere molehills. However, one of the party asserted that he knew of a hill, and sure enough he disappeared very suddenly. He had merely been bunkered. We at last came to a fairly steep place, and began to practice [sic] there. It was a fearful and wonderful sight, for a big storm was raging and the lightning flashes bore cruel testimony of the erratic manner of our going by lighting up the surrounding gloom and throwing into deep relief the many holes we made.
>
> The next morning was beautiful, and a hard frost had set in. Mr Harrison, the Club snow agent, very kindly directed us to an adjacent hill, on which we should find some good skiing. Then we heard a gasping and panting, and lo and behold! A man appeared with a very large camera. He had followed our tracks ... Such persistency was not to be denied, so after regaling ourselves of some excellent tea, we were photographed. Such is fame ... A blizzard of extraordinary fury temporarily blotted out the hills. But we were on ski, so what did it matter what the weather did?

Accompanying members of the fledgling Ski Club in the Scottish Highlands the following February, Wroughton soon found himself enjoying 'A Fortnight in the Cairngorms'. Again, the impact on the local populace was remarkable. 'Everywhere we went,' he wrote, 'foresters, keepers, gillies, farmers, and shepherds applauded the means of locomotion and expressed the wish that they had learned the art.' There was also clear evidence that, even then, ski runners enjoyed 'getting air' as we say today when skiers and snowboarders are airborne. 'What with dodging trees and bounding off hillocks,' he wrote, '(sometimes one's ski would not touch the ground for a space of 4ft or 5ft) we were thoroughly enlivened.'

A further and even more colourful example of getting airborne is contained in *Jumping On Tour. Its Educational Value*, by Hassa Horn (translated from the Norwegian):

> Up in the Norwegian hills, on clearings and on slippery declivities, the jumper's track is most frequently to be found. Here he has the finest slopes, to be taken at headlong speed, amidst tree and bush, with a rich variation of stumps and holes, dips and rises, over which he can perform the most different kind of jumps, and really 'air' himself thoroughly! ... Every considerable inequality in the ground is pressed into service. Over knolls and stumps, over heaps of stones and even dung-hills the take-off is to be found ... That more accidents do not happen seems often incredible; but that only bears out the proverb that fortune favours the bold – a truth which is specially applicable to all ski-runners.

The early Ski Club pioneers certainly lived a little dangerously. In an article entitled 'Around Sedbergh', G.H. Todd wrote proudly, 'We always make it a point of honour not to take off our skis, and this necessitated climbing walls, one of them surmounted by barbed wire, which does not provide a comfortable seat!'

Even more daring is this bizarre account of 'Near Manchester' by W.D. Worthington:

> We indulged in some skiing behind a motor and went along the road at a very merry pace ... One or two of us had some horrid tumbles, although nothing worse, luckily, than a shaking. It is essential ... not to be tied on in anyway, as it was most difficult to stop it quickly

in the slippery snow should one fall ... Still, I can cordially recommend it to those who are fortunate enough to have snow and a motor at the same time ... Already the days are drawing in, and it is not so long before we shall be overhauling the good old ash again.

Chapter 5

THE CONTINENT
BECKONS

*We found ablutions somewhat difficult as the
daughters of the house insisted on helping us.*

Although there were endless skiing permutations and
opportunities in Great Britain – the country enshrined in the name
of the club – ski-runners were beginning to cast a longing gaze at
sturdier mountain ranges, which they were already familiar with
through the exploits of generations of British climbers.

Writing about a 'Club Expedition to the Jotunheim, Norway,
at Easter 1905' (the first official overseas tour), the club's most
colourful founder member, E.C. Richardson, wrote with a hint of
hubris, 'The danger from avalanches is practically nil, and the
services of a guide are hardly necessary. As a matter of fact we
did have a guide, but he is not much of a ski-runner, and seemed
more familiar with the summer than with the winter aspect of
the country.'

By now, Richardson was experimenting with protective eye-
wear. 'I used a simple piece of leather with a couple of apertures in
it,' he wrote. 'I was not at all troubled with snow blindness, and
greatly prefer this arrangement to any smoked spectacles.'

Richardson had formed the opinion that ski-jumping and ski-touring were 'interdependent branches of the sport, and that it is almost impossible to be a first-class man in the woods or on the mountain sides without at the same time being a fairly useful jumper'.

It was Richardson who would later write of the Norwegians,

> In the past, it has been my good fortune to run into quite a number of really good Norwegian runners. Not a single one of them ever seemed to bother his head about *Open Christianias*, or *Closed Christianias*, or *Stem Christianias*, or *Lifted Stems*, or any of the long list of manoeuvres which seem to have been invented of late to plague the beginner. Their general idea seemed to be rather to get over the ground quickly and not to bother a bit about any particular 'style'.
>
> When they turned, which was, with them, rarely necessary, they always seemed to me to do it with a sort of body swing, and not by any noticeable placing of the ski in this position or in that. The body led the way, and the ski always seemed to follow quite naturally, and almost of their own accord, no matter what position they happened to be in at the time. What one noticed about them more than anything else was their extraordinary cat-like agility and general looseness and springiness. Let the ground or snow be what it might, they were always there and ready for it.
>
> The Norwegians as a whole are a loose-shouldered, loose-kneed race, rather like ourselves. The ordinary run of Germans and Swiss are stiffer and more clumsy.

Arnold Lunn had an explanation for this, which, not for the first time, rather took the wind out of Richardson's sails:

> This is an accurate description of the unconscious ease with which an expert performed a difficult manoeuvre. In every sport, unconscious ease, and apparent absence of effort, is the result of long and arduous practice. An expert performs unconsciously and without taking

thought of the movements which, as a beginner, he had to analyse and think out. Mr Richardson here confuses cause and effect. An expert Norwegian does not 'bother about style' because his style has become unconscious.

Even in these early days, there was endless discussion about technique. The Davos English Ski Club had decided, for example, that

> there can be no doubt that on very steep, wooded ground, where straight running is impossible, the man who sits on his stick will come down faster than the man who runs curves.
>
> Accordingly, where all *must* stick-ride the good runner is severely handicapped, for a duffer can go as fast as he. We consider that good, level running is one of the most difficult branches of the sport. To keep going at the rate of seven miles an hour on the level requires a knowledge of the one-two-three shove action which very few continental runners possess.

V. Caulfeild was soon explaining to readers the mysteries of 'How to Learn to Run Without Using the Stick;

> A large majority of English ski-runners undoubtedly still look upon the stick as an indispensable aid when running downhill ... It is perfectly possible for anyone of average physical endowments to learn ... how to run easily and safely, on any sort of ground and snow, without ever using the stick at all. This sort of running does not necessarily even call for more nerve or dash ... though it certainly requires more skill and judgement ... Without being controversial, it is safe to say that no one who has not tried the no-stick plan, has ever experienced a quarter of the pleasure of ski-running.

Meanwhile, E.C. Richardson's perhaps equally opinionated brother, C.W., was reporting (also from Davos): 'The Schia Tobel

... is a gully filled with snow ... one goes down this from side to side, like a marble in a rain-pipe.' There follows a quaint but strangely naïve remark about avalanches on the Jakobshorn: 'Good weather is absolutely essential, as some of the ground near the top holds avalanches.' As if avalanches don't happen in good weather!

The British press has long had a reputation for 'never letting the facts spoil a good story'. But I must confess, I was surprised – perhaps a little shocked – to discover that they were at it a century ago. Under the heading 'Avalanche Accidents', we read that

> shortly after the Andermatt accident Major Bayly was interviewed by a reporter from one of our leading daily papers, who refused to be guided by the true facts of the case and, contrary to Major Bayly's express desire, wired home a sensational and absurd version of his own. Major Bayly subsequently sent a correct account of what happened to the journal in question, but this was not published.

In 1908, H. Archer Thomson described in some detail an extraordinary Ski Club visit to Montenegro:

> It nearly fell through owing to the annexation of Bosnia and Herzegovina by Austria. Troops were massed on both sides of the frontier. We were summoned to an interview by the Minister for War who, satisfied that we were English, welcomed us cordially.
>
> The Montenegrin is a magnificent fellow, ranging up to 6 feet 6 inches and more in height. He wears a picturesque costume of crimson, blue and white, and always carries loaded weapons. We enquired eagerly about snow conditions in the interior from wayfarers coming from that direction. One stated that the north wind had blown all the snow away, while another positively assured us it was lying to the depth of at least 200 metres!
>
> We put up in a wayside 'han' [a wooden shanty of which the ground floor is occupied by cattle]. *We*

found ablutions somewhat difficult as the daughters of the house insisted on helping us; sponges were a delight to them, and tooth brushes a mystery.

The following night, encountering difficult terrain, the party was forced to sleep outdoors.

We were led into a gorge with steep banks, covered partly with ice and partly with deep snow, into which we sank to our thighs; we plunged on till midnight, and then the moon set. It was impossible to proceed in the darkness, so we had to make a night of it. A strenuous hour followed, Adlercron burrowing a hole of sufficient size in the snow, while Harmer and I foraged for firewood, attacking dead trees with our ski poles. Aldecron conceived the brilliant idea of slicing up a ski so as to get dry wood, and nobly commenced operations on his own. Our hopes rose and fell as the flame blazed and died down, but, feeding it stick by stick, we triumphed at last. In turn we crawled out of our hole and did exercises to prevent frost bite. The silence of the night was only disturbed by the occasional howl of a wolf.

Other parts of Switzerland were now being explored and T. Smythe-Hughes reported, 'Adelboden is comparatively easily approached, being only about 26 hours from London,' adding darkly, 'Confirmed invalids are not catered for in the village.' And, reporting on a visit to St Moritz, J. Dodgshon and C.R. Wingfield noted, 'The tours mentioned are easy ones round St Moritz, and are suitable for beginners and ladies.'

Austria, it seems, did not meet with quite such approval. W.R. Rickmers, another of the club's founder members, observed in a feature entitled 'The Eastern Alps and the Black Forest', 'Unless the adventurous Englishman be a good runner, capable of living the strenuous life, and surviving strange though sound food, the Arlberg cannot as yet be recommended for a long stay.' On the plus side, however, Rickmers noted that on the Arlberg ... the traveller ... will find it difficult to spend more than 6s [30 pence] per day unless the wine of the country has special attractions for him ... The expenses of a fortnight's holiday can be screwed down from a liberal margin of £17 to close upon £14. Less than two weeks are not worth one's while if one is obliged to economise, for the long distance tells rather heavily upon the exchequer.

However, there is a surprising note on Kitzbühel, which, because of its low altitude, sometimes struggles for snow: 'Kitzbühel,' writes Rickmers, 'has more snow than any place I know.'

As well as appearing in the Ski Club's *Year Book*, accounts of ski excursions were sometimes 'read before the club' by those taking part. In 1905, Harry W. Chubb (a Christian name which for once we are made aware of) was telling members, 'The art of ski-running as a sport is new, and, like the violin, can only be properly learnt in youth. As a new experience for a man over 35, it can be nothing more than a pleasant exercise, resulting chiefly in the discovery of certain dormant muscles.'

Mr Chubb seems to be a military man. He also writes eloquently of what later generations would recognise as 'tree skiing'. 'Few things are more effective than a company of men passing through a sloping wood. They glide rapidly in extended order, through the close-set pines, swerving and swaying to clear each obstacle, and disappear as quickly as the ghost in the first scene of *Hamlet*.'

But troops on skis did not always conjure up such a poetic scene, as this report from Austria shows:

> From Birgitz Alp the route taken by the Innsbruck garrison during their winter march could be seen. There were ... five or six bad cases of frostbite, and not only did the men have to carry machine guns and saddlery, but they were obliged more or less to carry the mules as well.

Ski Club 'readings' were usually greeted with 'noises off'. At the first annual Club Dinner in 1904, Captain F.J. Jackson, of the Jackson–Harmsworth Polar Expedition announced, 'If the late

Thibetan [sic] expedition had been furnished with ski, their difficulties would have been reduced considerably. [Hear, hear!] The unfortunate men ... were often up to their waists in snow; with ski those tiresome marches would have been as nothing at all ...'

'In conclusion,' said the report, 'Captain Jackson wished the Club every success in advancing the interests of a most useful sport. Ski-running was a vigorous, wholesome and manly exercise, and could only prove of benefit to the people who indulged in it. [Applause.]'

Skiing within the confines of the United Kingdom, of course, meant that ski-runners were never in much danger from wild animals. In more remote regions of Europe, however, there were wolves to consider. In 'A Tour in Norway and Sweden', Frank Hedges Butler wrote, 'Our idea was to shoot bears and wolves, but we only succeeded in capturing one wolf, which the Lap guide knocked on the head with a stick close to our hut on the borders of Russian Finland.'

And in his account of skiing in The Kebnekaise, Lapland, J.H.W. Fulton wrote, 'I had a .32 Colt automatic pistol in case any wolf, wolverine or fox was foolish enough to come within range.'

High adventure indeed!

There is another insight into the Lappish culture in 'Through Lapland with Skis and Reindeer':

> It appears that the Lapps, owing to the difficulty of getting to and fro, only go to church twice a year, once in winter (on the first Sunday in December) and once at Easter; and consequently all those ceremonies which require ecclesiastical sanction can only be performed on these two occasions. The result is that weddings, christenings, confirmations and burials have all to be saved up for these occasions.

Chapter 6

HALCYON DAYS

*Could it not be made a point of etiquette that all
persons would be expected to fill up holes made by
falling on practice grounds? If this were done, the
latter places would not be rendered unfit for ski-ing
after about one hour's practice ... and many
unpleasant falls would be avoided.*

'Will contributors kindly write proper names in capital letters, and
so save the Editor a deal of worry?'

The correspondence columns and feature articles of the *Ski
Club of Great Britain's Year Book* continued to flow – as usual with
more answers than questions.

G.J.G. – We think you were quite right to make your
will before going on the mountain with him. He is a
dangerous fellow.

G.A.N. – Had you made a Christiania swing you would
have avoided the bush. The only way to get out was to
shout for help.

K.R.S. – A broken binding that doesn't hold the foot adds a sense of glorious uncertainty to a run.

H.A.T. – As he eats only cheese, you would be quite safe in placing your lunch in his rucksack.

And, under 'Tips and Dodges', members read of the dangers of Yorkshire and Derbyshire potholes:

A correspondent writes to warn ski-runners against inadvertently falling into these, which in winter are often corniced, or even completely covered. Sometimes the holes are only a few feet wide, but many nevertheless attain a length of fifty feet, and a depth of two or three hundred ... After a heavy snowfall, enquiries should be made locally as to the dangerous areas.

Among the 'Letters to the Editor' was this from Walter Larden in Adelboden, Switzerland, concerning the Alpine distress signal:

Sir,

Lately a man who was with me and another, high up, had a bad accident and nearly killed himself ... My 'Alpine distress signal' failed to bring to our help another party; I found that they did not know what it meant. May I suggest that, by means of clearly printed notices, posted in hotels, club-rooms, etc., all skiers should be made aware of this recognised signal and of the proper answer, 'We see you and will help'?

The recognised Alpine signal of distress consists of any signal (as waving, whistling, shouting, showing a light, etc.) repeated six times ... being repeated after a distinct pause, until answered.

The *Year Book* returns to this subject in 1910, with a fuller description of the procedure in 'Alpine Signals of Distress', including day-time and night-time signals. To our ears it seems like pure Monty Python. But at the time, no doubt such signals served their purpose:

Optical signals By Day. Wave six times a minute, describing a semi-circle away from the sun, any object whatsoever, preferably a rag or a garment tied to a stick. Then pause a minute and repeat.

By Night. Display a light (lantern, fire &c) six times a minute. Pause a minute and repeat. Acoustic signals: Repeat a short, shrill cry six times a minute, then pause a minute and repeat.

The reply to a signal of distress is given by means of an optical or acoustic signal, repeated three times a minute and followed by a minute's pause.

The subject cropped up yet again the following year in *Ski Notes and Queries*, a new quarterly publication to keep members up to date throughout the year. In a reply to H. Gandy about the advisability of carrying a whistle on tour, 'for signalling when the party is broken up', the editor replied,

A jodel [sic] carries further than anything, but we (fortunately?) cannot all jodel. I have tried a powerful 'Rouser' whistle, warranted to kill a taxi at 200 yards, but found it very feeble and inefficient among the mountains. The same applies to siren whistles. Certainly the leader of every high tour, where fog or snow are possible, should have a method and code of signalling. It has been suggested that a little horn with a low pitch would carry further than anything. I will try to find where such things can be got, unless some member can inform us.

G.H.F. was kind enough to respond, 'Signalling horns, such as are used on railways, with a reed of low pitch, weight 2½ ozs, length 6½ inches, price 5/6, can be obtained from Messrs Besson, 198, Euston Road, London N.W. They seem likely to be far more useful than a whistle;

But W.E.H., it seems, was the man for the job:

I am sending two horns, such as are used by the Valaisian goat-herds. The sound, although hardly more musical than the average British jodel, carries a tremendously long way. When you have examined them, please send them back, because I sometimes return with a feeling of relief to their harmony after listening to the antics of our local Band, therefore they are to me most precious.

Unfortunately the horns never arrived. 'Alas,' quoth the editor, 'they have never reached us.'

Meanwhile, distress signals of an altogether different nature were raised in this reader's letter:

Sir,

Could it not be made a point of etiquette that all persons would be expected to fill up holes made by falling on practice grounds? If this were done, the latter places would not be rendered unfit for ski-ing after about one hour's practice, as they are at present, and many unpleasant falls would be avoided.

Yours truly,

Edward J. Dobson

Skiing was becoming more and more popular around the globe. In 1906, Ski Club members were rewarded with a fascinating Club Tour of Sweden. It was organised at the end of May when, of course, the mountains would have already been enjoying generous daylight hours. In a 'paper' read by E.C. Richardson to members on their return, the great man reported, 'We had for some time the advantage of the company of Captain Müller, the well-known African explorer, who is just as doughty a man on the snow as he is on the sand.' He would doubtless have been able to put their minds at rest about a slightly alarming incident when 'the slumbers of some of us were disturbed by certain weird noises, which we subsequently discovered proceeded from a cow who shared the same establishment as ourselves.'

In Åre, Dr Hoek (the early racer) and 'the professor' spent nearly half an hour looking for the hut on the summit before they discovered that they were standing on top of it. It was completely buried in snow.

C.H. Kerry, writing from Sydney on July 27, 1907, quoted from an inspirational article entitled 'Across the Alps in New South Wales',

> Free-wheeling down a mountain on a bolting bicycle is exciting; motoring at a hundred miles an hour ... has its own peculiar sensations; ballooning is by no means tame; and riding on the front of a flying express locomotive makes the wind roar in your ears and puts a tingle in your blood. There's a spice of real danger in these pastimes. I've tried them all; but, without hesitation, I place ski-running over a snowbank that drops away at the rate of one in two and a half, far before the best of them.

Meanwhile, in the same year, there was 'good news from India'. Members were told,

> The new head of the telegraph department in Kashmir intends to introduce ski for the purpose of keeping the line open between Srinagar and Gilgit. The line is some 250 miles long, and crosses two passes of 12,000 feet and 13,500 feet. In the last 15 years, over 200 lives have been lost through avalanches.
>
> Hitherto, the rate of progress through the snow on foot has been about six miles a day, but it is anticipated that the greatly increased speed which will be obtainable on ski will, in future, lessen the risk.

Only three years earlier, in 1903 – the very year the Ski Club of Great Britain was formed – Lord Kitchener had been assessing the use of skis and snowshoes for military purposes in the Himalayas. It was premature. In 1905, Kitchener pronounced: 'As regards the present frontier of India there is little probability that ski will be of use.'

One of the most enthralling and descriptive accounts of a skiing adventure comes from Olive Hockin – a brave woman who, at the Club Meet at Gstaad, 'pluckily went over the jump, covered 25 feet, and stood'. She had obviously earned the right to be allowed to grace the pages of the *Year Book* with the following graphic account of 'Racing a Mountain Mist on Ski'.

My companion consulted his aneroid and noted the height, in order that, should we be compelled by mist to return by this route, we might ... have some idea when to alter our general course; and he also took careful compass observations of St Cristof [sic], the summit and St Anton. Thrilling at the prospect of the glorious glissade of 3,000 feet ... we were tightening our straps and adjusting our gloves before taking the plunge, when suddenly we found ourselves blotted out from each other. A cloud had descended on us vertically. Our foiled enemy [the mist] had called an ally to his assistance. We were cut off from any connection with the world below ... I began to feel really scared ...

It was now getting dark and I personally had quite given up all hope of being able to reach the valley that night, and was occupied solely by devising the best methods of warding off frost-bite and such horrors. The howling wind swept through us, and the driven snow crystals stung like sparks of fire as they beat upon our faces ... My companion decided that we must dig a hole in the snow, which was in some places quite ten feet deep ... It was absolutely necessary, whatever the risk, to get to a less-exposed spot ... My companion produced a large, flowing, windproof coat. He is renowned for his capability in the commissariat line, but on this occasion, his sack, usually a veritable Pandora's box in the way of victuals, failed him.

Among the debris at the bottom we found half a grimy roll, one gingerbread biscuit, one egg (worth its weight in gold, I thought) and joy! A small jagged piece of dusty chocolate. I – alas! – had absolutely nothing. The egg, which I thought so precious, he could not account for; he knew, however, that it must be this season's, for he had brought his sack out empty from England! He fondled it tenderly and sadly, grieving that was not like Caesar's wife (above suspicion) ... Every crumb was swallowed ...

Suddenly we espied a thin faint line in the snow and hailed it with joy. Here was a ski track ... which would surely lead us back to the valley. Alas for our hopes! It was merely a wind ridge. Presently we found another such line in the snow. This time it was unmistakably a ski track. Lovingly we followed it ...

But now the wind increased again; our enemy, balked of his prey, swooped down on us ... The next thing we saw was a star; I had never felt such an affection for a star before. Presently the lights of St Anton showed up some 2,000 feet below us ... a last run down the home slopes ... a clatter down an icy road, and we emerged into the full glare of the hotel lights and scented the delicious fragrance of cooked dinner!

Archer Thomson (of Montenegro fame) seems to have been involved with and enjoyed many of the Ski Club of Great Britain's earliest and most dramatic adventures. A year or two later, he is back with his latest exploits in 'Skiing in the Balkans'. He writes:

In North Albania, the 'Albanian Alps' rise to a considerable height and probably include a number of virgin peaks. As this part of the country is inhabited by wild tribesmen, a tour there should not be lightly undertaken, and introductions to the chiefs of the tribes should be obtained beforehand.

One must be prepared to put up in the peasants' cottages and sleep in the same room with husband, wife, sons, daughters (generally fairly numerous) and stray uncles, aunts, cousins or friends who may happen to drop in, and an occasional calf or two.

By 1908, in Montana, Switzerland, we are beginning to hear more of another prolific young writer:

Arnold Lunn ... who, though only 19 or 20, made some difficult expeditions last winter, notably one over the Grand St Bernard, and another to Villars via the Wildstrübel, Lenk, etc. Arnold Lunn is already an experienced winter mountaineer, but should not take the risks he does in visiting the mountains alone.

A year later, he would suffer a terrible accident. He escaped death by a narrow margin in a terrifying fall while climbing in Wales. It left him with an open wound in a leg now shorter than the remaining good one but, although it restricted his movements, he continued to climb and ski as best he could, and indeed managed some Herculean expeditions in spite of it. It also prevented him fighting in the Great War, which embarrassed him considerably, but possibly by almost losing his life in 1909, he might have saved it a few years later.

It had been a perfect day. He later wrote,

> The burnished silver of the sea melted into a golden haze. Light shadows cast by scudding clouds drifted across the blue and distant hills ... on that glorious afternoon I longed to spin out the joys of Cyfrwy, and I found a direct route from the top to the bottom of this wall, a steep but not very severe variation ... I was glad to be alone.
>
> I revelled in the freedom from the restraints of the rope, and from the need to synchronise my movements with the movements of my companions.
>
> I have never enjoyed rock-climbing more. I have never enjoyed rock-climbing since. But at least the hills gave me of their best, full measure and overflowing, in those last few golden moments before I fell ...
>
> There was no suggestion of danger. Suddenly the mountain seemed to sway and a quiver ran through the rocks. I clung for one brief moment of agony to the face of the cliff. And then suddenly a vast block ... separated itself from the face, heeled over on top of me, and carried me with it into space. I turned a somersault, struck the cliff some distance below ... and after crashing against the ridge two or three times, landed on a sloping ledge ... The thunder of the rocks falling through the 150 feet below ... showed how narrow had been my escape.

Lunn's friend C. Scott Lindsay, who was with him in Wales but not climbing at the time of the accident, revealed during the Golden Jubilee celebrations of the Alpine Ski Club in 1958 that Lunn had come very close to having his shattered leg amputated.

He wrote,

> At about 11 o'clock that night, when the rescue party were approaching Dolgelly with Arnold on a stretcher, I met them on the road, to find him conscious and lucid, though in great pain. His first words were: 'Do you think I shall ever climb again?'
>
> A grim sequel to that question soon pressed upon me at about 2 a.m. next morning. In the hotel at Dolgelly, in which we had improvised an operating table, Dick Warren, the surgeon who was to do his best for him, came to me with a grave expression on his face to say that in view of the dirty state of the wound, and of the time which had elapsed since the fall, it was strictly his duty to amputate the leg on account of the danger of gangrene. He could only fail to amputate if a third party, responsible to the family, were to ask him to do so.
>
> It did not take me long to reflect that Arnold without that leg would find life intolerable, and that the risk should be taken. Luck was with us both, but at 21, the decision was not easy to make.

When the Swiss newspapers announced that Arnold Lunn was dead, they were, of course, quickly told that such reports were greatly exaggerated. He began to ski again 15 months after the accident, but now found it easier to make Telemark turns with his left leg and stem-Christiania turns with the right one. Elisabeth Hussey believes it was probably this injury which 'turned his energies from ski racing to organising ski races'. If one cannot exactly call such a fearful injury a blessing in disguise, it was certainly a stroke of luck for the development of downhill racing.

Chapter 7

SCOTT AND SHACKLETON

Captain Scott, who, if all has gone well, should now be somewhere near the Pole, took nearly 100 pairs of ski with him to the Antarctic.

Captain Scott, a reluctant skier by all accounts – at least in terms of Polar Exploration – had finally accepted that he would have little chance of realising his dreams unless he took 'ski' to the South Pole.

'On previous Antarctic Expeditions, ski have not formed an important part of the equipment,' Ski Club members were told, 'and it would seem that neither Captain Scott nor Sir E. Shackleton are experts in their use. All ski-runners have felt that this has been a serious blunder, and all will be glad to hear that it is now to be rectified.'

It is 1910 and Dr Wigner of the Scottish Ski Club is writing,

Dr Bruce, our President, retires by his own wish in November. It was mainly owing to Dr Bruce that the Post Office authorities have provided ski for postmen in some Highland districts, an innovation which may

59

be of great benefit to those who live in the wilds. Dr Bruce has been the most popular of presidents, and we all wish him success in his expedition to the Antarctic.

Ah, the Antarctic. Yes, this is the era of Scott and Shackleton – both honorary members of the Ski Club of Great Britain – which produces the following editorial in its *Year Book*:

> Montenegro, Albania and Turkey were invaded three years ago by some of our members on ski ... It is remarkable how this snow-sport of the north has steadily pushed its way southward ... and has even gained a footing beneath the rays of the African sun. For several years past, it has even flourished in Algeria.
>
> Captain Scott, who, if all has gone well, should now be somewhere near the Pole, took nearly 100 pairs of ski with him to the Antarctic.

There was no hint yet of the war that would destroy the youth of Europe. The world, at least through the eyes of the West, still seemed a peaceful place, and for those who could afford it, skiing was becoming an exciting if elitist prospect.

Yet the recently formed North of England Ski Club reported that 'Skees' (as they were called locally) had been in practical use in that part of the country for scores of years, but they were described as being 'cumbrous, weighty, and dangerous withal' and unsuitable for, say, crossing the Cheviots.

The Cheviots were certainly not the Antarctic, but even they had their fascination. And there were other places, more distant, that winter travellers were investigating.

In 'Elia-Tau: A Ski Expedition in the Caucasus' (we believe that this is the first time ski have been used in the Caucasus – Ed.), F.A.M. Noelting wrote,

> In the Caucasus it is always safe to carry arms in a *visible* way, as the natives themselves are generally armed to their very teeth, and an unarmed man is looked upon as a beggar or something of that sort. My

guide, Isaac Bezoortanoff ... was a splendid Ingooshi, well over six feet, and he looked more like an oriental prince. His get-up consisted of a big karakul fur cap, a smart Tcherkessian coat with silver cartridges on the breast, a silver-plated belt from which hung a kindjal (small dagger) and a revolver ... baggy breeches, soft leather riding boots, and last but not least, a Mauser rifle completed his outfit.

And then there were the slopes at Finse, Norway, described thus by W.A. Cadby:

> One might be at the North Pole or on the moon. And this is April, when Swiss skiing places are smelly and snowless, when Christiania (Oslo) is sloppy and wet, and far-famed Holmenkollen a depressing sight because of the luncheon papers of the thousands who visited the jumping there in February – squalid ghosts that the disappearing snow has revealed to us.

Mürren, synonymous in so many people's minds with 'the birthplace of skiing' – or at least one of them – was, it seems, nothing of the sort. In 1910, it was just putting itself on the map of 'Ski-ing Resorts; New or Little-known to English People'.

> Mürren ... is said to be a very fine ski resort. The railway can be pressed into service; for instance, one can take the train to Wengern and make an expedition to the Aletsch Glacier; or else, having climbed to the Sefinenfrugge, one can enjoy a very fine run down to the Kienthal, returning to Kandersteg next day by rail. The Shildhorn [sic] (9,747 feet) is another good climb.

Could the following early version (in the *Ski Club Year Book*) of the German habit of hogging poolside seats by covering them with beach towels possibly be an example of the British sense of humour? Sadly, I fear not. I could be wrong, but it's too close for comfort and I rather think it must be genuine.

Herr H.B. Wieland complains of the behaviour of the English ladies and gentlemen who were at Bessheim last Easter. He says that 'with the naïve egoism of their race' they always occupied the best places by the fire, and that in the evening in silk blouses, stand-up collars, and stiff demeanour, they ruled the roost from the top of the table.

Much might doubtless be urged in extenuation of some at least of Herr Wieland's charges. There are people of all nationalities who think that a change of clothing is, in the interests of cleanliness, desirable after a hard day's skiing ... Herr Wieland, with a temerity bred of ignorance of the true character of our race, is striving to encroach upon the most sacred of our national privileges. Does he not know that it is the prerogative of the true Briton in all parts of the world to stand with outstretched legs and parted coat-tails in front of the fire? How dare he talk about naivety in such a connection? Egoism, stand-up collars, silk blouses, top of the table and so forth, we will give them up if he wishes, but the lion's share of the fire is our birth-right, and for that we shall fight to the bitter end.

War broke out four years later – not surprisingly, if episodes such as the one chronicled above can be taken seriously! It would be, without doubt, the end of an era. And, temporarily at least, the end of recreational skiing.

Chapter 8

PLEASE WIRE
IF POSSIBLE

Towards dawn I fell sound asleep, only to awake
when someone announced it to be 8.00 a.m. At first I
could not account for the darkness which surrounded
me, then suddenly remembered my head was in the
rucksack.

It is 1911 and there's a song in the air: the Ski Club song. It is first
sung on the occasion of the club's Summer Dinner at the Café
Imperial on May 31. The women are on song, but struggle a little
to make themselves heard – unfortunately, the status of women in
the club is not making huge strides. Under the latest 'Rules and
By-Laws &c',

> the total number of lady members shall not at any
> time exceed twenty per cent of the total membership.
> Ladies shall be entitled to participate in all the
> activities of the Club and to enjoy all its privileges
> subject to the restriction that their participation in
> Club Tours and Dinners shall be at the discretion of
> the [all male] Committee. Ladies shall pay the same
> subscription as men.

But are members – of both sexes – being a little too regimented, perhaps? One correspondent of the day obviously believes they are:

> Winter sports are tending to become over-organised. We are apt to forget that their end is health and holiday, that the sport is only a means to this end, not a profession or a life's work. There are certain bacteria which are ultimately stifled by the products of their own activity; it seems as if some of the older sports were beginning to suffer in the same way.

To deal with such healthy discussion, the club started its new publication, *Ski Notes and Queries*: '... hitherto, members received no account of the club's doings until the appearance of the *Year Book* the following winter. The new quarterly publication serves to keep them posted.' Meanwhile, there was an appeal from the editor of the faithful old *Year Book*: 'In order to facilitate the earlier appearance of the *Year Book* in future,' wrote the hard-pressed editor of the day, 'members are specially requested to send in their contribution early in the year, while their experiences are still fresh in their memory. Photographs should be of black or purple colour, not red or red-brown.' The unfortunate chap, predictably, is doomed to disappointment – as is his *Ski Notes and Queries* colleague: 'The editor of *SN & Q* records with regret that up to the present it has received very little support from the general membership of the club in the shape of contributions. He only hopes that he may be overwhelmed with manuscript about January next.'

Ten years later, nothing much has changed and Arnold Lunn, editor of the now renamed *British Ski Year Book* writes, 'So far we have received for the first two issues precisely three unsolicited contributions ... The alternative of not publishing a *Year Book* or writing the bulk of it ourselves is becoming tiresome.'

There are, however, always book reviews to fall back on. *With Ski In Norway and Lapland* by J.H.W. Fulton goes down well:

> There are no wearisome descriptions of scenery, no long and tedious accounts of ski tours, and there is no

grandiloquence about the lofty nature of the sport. Mr Fulton ... writes like a reserved but observant Englishman ... Nothing very showy seems to have been accomplished. The error of spelling rucksack *rück-sack* should be corrected in the next edition.

But, inevitably, there are some who think yet another publication is overdoing it: 'There exist now in Great Britain a quarterly review, an Annual, and at least four Club *Year Books* ... all dealing with winter sports, involving by multiplication a terrible waste of brain and money; can no sort of amalgamation produce one really first class Annual?' (This would, eventually, come to pass.)

September 1911 brought exciting reports of two evenings of entertainment featuring magic lanterns. 'An interesting Lantern Lecture,' readers were informed, 'on *Ski-running in the High Alps* and *Winter Climbing* was given by Professor F.F. Roget.' And, at a joint meeting of the Ski Club, the Swiss Alpine Club and the Alpine Ski Club, 'some wonderful natural-colour lantern-slides were shown by Mr H. Roger-Smith.'

Meanwhile, C.R. Wingfield appears anxious to improve the organisation of ski-running in Great Britain. He writes,

I should be much obliged if you would notify me by Thursday evening's post when there is enough snow for skiing, four to six inches required. Should deep snow fall on Friday, or a thaw set in after notifying good snow, PLEASE WIRE if possible. Expenses will be refunded at the end of each winter.

Encouraged by this, W.D. Worthington was soon rhapsodising about an excursion to the Peak District: 'We chartered the only conveyance and calmly ordered the driver to drive to snow; we smoked our pipes in peace.'

Meanwhile, in Switzerland, night skiing of a sort seems to have started in Arosa and Lenzerheide. 'Moonlight expeditions with Chinese lanterns proved a popular innovation,' readers learned. 'The coloured lights gliding swiftly through the night produced a weird effect, and occasional sudden extinctions told their own eloquent tale.'

In Gstaad, a lecture on 'A Winter Tour Through Montenegro and into Albania with Ski', illustrated by lantern-slides, was given by H. Archer Thomson. In the Riesengebirge, on the borders of Prussia and Bohemia, children were now compelled by law to learn to ski.

On the racing front, progress was obviously still slow: Cecil Hopkinson, the winner of the Roberts Cup in the 1910–11 season at Montana, took exactly 61 minutes to complete the 11½-kilometre course. Roughly seven miles an hour!

In his feature 'Ski Tours in Norway, Sweden and Lapland', Hedges Butler reassured readers thus about the cold weather: 'Cold is never felt as you practically become a reindeer, the whole reindeer coat worn coming over one's head. The Lapps carry spears to kill the wolves, and can run faster on their ski than the wolves in the snow.'

The following, one must reluctantly assume, was rather a good contemporary joke, with a fine illustration to match. Writing about 'The Club Tour in Vorarlberg', H. Archer Thomson, seizing his opportunity as editor of the *Year Book*, described the following delightful suggestion for a novel way to sharpen the edges of a ski.

> A rigorous censorship was exercised over the contents of each man's sack, and many articles, such as razors, brushes, etc. were disallowed and sent away by post ... Among other economies of weight we discovered a method of dispensing with the steel shavings which one usually carries for removing superfluous wax from ski; to wit, choose the man with the smallest stature (and preferably the most stubbly beard) ... lay him on the table, and proceed as shown in the accompanying illustration.

The picture shows the man's chin being used, like a Brillo pad, to smooth the edges of a ski.

There was other intriguing advice to be found in 'Tips and Dodges', concerning 'Under-garments made of Japanese Waterproof Paper':

> These under-garments are extremely warm, very light to wear and take much less room than woollen undergarments. It is claimed that it is by wearing them that the Japanese soldiers are able to stand their winters

better than their European comrades, and that during the Russo-Japanese war, the number of sick men was remarkably low in the Japanese army.

Readers were also treated to a useful early insight into the prospects of 'Winter Sport in North China and Japan':

> On being ordered to the North China command, with its arctic winter temperature, I looked forward to getting good winter sport, including ski-running. This hope was not destined to be fulfilled. The country from the coast to the walls of Pekin is so flat and so little above sea level that a very moderate tidal wave would place the whole surface under water ... It was distinctly aggravating to the mind of a ski-runner to find no elevation higher than a Chinaman's grave. Beyond Pekin there are hills which could be reached by train, where probably skiing would be possible, but the absence of accommodation for a white man would be a great difficulty, and only those members who joined the Club Tour in Montenegro could be expected to brave the horrors of a Chinese inn in the winter!

Closer to home, Mr W.R. Rickmers proposed 'a tour through Alpine Austria. The tour is for good runners only and, owing to the possibility of rough quarters at times, ladies are not invited!'

As skiers bade farewell to 1911, there was a rather heartbreaking letter from E.W.H., who was evidently struggling with the absurd anti-'carving' technique of the day. 'According to the usual instructions, one must never edge the ski,' he lamented. 'Well, if I try to keep the ski perfectly flat on anything like a steep slope, if the snow is at all hard, or even moderately firm, I go slithering sideways down the slope and cannot stop until I do edge the ski. What is the remedy for this?'

The remedy, of course, was to tell his instructors that they were talking tosh. Poor chap. He was born too soon. If only he could have persuaded his peers that he was right and they were wrong, it could have revolutionised the sport. Today, everyone tries to carve.

Early in the spring of 1912, a group of members suffered one of the most harrowing and – literally – chilling experiences ever recorded in any Ski Club of Great Britain publication. It was interspersed with moments of sheer farce, which somehow made a desperate situation almost bearable – at least to the reader. It appeared in the *British Ski Year Book* for 1920 under the innocuous title of 'A Winter's Night on the Tödi'. The author was Maxwell Finch. It starts harmlessly enough: 'A party of five, consisting of Obexer, Morgenthaler, Weber, Forster and Maxwell Finch, boarded the 1.30 p.m. train for Linthal.' But almost immediately came an event – seemingly trivial – which would have a disastrous effect on the success of the expedition. 'At Zürich-Enge,' Finch noted, 'the first stop of the train, we were reduced to four, since Forster left us to chase after a porter to whose care he had entrusted his skis and rücksack, and who, of course, failed to put in an appearance at the right moment.' Leaving Forster behind would have severe repercussions.

Finch continues his account, 'Two members of our party were comparatively inexperienced mountaineers; Obexer and I were therefore disturbed when Weber, one of the two novices, led ... rather too energetically, for a killing pace on the first day often means a winded man on the morrow ...' All goes to plan, however, until the weather turns nasty:

> Once the decision to bivouac has been definitely arrived at, the next question was how best and quickest to protect ourselves from the biting wind. Obexer proposed to dig a hole, but a prod with the axe revealed ice under a layer of barely two feet of soft, powdery snow. Another suggestion was to seek the shelter provided by some shallow or otherwise suitable crevasse. This was my idea, so I promptly proceeded to look around for something after the nature of a harmless crevasse. Hardly had I moved a few feet downwards when, with a dull thump, there I hung, with nothing but empty space under my skis. I clung to two ski-sticks, up to my shoulders in a bottomless crevasse.
>
> As I began hauling myself out by the sticks, Weber noticed my disappearance, and pulled wildly on the rope. An unfortunate move on his part, for it jerked me

away from the sticks and threw me into the crevasse, where I hung with my full weight on the rope, some four feet below the surface. In falling, the sudden jerk of the rope on my ribs winded me thoroughly.

Even the united forces of all three of them could not pull me up on that rope, for it had cut deeply into the frozen overhanging snow edge of the crevasse ... Propped with my feet against one wall, and my shoulders against the other, I could relieve the pressure on my ribs, and was able to sling the rücksack, on which I carried my ice-axe, off my back, and unfasten the axe ... the rope suddenly slackened, and down I rattled another couple of feet. The poor old rücksack, a dear friend, failed to gain the safety of the upper world, and fell thud – thud – thud, far out of all reach down into the invisible depths of my grim prison. Gone with it, and most regretted, was one glove, which had frozen to the strap which I had been holding.

With my axe, I managed to cut steps up one wall of this troublesome crevasse, knock a breach in the corniced edge, and work with my head above ground. Then I shouted to the others, who stood some distance off, to throw me an end of the other rope. Between us yawned the wide-open mouth of another crevasse, which prevented them from approaching any nearer to me.

The wind flung wide three casts of the second rope, but the fourth succeeded. After a few minutes more of hard struggling, we were once again all united. We no longer felt inclined to hunt after safe crevasses.

Wisely, the party settled instead for digging a snow-hole in which to shelter. But the first few minutes of inaction, wrote Finch, revealed two facts.

Firstly, for all the protection from the wind our 'Palace Hotel' (as Oxeber named the happy home) afforded us, we might almost as well have camped out on the normal unprepared surface.

Secondly, my head was covered with an inch of ice and snow, icicles pendant from eyebrows and eyelashes, and one half of my face dolefully sore as if commencing frostbite. So I borrowed the nearest rücksack, and tucked my head into it. It was full of snow in the dark interior, but by now I was accustomed to snow, and the storm at least was outside.

The usual manner of whirling away sleepless bivouacs by songs, jests and yarns was out of the question, as the storm howled louder than any or all of us together. Towards dawn I fell sound asleep, only to awake when someone announced it to be 8 a.m. At first I could not account for the darkness which surrounded me, then suddenly remembered my head was in the rücksack. Outside this 'abode-à-la-ostrich' was broad daylight, but grey white, and no signs of any abatement in the fury of the storm.

In our soaked condition, the cold was doubly penetrating ... We decided to attempt further descent on foot, leaving our skis to be recovered on some later occasion ... Almost at once, the steepness of the ground increased rapidly, and it was soon necessary to cut steps ... It became all too evident we could not descend the ice-fall as long as the storm held on. For every few minutes, terrific gusts would force us to our knees, all but sweeping us off our steps. So when we came to a fallen ice block, and found a four-foot-deep hollow in the snow beside it, we decided to camp here anew, in hopes the gusts were but a final effort and sign of approaching exhaustion on the part of the storm.

Later in the morning, deceived by lengthy pauses between the shrieking blasts of the gale, we made two more vain attempts to continue the descent. Soon after noon, it commenced to snow very heavily. At 3 p.m., satisfied that no more fierce gusts were likely to surprise us, we resumed the descent, which had been interrupted by a total of nearly 12 hours in bivouac.

The walls of the Bifertenstock were alive with avalanches, invisible on account of the falling snow and dense mists, but ever crashing over the precipices and rumbling down nearly to the right. On the plateau below the ice-fall, the mist once became so dense that we had to steer for the hut by compass.

After some hours' vain stumbling, thereabouts, where we thought the hut should lie, we found it shortly before 9 p.m. On the table was a note from Forster, leaving word to say he had descended to see about a rescue party. Had we been in anything like undamaged condition, we should at once have continued our descent down to the valley of Lintal. As it was, we ate a frugal supper – then slept like logs till far in to the next morning.

The story's ending is none too happy. Having regained the safety of the valley,

Weber went off to bed at once and was more or less an invalid for the next six weeks. His hands and feet were badly frostbitten, due to woollen gloves, and tight, ill-fitting boots. Thanks to careful treatment his hands recovered completely, but most toes of both feet had to be amputated.

More serious was Morgenthaler's fate. Nearly all his fingers had to be amputated at the first or second joint. He also wore woollen gloves, but large, loose-fitting ski boots had kept his feet in perfect condition. Obexer and I suffered no serious consequences.

And now the role unwittingly played by the 'missing' Forster. Finch spells it out: 'The moral of this story is: Head your equipment-list for a winter climb with a reliable pocket-barometer! By bad luck there was none such with our party, and Forster's served us little, as he arrived in the hut some hours after we had left it.'

Finch added another moral: 'We should never have attempted a mountain like the Tödi with companions of whose equipment and experience we had no knowledge.'

Chapter 9

TROUBLE AT t'CLUB

*Are cows likely to feel comfortable, when standing
on this slope in summer? If an affirmative answer can
be given, the slope is not dangerous. It is, of course,
understood that gorges, ravines and steep declivities
will be avoided by Swiss cows just as much by
those of any other nationality.*

On June 15, 1912, Sir Arthur Conan Doyle – 'the first Englishman
to call public attention to ski-ing as a winter sport' – and Lady
Conan Doyle are honoured guests at the 'best-attended' summer
dinner at the Trocadero Restaurant.

Meanwhile Professor F.F. Roget is making a bizarre deduction
that might have floored Sherlock Holmes in an article entitled 'Ski-
Running in the High Alps'. He informs his readers that,

> As a general rule, snow that accumulates … on the
> grazings frequented by cows in summer affords a safe
> and reliable skiing ground. When in doubt, the ski-
> runner should ask himself: Are cows, as I know them,
> likely to feel comfortable, when standing on this slope

in summer? If an affirmative answer can be given in a bona fide manner, the slope is not dangerous. It is, of course, understood that gorges, ravines and steep declivities will be avoided by Swiss cows just as much by those of any other nationality.

It was in 1912, two years before the terrible conflagration of the Great War, which sought vainly to end all wars, that a serious conflict broke out in British skiing circles. It was an extraordinary battle in that the Ski Club of Great Britain – linked in so many members' minds with Sir Arnold Lunn, who would edit the *British Ski Year Book* for half a century and whose name would be enshrined in the club's eponymous library – found itself in almost total opposition to the entire Lunn family.

At the root of the trouble was the decision by E.C. Richardson to start a new holiday organisation called the Winter Sports Club. Because of Richardson's powerful Ski Club of Great Britain connections, Arnold Lunn's father, Sir Henry, viewed this as a threat to his own Public Schools Alpine Sports Club. This 'club' enabled skiers for whom a tour organised by a common-or-garden travel agent would have been 'non-U' to 'travel Lunn without appearing to Travel Lunn'. The Ski Club of Great Britain was anxious about the commercial implications – as well as the loosening of skiing standards.

Arnold Lunn could scarcely disguise a hefty element of snobbery when describing his father's club:

> It was a success because it catered for people who liked to preserve their social environment while changing their physical environment. Congenial society consists by definition of members of the same genus, and Englishmen may be divided into those who enjoy meeting other genera on their travels, and those who prefer to associate only with their own particular genus.
>
> Father catered for the latter class ... Sir Henry Lunn, Ltd. might have been described as a travel agency for the benefit of travellers who did not want to travel.

Nevertheless, E.C. Richardson, the principal founder of the Ski Club of Great Britain, later said of Sir Henry,

> He was one of the very first to realise that skiing was good. And, by way of the many 'centres' in Switzerland which were opened under his auspices before the war, far more people in this country became acquainted with all that skiing implies than would otherwise have been the case. Amongst other things, the application of the word 'Kandahar' to skiing affairs originated with him. The first race bearing that name was held under his supervision in 1911. And since then, in connection with the famous Club of that name, the well-known [ski] binding, and so on, 'Kandahar' is probably better known to most people rightly or wrongly, in connection with skiing than with the late Lord Roberts of Kandahar, and his victories in India ... Sir Henry was a great pioneer of skiing.

At the time, however, Sir Henry was anxious that Richardson might gain access to the ownership of his clients' names and addresses – his 'mailing list'. Lunn regarded Richardson's Winter Sports Club – and, by association, the Ski Club of Great Britain – as a commercial rival. It cut both ways: in 1912, there appeared in the club's *Year Book* an article entitled 'Steps to Safeguard the SCGB'. The article explained that the club was perceived to be under threat from Sir Henry Lunn's newly formed British Ski Association (BSA), which had 'thrown the committee into a panic'.

A campaign of some bitterness and not a little venom – with Sir Henry labelled a 'dictator' – was fought out between the two organisations, with considerable political in-fighting.

One significant area in which the Ski Club fought hardest was that its ski-members should be qualified skiers. The BSA placed no such qualification on its members. Ski-runners could be novices. They didn't even need to have skied at all. The Ski Club, meanwhile, resolved to 'stiffen' its qualifications for membership, emulating the celebrated Leander rowing club at Henley-on-Thames, which had by now 'eclipsed' its rivals.

The row continued. A new publication, *Ski-ing Magazine*,

featured 'an attack on the SCGB and all its works.' In a review, *Year Book* readers were told, 'We believe the magazine is edited by Mr Arnold Lunn.'

E.C. Richardson, caught in the crossfire, attempted a Solomon-like solution, and wrote a controversial letter to the 'Field' suggesting that 'people shouldn't join either club'. But the Ski Club's Mr Harmer did not think 'any member had a right to advise the public not to join his own club!'

The Ski Club decided it was faced with 'a body which might do serious injury to the Club' and 'gave grave and anxious consideration' to a course of action which was unanimously agreed – trying to get Lunn Senior to 'modify' his club.

'This mission proved ineffectual,' Ski Club members were told. As a compromise of sorts, the National Ski Union was set up. At the Ski Club, a referendum in favour of discarding the skiing qualification was defeated by 65 votes to 38. Life went on, and Arnold Lunn became, in a way, the Ski Club's prodigal son.

In 1923, looking back on the club's first 20 years in *Phoenix*, the editor of *Ski Notes and Queries* talked of 'a series of unfortunate happenings, internecine combats which wrought their useful havoc. These differences having been happily composed on a sound and permanent basis, there came the war' – a *real* internecine combat! After the AGM, 'an informal dinner took place.'

Afterwards, 'many of the diners danced in the Hotel Ballroom, which was considered an improvement on the merry discussions on bindings with which Ski Club dinners usually terminate.'

Ski-jumping was still very much a *force majeur*, particularly the celebrated Holmenkollen championships in Oslo. The *Year Book* hinted that the British, it seemed, were in need of some sort of contemporary Eddie the Eagle. A correspondent in Norway pointed out,

> No Englishman has ever competed at Holmenkollen.
> Surely there must be one or two amateurs in England
> up to international standard? The first British ski-
> runner who appears at this meet will be accorded a
> tremendous reception, and, whether he 'stands' or
> 'falls' at the jump, he will do so amidst a scene of

wild enthusiasm. Reasonable notice of the event should be given in order that the local Band may practise *Rule Britannia*!

In New Zealand, *Year Book* readers learned that, 'for the first time on record, the ski-runner has aroused hostility among those to whom the sport is a novelty. He will doubtless feel much as we do towards those infuriated predecessors of ours who condemned railways as newfangled inventions of the devil.'

This incident recalls difficulties encountered by the Scotsmen 'who took the first curling stones from their native country to Switzerland. The customs authorities at Boulogne took these strange objects for bombs, and the party were treated as suspects until one of them demonstrated on the Customs House floor how to play the game.'

Chapter 10

DISASTER AT THE POLE

*News of Captain Scott and the explorers is
expected early in 1913.*

Unfortunately, it was bad news – as Ski Club members would
discover all too soon.

In some ways, the year 1913 served as a grim *hors d'oeuvre* to
the terrible events that would start to unfold in the following year.
In others, it was an unwitting last 'hurrah'. Arnold Lunn took on
the Eiger – and lived to climb another day. Robert Falcon Scott
took on the South Pole – and perished. It was solemnly dealt with
in the *Year Book*:

> There is one event of the past year ... which cannot be
> passed over in silence: we refer to the death of Captain
> Scott and his gallant comrades. The Club has already
> recorded at its General Meeting in June the expression
> of its profound sorrow at the tragic fate that befell
> those gallant men ... losing one of our most
> distinguished honorary members ... and admiration,
> greater than we can express, for the heroic fortitude

and self-sacrifice with which he and his comrades met their death.

After his triumph, the great Norwegian explorer Roald Amundsen, who had beaten Scott's ill-fated expedition to the South Pole, was made an honorary member of the Ski Club of Great Britain, joining the illustrious ranks of Sir Arthur Conan Doyle, Fridtjof Nansen, Commander Peary, Mathias Zdarsky and, of course, Amundsen's tragic rival, Robert Falcon Scott.

But back in the dampness of England's pleasant land, there were more mundane matters to consider: 'There are some, perhaps, who may think the inauguration of the [British] Championship premature in view of the fact that there is at present no British ski-runner who has passed the SCGB second-class test.'

Arnold Lunn was having a run-in with a rather unpleasant-sounding colonel called E.L. Strutt, part of the 'old guard' at the Alpine Club who had described him as 'an offensive little cad'. However, Lunn was somewhat consoled by Strutt's grudging follow-up: 'I am bound to say that A.L. writes more sense than any other ski idiot.' Surprisingly, perhaps, Lunn says that 'many years later, Colonel Strutt and I became great friends.'

North of the border, up in the glens, they were having a good winter – and a late one. In 'Easter 1913 at Dalwhinnie', we read:

> It is rather a curious experience to leave London on a warm, muggy evening in the early spring, when all signs of frost and snow have long departed, and to wake up in the Drummochter Pass to find a foot of snow beside the railway, a keen bite in the air, snow-white peaks on both sides, and a clear blue sky overhead.

But, oh, to be in England now that Kenneth Swan was editing the *Ski Club Year Book*! There appeared the most wonderfully mischievous campaign against the ever-controversial E.C. Richardson. Swan, the previous year's club president, seized his opportunity for a little rapier-like dismemberment of the great man. Richardson must have done something pretty major to upset him. Or was it just that this particular 'father of skiing' had been such a constant irritant to the club?

How members must have chuckled when they saw E.C. getting his comeuppance in such spectacular style. This is how Richardson's 'The Arosa Meet' was dealt with in the *Year Book*. (Was it entirely malicious, or did Richardson see the funny side?) Readers were told straight away that this was to be a rare treasure. Below you can read not the article itself, but Swan's wonderfully delivered death by a thousand cuts.

The Editor began,

> This article was of a length of about 10,000 words, and we have had to subject it to pretty drastic excision. The ellipses denote passages which we have omitted – Editor. (Here follows a lot of other matter in the same strain about the arranging of his binding, the waking up of his comrades, etc., etc., of no interest to anyone but himself – Editor.)

And then this: '(As neither Mr Richardson nor Messrs Ayres have paid the usual rate for the insertion of an advertisement of this undoubtedly ingenious invention, we are reluctantly obliged by our trade union regulations to debar the former from further expatiating upon its merits – Editor.)' And this: '(Here follows a long and entirely unsolicited homily about jumping hills –Editor.)' And this: '(Here follow other remarks about jumping hills and competitions for which there is no room – Editor.)' Swan ended his diatribe thus: 'We regret that owing to pressure upon space we have had to curtail Mr E.C. Richardson's interesting remarks at this point – Editor.'

Delicious. If only we could have some way of going back in time to watch Richardson's face when he saw the tattered results of his labours for the first time!

One fancies that Arnold Lunn, who would become by far the longest-serving editor of the *British Ski Year Book*, would never have tolerated such liberties with his copy but, since he was in charge, it was not something he needed to be much concerned with. Thus, his wonderful 14-page account of 'The Eiger (Ogre) on Ski' – which starts with a dramatic and highly dangerous excursion undertaken on New Year's Day 1913, from which, it appears, he and his companion were lucky to escape unscathed –

also escaped the red pen when it was published in 1924. A decade later, a glutton for punishment, he would return to the Eiger to try to get his revenge. An unwise move, perhaps, but again he somehow survives.

For Lunn, the Eiger seems to have been almost what the Matterhorn was to its first conqueror, Edward Whymper (described in 1943 by Sir Claud Schuster, first secretary to the Lord Chancellor from 1915 to 1944, and a prominent member of the club, as a 'victor–victim' – a reference to the deaths of four of Whymper's companions after his initial triumph). Fortunately, over the years, Lunn's adventures produced no casualties except the injury to his own leg and, although, sooner or later, Lunn was determined to conquer the old ogre, even he had the sense to realise that the dreaded north face was not within his ability, especially because of his old injury.

Below is a portion of Lunn's gripping double-saga. The north face had yet to be conquered (and would not be until 1938), but Lunn's route was, nonetheless, an extremely stern test.

> The Eiger may extend a benign welcome to those who approach him with the due ritual of ice-axe and rope, but he resents as an impertinence the intrusion of ski-runners into the sacred preserves of the Alpine fraternity ... Maurice Crettex and I had dragged our ski up to the base of the rocks which are followed on the usual summer route. This insult was more than the old ogre could bear, and just as we reached the rocks, he gave a low growl and let loose one of the noblest avalanches I have ever seen. A curtain of ice thundered down the cliffs, and poured in a seething torrent across the slopes which we had just left. In that torrent our ski sank, never to rise again.
>
> The Eiger had missed us, but he still had a few shots left in his locker. As we started up the rocks, the weather changed. The wind wheezed fitfully round the ridges, dampish clouds streamed untidily across the sky, and the stars went out one by one. Very soon it began to snow, and the snow continued for the next eight hours. The slabs were soon coated with ice, and I

cursed my forgetfulness, for my crampons had been inadvertently left behind. [An early example of Lunn's lifelong problems with absent-mindedness!]

As we struggled up through the driving snow, I was haunted and depressed by an odd sense of being up against a very real personality. I felt convinced that the Eiger had some very offensive surprises in store for us. At last the final ice slope, black and dour, loomed up through the driving snow. The gale had dropped. Crettex swung his ice-axe with right good will, and the ninth hour of our long struggle somehow ended on the summit. We wasted no words, but turned downhill at once.

But the drama was only just beginning to unfold. Lunn continued,

The Eiger chuckled. He had lured us onto the ice, and only one of us had crampons. And then suddenly he released the full fury of his artillery ... A gale leapt on to the crest of the Eiger, and the heavens were filled with tumult. A stone whipped off the slope and whistled past my ear. A flood of loose snow and ice poured down the rocks. 'Take that,' screamed the wind, and out I went, at full rope's length. I fell back, breathless and bruised. 'And that! – And that!' shrieked the gale. Twice again I took the count. But Crettex held. His ten-pointed crampons had saved us, and the Eiger had lost the last trick.

As a ski trip, the Eiger had proved a failure. The blood of our murdered ski cried aloud from the ground. I was determined to avenge them, to return some day and humble the ogre by proving that, for all his proud panoply of rock and ice, he was no better than a mere miserable ski spitz, a slalom playground, a 'bus tour' suitable for those who have passed the Third Class Test (part A).

Lunn would, indeed, return. But it would be another decade before he finally got his revenge.

Chapter 11

WAR

*In 1914, of the 5,432 Ski Club members, 503 were
educated at Eton, 252 at Harrow, 186 at Rugby,
170 at Marlborough, 162 at Charterhouse, and 117 at
Winchester. There were 768 army officers, 79 naval
officers, 179 clergy and 311 members held titles.
The 57 MPs included the Prime Minister, the Home
Secretary, the Postmaster General and
the Lord Privy Seal.*

My good friend and colleague Peter Hardy, himself an old Etonian,
once bumped into his milkman on the slopes of Breckenridge,
Colorado. In rather less unlikely circumstances, I ran into the
owner of my local Chinese restaurant in Kent while skiing in
Whistler, Canada. Everyone goes skiing these days, but you only
have to look at the membership profile of the Ski Club of Great
Britain on the eve of World War I to confirm that, in its early years
at least, the sport was not taken up by many miners, market traders
or, for that matter, milkmen. In 1914, skiing was, without question,
an elitist sport.

Writing in the British magazine *History Today* (April 2003), E.

John B. Allen, Emeritus Professor of History at Plymouth State College, New Hampshire, observed in *The British and the Modernisation of Skiing*,

> In 1914, of the 5,432 members (which included 1,370 women), some 503 were educated at Eton, 252 at Harrow, 186 at Rugby, 170 at Marlborough, 162 at Charterhouse, and 117 at Winchester. There were 768 army officers, 79 naval officers, 179 clergy and 311 members held titles. The 57 MPs included the then prime minister, H.H. Asquith, the Home Secretary, the Postmaster General and the Lord Privy Seal.

Warming to his theme, the professor continued,

> Imperial governors of Australia, Bombay and Hong Kong could happily swap stories with field marshals and any number of major generals. The medical officer to the Sultan of Zanzibar could compare notes with the laryngologist of the royal household. An international polo player, a cycling champion, an Olympic oarsman and a world-record holding skater could discourse on the merits of their sports with international cricketers, association footballers, and rugby enthusiasts, not a few of whom were 'sporting parsons'.

This was 'the top drawer', said Allen – 'just one big English family'.

Arnold Lunn had some interesting thoughts on all this – and the gradual skiing emancipation of women, particularly in Norway. Writing much later, in 1924, he said,

> Skiing is responsible for something like a social revolution, which, unlike most revolutions, has damaged nobody and benefited all those who have been infected by the passion …
>
> Those who have penetrated in winter to the remoter valleys whose inhabitants have not yet taken to skiing must have noticed the contrast between the listless natives and the keen, happy energy of those

who live in happier vales where the ski have found a home. The same change was observed in Christiania [the old name for Oslo]. The improvement in general health and physique was striking, and the effect was perhaps most marked on Norwegian womanhood. Norwegian women had conformed to the best Victorian models until the ski came and crochet work lost its charm. The ladies were not slow in deserting the fireside, and in insisting on accompanying their menfolk into the hills ... The outlook and the status of the sex was radically changed.

There were other issues. What exactly should the relationship be between ski-runner and mountain guide? It was eloquently summed up by Geoffrey Young in a feature entitled 'Mountain Craft'. He believed that

It is a mistake to allow the relationship to become too personal, to expect a guide to act as valet or to perform small menial services in bivouac or hotel ... If possible, laugh him out of the common trick of dropping behind and making a sort of tail to your triumph as you return into the village or meet another party. He is taught that this is good manners, and will please your touristship; but it is really insulting to both, if a man has been your companion or leader during a great climb of united effort, to accept this mock tribute to your poor dignity when there is no longer any chance of going a step wrong ...

In the valley, let the guide see that, as between yourselves, you consider that the fellowship remains unaltered, that you do not barter your right to be treated as his equal as a mountaineer for the sake of posturing as his 'Herr' ... You will soon find out what you can and cannot do. You cannot traditionally invite him to dinner at the same table with other strangers in a large hotel, but he will join you for coffee at your separate table.

But what of the ski-runner himself? Did he deserve any reverential treatment in the first place? Arnold Lunn quoted a mysterious 'well-known ski-runner' in the following extract:

> I must say I think a little less strained gentlemanliness and a little more personal criticism would make things a dashed sight more interesting. In no other sport is there such deadly public politeness (nor perhaps such deadly private impoliteness) as in skiing. Boxers, for instance, are called fools, cowards, clumsy brutes or physical wrecks every day in the papers (and have dinner quite happily with their critics the same evening). And the well-known figures in tennis, cricket, *footer* or any other sport are criticised with the same disregard for their feelings. Why not also in skiing?
>
> Think how delightful it would be for A to be able to print his candid opinion that B was a blundering lout with nothing to redeem his (or her) running but a courage born of total brainlessness, and for B to be able to say that A was a poor worm suffering from incipient senile decay, who thought himself (or herself) clever on the strength of being able to do a pretty turn or two on a practice ground. I suggest a new symposium for the *Year Book* – 'Home Truths about Well-known Skiers' or 'Your Favourite Runner and What I Think of Him'.

And then there was the vexed question of whether or not ski-runners should dress for dinner.

Arnold Lunn suggested that, during the first decade of the 20th century, it would have been 'unthinkable for an Englishman not to dress for dinner at any of the leading winter sports centres'.

He continued, in whimsical mood,

> Such luckless guests as had lost their luggage *en route* slunk about with miserable and apologetic *mien*. It wasn't their fault that they had to dine in their ordinary clothes. We knew that. Still, they were

under a cloud – the tainted wether [castrated sheep] of the flock.

I remember one miserable outcast whose registered luggage did not arrive for a week. Everybody was kind to him, but he lost *caste*. He was slipping. He knew it. We knew it. The head waiter knew it. And then the cloud lifted.

His luggage arrived. I shall never forget the expression on his face when he appeared for the first time in evening dress. He looked like a man who has just been cleared by court martial of a disgraceful charge.

But things were different, it seems, for the Alpine Club. Lunn recounts how he overheard a member explaining,

> They have to send round their bags by post while they cross glacier passes from one valley to another, so they can't be expected to burden themselves with dress clothes. It isn't that he hasn't got dress clothes. It's a tradition of the Alpine Club not to dress for dinner in the Alps.

'The Alpine Club man in his brown serge suit was terribly impressive,' thought Lunn, with just a touch of mockery. 'What risks these heroes ran! In summer they defied the avalanche and the storm; in winter the peril of social ostracism.'

But that, said Lunn, was in 1903.

> In 1939, the revolt against form had gone so far that hotels which were still fussy about evening dress were finding it necessary to provide dining accommodation for those who could not be bothered to change into ceremonial garments. The English began to show a distaste for evening dress in Alpine hotels when ski teachers began to dress for dinner.

In November, 1914, Arnold Lunn's first son, Peter, was born in London. But he would spend his early years in Mürren, where, 88

years later, in March 2003, we chatted for a video which Chris
Tizzard and I were producing to mark the Ski Club of Great
Britain's centenary.

'What happened was that after my father had had this appalling
fall in Wales he ended up with one leg five centimetres shorter
than the other, and was rejected for a military service,' he said.
(The wound took many years to heal.)

> He said to the doctor who rejected him, 'But I've been
> up the Eiger in winter on this leg!' And the doctor said,
> 'For your own amusement, perhaps.'
>
> And then he was sent here to Mürren to look after
> the interned. They were put up at the Palace Hotel
> which then belonged to my grandfather [Sir Henry].
> And somebody once said they were looking forward to
> a nice restful time in Switzerland – and waiting for
> them was Arnold Lunn determined to teach them how
> to ski!
>
> That internment period has left just one relic in
> Mürren: the Hindenburg Line on the Schiltgrat. I have
> met Germans who believed it got the name because
> their Field Marshal Hindenburg skied down it.
> Hindenburg never visited Mürren. In any case he came
> from East Prussia – more suitable for cross-country
> than for downhill skiing. In the Great War there was,
> ahead of the Allies, a Hindenburg defence line. Some
> of the interned skiers had persuaded themselves,
> optimistically rather than rationally, that this would
> prove an easy target. So they gave the name
> Hindenburg to the easiest of all the Schiltgrat descents.
>
> Of course things were so different in those days.
> There were no snow ploughs and, if there were heavy
> snowfalls, my father would stand up and say to all the
> guests, 'If you want your Christmas dinner to arrive
> from Lauterbrunnen you will all have to come down
> and help clear the line.' So all these people went down
> with spades and shovels and cleared the line.
>
> Before I was two years old I was put on ski and I used
> to shuffle backwards and forwards beside the ice rink,

and when I got to the end I would fall over and wait for somebody to come along and then I'd say, 'Pick I up and turn I round!' Then I'd go back in the other direction. My very earliest memories of ski are here in Mürren.

In the Süd Tirol, much of the fiercest fighting between Austria and Italy in the Great War took place at altitude. The fierce cold and risk of avalanches made the suffering even more harrowing. Sometimes the opposing forces managed to kill the enemy by bringing down avalanches with their weapons. A poignant account of a tragic Christmas – 'Christmas Trees and Machine Guns' – appeared in the *Year Book*, in a review of *Der Kampf über den Gletschern* by Walter Schmidkunk.

It is pleasant to record that, almost a century later, the old enmities have long since vanished, and the Süd Tirol today is a hospitable and fascinating melange of culture, cuisine and courtesy.

It was all very different during that terrible mountain war. 'Mountaineering and war make a most unpleasant mixture,' wrote the unnamed reviewer (probably Lunn).

Those trenches on the Italian front, which were buried in snow for many months in the winter, trenches where the temperature sank sometimes to 20 degrees centigrade below freezing, where the sentries crept from the little wooden huts to do 'sentry go' in all the horrors of a winter's storm, and you will begin to feel that even Flanders mud had its points. Carrying a heavy rücksack is no joke, but it is, at least, preferable to carrying a machine gun.

There is an account of a raid across a glacier pass into the heart of an Italian camp, which is one of the grimmest bits of war literature I know. No sentiment is wasted on the foe. You can hear the Tirolese grunting with joy as their machine guns begin to play on the unsuspecting Italians. The author ticks off, with dour satisfaction, each Italian corpse. Of course the fighting on this front was very bitter, for the Tirolese are magnificent at a defensive war. They do not love the Italians, and as most of them were expert chamois hunters, they derived much satisfaction from sitting up among the cliffs and sniping the enemy.

For days a terrible snowstorm had raged, and at last the storm lifted, and a telephone message came from the outer world that a party of eleven men were coming up on ski, burdened with all manner of Christmas presents – food, tobacco, and gramophone records. But the thing that excited these bloodthirsty Tirolese even more than the presents was the promise of a Christmas tree!

Next day, a ski-runner struggled up through the drifts, but the tree had been left some distance below. Half a dozen men promptly went on a search party for the missing tree. They found it, but the presents never arrived. Those who were bringing them were swept away in an avalanche, and the description of the finding of their corpses has the dignity of genuine emotion.

They dug them out. Their sacks were still full of succulent sausages and other Christmas fare. But the gruff old Tirolese Landsturmer would have none of them. 'We've lost all gusto,' he said. 'We couldn't touch the stuff. Perhaps the grave diggers would like it.' The death toll from avalanches on this front ran into hundreds.

Meanwhile, not so far away from this terrible winter battlefield, in another part of the Alps, things were considerably more civilised. What wouldn't those Italian and Austrian troops have given to be in Mürren?

Arnold Lunn wrote,

Thanks to the intervention of the Swiss Government, an arrangement was arrived at to intern in Switzerland prisoners-of-war who were suffering from certain specified diseases and disablements, an agreement which was later extended to cover all officers and NCOs who had been in Germany for more than two years. The first parties of British interned began to arrive early in 1916.

The British Tommy did not take to skiing in any very great numbers. The rest tobogganed and skated.

Some of the men suspected that their officers wished them to ski in order to keep them out of mischief, which was quite sufficient to prevent them skiing. 'What use is skiing to the British working man?' asked another gentleman with Bolshevist tendencies.

I once persuaded a very sceptical Tommy to take up the sport. For a day or two all went well, and Thomas began to fancy himself as a ski-runner, so I took him on a run which would end up with a little easy wood-running. Halfway through the wood I heard a loud crash, and the tardy convert was discovered with his ski imprisoned in the low-lying branches of a tree and his head submerged in snow. 'I say, Mr Lunn,' he exclaimed, 'do you call this ski-ing? I call it ... bird's nesting.'

In 1917, Lunn made the first ever ski ascent of the Dom, at 4,545 metres (14,912 ft) the highest mountain entirely in Switzerland. The following May, with the war reaching its climax, he undertook a memorable and idyllic ski tour from his beloved Mürren with three officers recovering from the ravages of war: Bob Middleditch, Ralph Evans and Tristram Carlyon. To say it was idyllic might even be an understatement. It is almost as though, with the war rumbling on, it is a final journey into the past, for, until the sounds of that terrible conflict had finally died away, the Alps were still as pristine as they had been in 1914. More so, perhaps, because the tourists were preoccupied elsewhere.

Lunn writes,

We breakfasted at the Concordiaplatz and smoked the best pipe of the day, observing with pleasure that the last clouds had been hunted from the sky. We fixed string to our ski and prepared to drag them up to our pass. In spring, one climbs on foot, dragging one's ski on string; on moderate slopes, one scarcely notices their weight, and one climbs about fifty or even a hundred per cent quicker than in winter, where height has to be gained by long gentle zigzags in soft snow.

There are few jollier sensations than skiing in the

early hours of a May morning. A glorious sense of freshness haunts the hills. By noon, every rock will be sweating in the sun, the snows a wet, soft swamp. But night restores strength to the hills. Night cools the hot surface of rock and snow. The peaks washed in the lucid light of dawn suggest cheerful giants emerging from a morning tub. The snow is clean and firm underfoot, its surface catches a thousand stars that the low-risen sun scatters on the film crust. The long, glinting shadows – so harsh and black in the hours of the sun's supremacy – seem half transparent, like the shadows of light clouds on still waters.

We crouched down, the wind sang its last song, the steepness relented into a long, unchanging gradient; the breeze died away, four rapid swings and four breathless ski-runners faced the slope whose swift joys they had squandered all too soon ... As the speed dies, the hills adopt a sedater measure ... The wind that thunders in one's heart melts into a fitful breeze.

The snow in front of the ski hunches itself together, and thrusts the ski backwards. Suddenly the world gives a little jerk, the mountains stop moving, and you know that you are a creeping thing once more.

There is a subtle joy in doing something delightful not as an individual, but as a member of a team, a pleasure which is nowhere greater than in skiing, especially when you know your friend's skiing as thoroughly as you know his jokes, his best swing as well as you know your own virtues, and his weak turns as completely as he knows your vices ...

But like most skiers, if they are honest, Lunn – who cannot wait for each winter's snow to arrive – is finally glad to see the back of it when the time finally comes. With a sudden change of mood, he writes,

We were more than sick of snow, sick of the stubborn winter which still held out in her mountain fortress. We longed for colour, for cool places, for running

streams ... We turned a corner and discovered an oasis
of green in a desert of burning snow. The hut ... stood
in a little meadow of emerald turf, dotted with sulphur
anemones and the bluest of gentians, and splashed by
the spray from a little stream that had just woken from
the long sleep of winter ... We lunched in the open,
and throwing off our superfluous clothes, lay down
half naked in the grass ... We lit our pipes and watched
the smoke coiling idly upwards to a windless sky, and
as we lay, we listened to a chuckling stream (without
running water an Alpine siesta is sadly incomplete), a
stream which sang a cheerful thanksgiving to the great
Sun God who had burst the prison bars of the frost and
restored to the hills their heritage song ...

Slowly, the afternoon passed away. We dozed and
gossiped and listened to the stream singing the same
song that it sang before the world went mad, the same
song that it will sing when the world of men has ceased
to be. Slowly the shadows gathered the mountains into
their arms. Slowly the light faded from the snowy
crests. We knocked out our pipes, a little sadly, for a
perfect Alpine day was on the way to become nothing
but a memory.

There are many references to the war in this essay, and another I
particularly like is this little gem:

We lay on the pass for an hour, and devoured the
remains of a plum pudding sent out to Carlyon by his
aunt, a pudding made before the Food Controller's
voice was heard in the land, one of that rare old
vintage of 1912 plum puddings which we shall never
see again.

What sums up Switzerland's role in the scheme of things at the time
is poignantly expressed by Arnold Lunn's portrait of Ralph Evans:

When Evans first arrived from Germany, he could
hardly manage an hour's climb. At the end of his first

season he all but collapsed on the Great Scheidegg. As I write, many memories come back to me of Evans supporting himself on two ski sticks, his head drooped, his whole attitude suggesting prayer, an illusion, however, which could only be maintained by keeping well out of earshot. But he never gave in. As I watched him striding down the road, I realised the great debt many and many an Englishman owe to the little country which rescued them from barbed wire and restored them to health and the joy of life.

Lunn later received a letter from Evans in Mesopotamia. It said, 'Perhaps the four of us will get together for another May run when we have gone over to the "other side" ... We shall never get all the conditions right again in *this* life.' A prediction which, as Lunn put it, 'proved only too sorrowfully true'. Almost half a century later, as he celebrated 70 years of skiing, Lunn would write,

> Few friends have meant more to me than Ralph Evans, Tristram Carlyon and Bob Middleditch ... and few mountain memories, if any, mean more to me than the memory of a perfect May tour in the Oberland glaciers ... The four of us never skied together again, and in this life will never again meet, for my three beloved friends all died between the two world wars. One of the penalties one pays for living to an advanced age is that one survives most of one's dearest friends.

Chapter 12

A BRAVE
NEW WORLD

*A sudden intrusion of sound invaded the silence of
the glaciers. We looked up; against the sky an arrogant
aeroplane circled round and then swooped past the
Jungfrau, a horrible reminder that the aerobusses of the
future will doubtless invade these Alpine solitudes. We
felt like the last survivors of a disappearing race.*

The 1919 Roberts of Kandahar race was one of the most dramatic
ever held. 'Very soon the slope leading down to the valley
resembled a picture of German atrocities,' *Year Book* readers were
told, with 'countless little black figures, like the victims of a
submarine attack, drowning in a sea of snow'. The race was won
by Chilton — 'a very fine racer; it is a pity he does not bother to
master turns.'

The Ski Club of Great Britain has, inevitably, always attracted
its fair share of eccentrics — or members who skied with eccentrics.
In 1921, 'Continental Reports', which appeared regularly in the
Year Book, produced this hilarious letter from a correspondent
called Shaun in Lenzerheide. Unlike many Swiss resorts,
Lenzerheide had enjoyed a good winter, and Shaun commenced by
noting that it had been a relief not to ski on bare slopes as some of

his contemporaries in other resorts had been forced to do. His drift, as it were, then ... drifted, in a most delightful way.

You have asked me, Mr Editor, to give you some account of last winter's season at Lenzerheide. Have you ever tried skiing on grass, sir? I have, and though the ski will run quite fast if steep enough, it is a very poor substitute for snow, and turning and falling are both very 'hard'.

I knew a man once – at least I still know him, although he really should have broken his neck years ago – who was so keen on skiing that he often got some practice in England by skiing on hoar frost in his garden. He told me it was quite exciting and the ski ran fast; but that the last time he tried it they ran away with him, and in the end he was deposited in a heap of manure – the only advantage being that the fall was softer than he was expecting. When particularly bored he used to try skiing down his front stairs and doing Christianias in the hall.

He was a bold, bad man and has often nearly got me into trouble in Switzerland among the trees. He and I used to be keen on going through the trees, and the way he did not get killed, trying to squeeze through small spaces at top speed, was very remarkable. He did not even take the precautions of a man I met in the Black Forest, who, being a German, was very thorough, though somewhat eccentric.

This man was not particularly keen on skiing through trees, but there are so many in the Black Forest that sometimes it had to be done. So on these occasions he used to fasten a thick piece of rubber round his head to save his brains from being spilled in any argument with a tree; in so far as I know, they are still 'reposing in peace in his skull'. But then he *was* odd. He was always supposed to wrap up each toe separately in brown paper to guard against frostbite, and had his skiing coat lined with dried figs in case he got lost in a fog, of which they get a fair number in that district.

With the First World War finally over, the Ski Club of Great Britain burst back into print. The *British Ski Year Book*, edited by Arnold Lunn and Captain H.C.H. Marriott, was published by the Federal Council of British Ski Clubs.

The Council had been formed in March 1914 to co-ordinate the activities of the existing skiing clubs (Davos English Ski Club, the Ski Club of Great Britain, the Scottish Ski Club, the North of England Ski Club, the British Ski Association and the National Ski Union) and, in particular, to control tests, championships and 'other matters affecting the general interests of all British ski-runners'.

(Intriguingly, the Council had met once after the outbreak of war – on November 7, 1914 – to discuss the possibility of raising a skiing battalion or company to co-operate with the French in the Vosges. For various reasons this scheme was considered 'quite impracticable'.)

In 1920, Arnold Lunn announced, 'Whatever sentimental regrets one may feel for the disappearance of various year books, each with their own history, associations and individuality, all ski-runners are agreed that the cost of printing renders a single *Year Book* essential.'

(By 1925, Kenneth Swan, the club's Honorary Secretary would be describing the Federal Council as a 'mule with no pride of ancestry and no hope of posterity' – cruel words, but possibly ultimately true.)

Gradually life was returning to something like normal, and there to record these golden moments was an artist who, more than any other, captured the spirit of the age – Alan d'Egville, known to all as 'Deggers', who also edited *Ski Notes and Queries* and jokingly described the *Year Book* as 'a little grey tombstone, mostly written in Greek'. (This was a reference to Arnold Lunn's habit of sprinkling his articles with not only Latin but Greek quotations. Quite how the printers coped with this – in addition to Lunn's appalling typing – is hard to say.)

Members sought out old friends. 'Many British ski-runners,' *Year Book* readers were told, 'will be glad to hear that Mr Rickmers and his English wife have survived the war.' Rickmers, though fluent in English, was German.

Dr H. Hoek [who had dominated the Ski Club Schwarzwald's championships in the Black Forest, at the opening of the century] is also well. He went up on two successive days as an aeroplane observer, and on both occasions the machine crashed and the pilot was killed, Dr Hoek escaping without a scratch.

It was decided 'not to require payment of subscriptions during the war ... during which period all activities of the SCGB have been in abeyance'.

The *Year Book*'s advertisement rates were fixed at £12 for the outside back cover, £10 for the inside back or front cover, and £8 each for the pages facing the inside back cover or the last page of text (£5 for half a page on these) and £6 for all other pages. Half-pages were £3 10s (£3.50p) and quarter-pages £2.

Inside the *Year Book*, there was also a call for new blood. 'This Club is getting old,' readers were told. 'We must study youth. Caution can be overdone. We must search out, encourage and bring on young men, into the club and onto the Committee.' In spite of this, the average age of the members of the Federal Council was under 30.

This sentiment would be echoed by E.C. Richardson, who, responding to a toast at the Federal Council Dinner in March 1921, would cause a peal of laughter with his opening remarks, 'Mr Chairman, Ladies and Gentlemen – Whatever else I may be the father of, I am certainly not the father of British skiing. Sir Arthur Conan Doyle, and many others, put on ski before I did.'

Later in his speech, Richardson says, 'Some of us are getting pretty long in the tooth, and we must be careful not to regulate championships for the convenience of middle-aged folk.'

Even Arnold Lunn, by now in his early 30s, was not as fit as he had been – partly because of his old leg injury. He shared this modest decline in his stamina with readers of the 1920 *Year Book*, where (in the previous chapter) we found him undertaking 'A Ski Tour In May' – a month when the sun 'has cut wrinkles into the ageing forehead of winter'. He wrote,

> We slept at the Jungfraujoch. I was very tired, for I had rashly decided to dispense with a porter and to carry my own kit. Alas! The art of carrying heavy sacks seems to have vanished with other accomplishments as the result of my tumble. Certainly 30 pounds in one's sack, and ten pounds' weight of ski on one's shoulder, proved more than I could comfortably manage.

Having unloaded my sack, I offered a large and heavy tin of preserved meat to Carlyon, and half a dozen tins of sardines to Evans and Middleditch. 'Help yourselves,' I murmured with the bland *bonhomie* of a curate at a Sunday school treat.

'No thanks, Lunning,' said Carlyon coarsely, 'we've got plenty of our own stuff, and we mean to see you carry your old sack for a bit. We'll learn you to swank about feats of strength in the High Alps.'

The appearance of an aeroplane, however, made the party realise that these halcyon days would not last for ever.

As we neared the pass, a sudden intrusion of sound invaded the silence of the glaciers. We looked up; against the sky an arrogant aeroplane circled round and then swooped past the Jungfrau, a horrible reminder that the aerobusses of the future will doubtless invade these Alpine solitudes. The thought saddened us. We felt like the last survivors of a disappearing race, the race of men who climbed on foot.

Lunn was, however, happy to use dramatic new photographs of the Alps taken from such flying contraptions in the *British Ski Year Books*.

Whatever the shape of the new *Year Book*, it was soon obvious that a generous vein of humour, as ever, would run through its contents, as the editors explained,

And now we venture to make an earnest appeal to all ski-runners to assist in making the *Year Book* worthy of British skiing. The work of editing the *Year Book* ... is very heavy. All this work is purely honorary; the FC [Federal Council] has at present shown no anxiety to reward the Editors with a handsome pension. We scan the Honours List in vain for any recognition from the King. We are not even MBEs.

A little perversely, perhaps, Lunn would sometimes steer

determined ski mountaineers away from their normal routes and pressurise them into remaining on a marked run – to show them what 'good skiing' was like. A case in point was his invitation to Marcel Kurz, the most famous ski mountaineer of his day, to ski in Lunn's beloved Mürren. Middleditch, one of Lunn's ski-touring partners, recalled, 'Kurz likes to climb 8,000 feet with an infernal great sack, to crash down on trap crust, and then to wind up with a good, steady sweat up to a hut. If he missed that, he'd think he hadn't earned his dinner.'

Sometimes Middleditch could be equally hard on Lunn:

> I'm as happy as a bumble-bee as long as I'm on my faithful ski, and I enjoy looking at these old hills from a safe and comfortable distance. But, my dear Lunning ... I loathe and detest crawling up your infernal *spitzes*. For God's sake let's confine ourselves in the future to things one can ski down. Every time you hale me up one of those cursed horns, I vow never to be trapped again. Do, like a good chap, impress on me next time that my mother never raised me to be a blinking mountaineer!

Lunn and Middleditch had endured many tough days of ski mountaineering with Kurz. And Lunn was anxious to introduce Kurz, who disdained anything but *ski sauvage*, to more conventional skiing. Kurz was all for striding off to the top of the Schilthorn. 'Forward!' he barked.

'Not so fast,' said Lunn, and turned downhill. 'If you run down the shortest route, you can just catch every train [the Almendhubel funicular], for there is an interval of about five minutes between successive trains.'

Lunn reports that 'Kurz followed, complaining bitterly.' The two men spent the rest of the day skiing the same run, until Kurz – hard man that he undoubtedly was – unexpectedly burst into tears, complaining, 'But we must make a *petite* course, *une toute petite course, vous savez*!' Lunn wouldn't hear of it. 'The countless days of vile skiing and hours of climbing were avenged,' he wrote. 'Kurz spent the whole day running up in a lift and running down on perfect snow. But he never quite forgave me.'

Chapter 13

BATTLE WITH AN OGRE

We seemed to be looking down not on a green carpet spread above the solid foundation of the earth, but on to a phantom valley built from the fabric of dreams and haunted by a loveliness which is not of this world. Old memories of boyish rambles among the lower hills came back like stars after a storm.

Although Peter Lunn and Jimmy Riddell would captain the British team at the Garmisch-Partenkirchen Winter Olympics in 1936, in the 1920s, the development of downhill ski racing was yet to have any impact on the Games. The Norwegians, venerated by the British for their excellent cross-country and ski-jumping prowess, were also villains when it came to the development of Alpine events. Lunn wrote,

> I have before me the Norwegian rules ... three pages are given up to detailed instructions on the best method of training for distance races ... almost every line is concerned with the art of getting uphill and along the level. Downhill skiing merely gets a passing reference:

'When going downhill, one should regain breath and rest as much as possible. Avoid falling as it both fatigues and lowers the spirits.'

'In other words,' wrote a frustrated Lunn, 'the downhill part of the race is mainly useful because it gives you a much-needed breather. Don't try to run downhill too fast. Rest as much as possible.'

It would be a full 12 years before Lunn's dream of having Alpine (downhill) skiing at a Winter Olympics would be realised. There was a lot of waiting in Lunn's life. He had already waited a decade for another opportunity to take his skis to the top of the Eiger.

The prospect of newly discovered touring routes inspired Lunn's great Swiss friend Walter Amstutz to write, 'There is always an element of secrecy about a new tour, even the preparation is delightful. A flapper [then a current term for a brazen young woman of the 20s Jazz age] devouring her first sentimental novel is scarcely less enthralled than a mountaineer canvassing the possibilities of a new ascent.'

Amstutz would soon join his old friend on what would turn out to be perhaps the greatest challenge the pair would face together. During the long years since Lunn's abandoned attempt to reach the summit of the Eiger, he had never given up his dream. He wrote,

I spent my winters in full view of that great curtain of snow which falls from the Eigerjoch to the Scheidegg. The sight irritated me. I knew that I should have no peace of mind until I had imprinted on these snows the signature of my ski ... It is not until you have rubbed your nose against the seracs of an icefall that you really realise the resources of the defence ...

The reader may perhaps wonder whether much is to be gained by taking ski up the Eiger. 'Why not climb it on foot if you want a climb, or chose some easier expedition if you want to ski?' Well, I happen to enjoy mountaineering, especially ice work, not less than skiing, and an expedition which provides the ski-runner with some excellent sport, and the mountaineer with ice work as interesting as he could possibly desire, seems to be better worth doing than an easy glacier pass on ski or a difficult ice expedition on foot. Moreover, one of the charms of this particular tour was the fact that it had not yet been accomplished on ski ... I had come to regard this pet scheme as my private property, and I was in no hurry to put it into execution.

I had no fear of being forestalled until I met Lauper at Mürren. Lauper is one of the leading spirits in the Berne University Alpine Club, which has a fine record for daring first ascents, none more daring than those which stand to Lauper's credit. So when I saw Lauper busily engaged in conversation with a friend, Hermann Gurtner, I felt a queer telepathic foreboding that Lauper had designs on the Eiger. My instinct was sound, and I felt vaguely nettled when I discovered that my plans were in danger of being forestalled. However, the Eiger is not my private property, and I was honoured when Lauper suggested making a joint attack the following spring.

Unfortunately, Lauper could not get away, and that summer he left for America. I did not feel entitled to make an ascent of the Eiger so long as the possibility that he would join me had not been definitely excluded, but when he went to America, I determined to make an attempt in the following spring. Walter Amstutz, who was also at Mürren that winter, promised to join me.

'Walter Amstutz and Richardet arranged to meet me in Grindelwald on the evening of May 16,' says Lunn. 'Amstutz and Richardet are students at Berne University. They are brilliant and daring mountaineers and first-class ski-runners.'

But not, apparently, brilliant timekeepers. The pair failed to arrived until the following morning. 'I begged him [Amstutz] not to waste energy required for the climb in inventing an ingenious excuse for his delay,' said Lunn.

Those who, like Amstutz, are born among the mountains, where a million years or so are required to carve out a valley, often imitate the more leisurely geological processes in answering letters or keeping appointments. It is with difficulty that he resists the chance of leaving a letter unanswered, an appointment unkept, or a train uncaught.

On the eve of their departure, Lunn, Amstutz and Richardet, plus a porter, Fritz Amacher (described by Lunn's great friend Commodore Hugh Dowding as 'the possessor of an imperfectly expressed sense of humour wasted – and indeed misplaced – in a porter'), dined at the next table to three tourists who, over a four-course dinner washed down with two bottles of champagne, irritated them by suggesting that their planned excursion was '*sehr, sehr gewagt*' – very reckless. Earlier, the three had witnessed Amstutz and Richardet narrowly miss being killed by an avalanche while reconnoitring the route they would take later that night.

Lunn recalls,

> The charge of recklessness can be met with equanimity after a climb is safely over, but it has a remarkably depressing effect just as one is starting on a new and difficult expedition ... I could stand no more. Seizing an empty champagne bottle I remarked, 'that is also *sehr gewagt*. More people die of over-eating and over-drinking than ever died on mountains.'
>
> I had meant to be offensive, but only succeeded in being amusing. The hearty laugh with which my remark was greeted proved its failure ... We were all relieved when the moment came to leave. We roped up and left the Eiger Glacier station at 10.15 p.m. followed by tearful forebodings. But the jeremiads of our fat friend ceased to trouble us once the rope had been uncoiled. The lassitude which paralysed mind and body before the possibility of a night in bed had joined the limbo of dead options, disappeared with the first upwards step ... Weeks of anticipation seemed telescoped into one vivid moment of expectancy. The opening phase of a great climb is never more charged with suppressed excitement than when the issue is in doubt and success at the best problematic ...
>
> At last, to our great relief, the moon shot over the

intervening buttresses, and flooded the foreground
with light. The light did not seem to be poured out on
to the slopes from above. It was more as if the moon, an
ardent lover, had stripped from the body of the glacier,
a close-fitting veil, and revealed all the beauty that had
been hidden below. The wilderness of ice through
which we forced our way displayed a marvellous
variety of form. The towering cliffs of ice were barbaric
in their splendour, but the soft moonlight lent them an
air of unreality, as if they were formed not of solid ice,
but of frozen moonbeams ... We climbed rapidly,
threading our way through countless crevasses. The
false corridor which I had spotted from below did its
best to lure us to a cul-de-sac, but we avoided the
temptation and pressed steadily upwards.

After endless adventures and struggles across seemingly
unconquerable crevasses, the party reached the top.

We reached the summit at 9.30 a.m., eleven hours after
leaving the Eiger Glacier station. We had our reward.
Our toil was a small price to pay for one of the loveliest
views I have ever seen. The monarchs of the Oberland,
lording it above their great ice-streams, served as a foil
to the quiet charm of the most beautiful of all
conceivable valleys in the divine habit of May. From
Schwendi to the Great Scheidegg, Grindelwald lay at
our feet, dreaming of the summer that would hunt the
last of the snows from the friendly cow Alps of Bach,
Buss and Holzmatten...

From our lofty perch we saw a valley very different
to the valley in which I had been living. The familiar
fields seemed transfigured. In the valley you are
conscious of too many details, individual flowers, and
blades of grass, but from the heights these details are
lost in a flood of dominant colour. The sheets of
buttercup are transformed into a woof of gold, the
cherry blossom into a thread of silver.

We seemed to be looking down not on a green carpet

spread above the solid foundation of the earth, but on to a phantom valley built from the fabric of dreams and haunted by a loveliness which is not of this world. An hour slipped by in a dreamy mood of comatose enjoyment. Old memories of boyish rambles among the lower hills came back like stars after a storm.

One lived for the moment and refused to remember that the descent might still prove troublesome. Time stood still and the future ceased to exist. Mind and body relaxed in the perfect peace of inaction. Lazily content, one drowsed away the precious moments. Beauty poured in uncatalogued, a surge of impressions which defied analysis and which rendered futile the attempt to disentangle the separate chords of the great harmony of glacier, lake and valley. But alas! Time does not really stand still. Grudgingly, we returned to the matter-of-fact world where avalanches fall and where an hour's delay may make the difference between safety and danger. One last long look and then away. The hour in dreamland had passed all too soon.

On the descent, however, things almost took a tragic turn. Lunn and his party overcame numerous obstacles – principally myriad crevasses made more dangerous by snow that had been progressively melting as the sun rose higher in the sky. Inevitably, there was drama:

I had just taken a peculiarly nasty bridge with a rush when the ground collapsed below me and I disappeared with a hearty bellow of warning to Amstutz. But the hole was only eight feet deep, a welcome if ridiculous anti-climax. 'Can you get out?' asked Amstutz. I detected a touch of merriment in his voice, and I replied, with sulky determination, 'No, I can't get out and I won't.'

This was untrue, but I saw no reason why Amstutz, who had had all the fun of seeing me fall in, should not do a little work in pulling me out again.

At last the party returns safely to Grindelwald, where, Lunn reports,

> the air was fragrant with the scents of growing things, very welcome after the long hours among the barren hours.
>
> The valley was full of music, the melody of running water with which Spring welcomes back the wanderer from the silent heights. May at her best, a perfect ending to a perfect day.
>
> The Eiger on ski by the Eigerjoch is a magnificent expedition ... The icefall by moonlight stands out among a host of Alpine memories, unique in its severe beauty. We enjoyed in all some 4,500 feet of running, of which about 2,000 feet was easy and pleasant, and the remainder difficult but intensely interesting.
>
> None the less, I can hardly recommend others to follow our example. Risk is inseparable from mountaineering, but the Eiger on ski is a shade too dangerous to rank as a justifiable expedition. Half an hour after we left the Eiger Glacier station, a tremendous snow avalanche peeled off the buttresses of the Mönch and swept right across the slopes which we had been descending. Had we been half an hour later, we could not possibly have escaped. It is difficult, if not impossible, to time one's programme so as to reach safety by midday ... It is with real sorrow that I record my agreement with the verdict of my two friends: '*Der Eiger ist kein Ski Gebirg*' – [the Eiger is not a ski mountain].

While Switzerland started once again to enjoy the patronage of British ski-runners, Austria was not so lucky. Financially, as in Germany, things were rapidly getting out of control. Even worse, there were rumours that the British were not welcome. Hardly encouraging for a country desperate to encourage tourism, and this appeal reached the Ski Club:

> A correspondent sends us a letter from an English lady resident in Thierberg bei Kufstein, Tirol, the following

being an extract: 'Please tell anybody you meet that there is not a word of truth in those malicious reports that have got into English papers about Austria objecting to foreigners. It would be jolly if you came out and brought a few of the old lot.'

However, with Austria going through similar financial problems to Germany (where, by 1923, rampant inflation had made the dollar worth 2.5 trillion marks!) it was difficult to budget for a holiday there. 'The experience which two of our party encountered with Obladis may be briefly recounted,' reported Lieutenant-Colonel H. de Watteville in 'A Winter in Tirol'.

In August, a letter to Obladis obtained a promise of pension at 2s [10p!] per day. In late September, another letter was received, raising the price to 4s a day. In early December, yet another communication raised that figure to 6s 6d [32½p]. The result was than none of us went there.

It was estimated that during four weeks in 1922, the cost of living in Austria had risen 124 per cent!

Poor old Austria, back in the 1920s, was not getting a very good press, and was very much viewed as Switzerland's poor relation. Things were not helped by a newspaper report that some members of the Tirolese human population had succumbed to foot-and-mouth disease!

In the late summer of 1921 came a catastrophic event that robbed the Ski Club of Great Britain of its President, Air-Commodore E.M. Maitland. On that August day he was piloting a giant airship when it broke in two off the coast of Hull. Like a sea captain, he went down with his ship.

Altogether, 44 people were killed when the R38 (ZR-2) disintegrated during a training and test flight. There were just five survivors. The Air-Commodore, who had only been elected President of the Ski Club the previous year, had recently become President of the Federal Council too. During its fourth trial flight, the rigid airship built for the Navy by the Royal Air Force, broke into two parts and fell into the River Humber. It carried to their deaths 28 British nationals and 16 Americans, including Air-Commodore Maitland and Commander L.H. Maxfield, the prospective commanding officer, an American.

The Air-Commodore, who was 41, had taken up ballooning in 1908, and that year he had been aboard the *Daily Graphic*'s Mammoth airship from London's Crystal Palace to Meeki Derevi in Russia – a distance of 1,117 miles, achieved in just over 36 hours. While attached to the Balloon School, he undertook experiments with powered aircraft but, following a bad crash, decided to concentrate on airships.

> On one occasion, he took two young women aloft in a balloon, only to come down on the rooftops of Kensington, necessitating rescue by the fire brigade. In 1913, he undertook the first parachute descent from the airship Delta. He continued to experiment with parachutes, which he considered to be a vital adjunct to the airship, making a descent from a balloon at a height of 10,000 feet.

Awarded the DSO, his citation read, 'In recognition of valuable and gallant work in connection with airships and parachutes. He has carried out experiments at his own personal risk, and has made some descents under enemy fire.' In 1919, he had been chief observer on the first transatlantic crossing aboard the R34.

The 1921 *British Ski Year Book* reported,

> As a first-rate ski-runner and an ardent lover of this finest of all winter sports, Commodore E.M. Maitland was known to many of those who belong to the great and growing fraternity of the ski. Those who have skied with him in Switzerland or Norway will always retain pleasant memories of his prowess and delightful companionship upon the snows ... He seemed to regard the downhill part of the journey as a precious asset, no single yard of which was to be wasted. I have never seen a finer exposition of the Telemark swing ... How pleased I felt ... that at least one Englishman had mastered this most graceful of turns.

His faith in the ultimate development of the airship as a safe, practicable and even economical means of transit was absolute; and he threw himself into the task of attaining this aim with all the devotion and ardour of an enthusiast; and, alas, we must add, with the sacrifice of a martyr. But his labours, though unfinished, have not been in vain. Others have caught the kindling flame of his enthusiasm, and will carry on his work.

He was the first Army officer to build an aeroplane at his own expense, and it was subsequently sold to the War Office. It was the forerunner of our army of aeroplanes today, and was styled 'No. 1.' It was on this machine that he had his first spill, breaking both ankles.

His enthusiasm for flying, whether in an aeroplane or airship, was a by-word among all who knew him, while the thoroughness of his methods was shown by the fact that on one occasion he made a vow, which he faithfully kept, never to land from an airship otherwise than by parachute whenever such an apparatus was available ... his argument being that parachutes would never come into general use, in connection with airships, unless an example was set by constant demonstrations that they were a safe means of descent.

Maitland was always one who put duty first and, when the end came, it found him calm and unperturbed, not caring one jot about his own safety, but thinking only of that of those under his command – with his hand upon the control of the giant airship as, with her back broken, she hurled downwards to her doom.

Chapter 14

THE LADIES
FIGHT BACK

*Up till then, women skiers had been baggily
clad, khaki figures with cold cream streaked across
their sunburned noses, and rucksacks on their
strong backs.*

In 1923, the world's first women's ski club was formed by Arnold
Lunn. Until then, the role of women in skiing had been to 'stand
and wait', said Lunn, 'to follow with respectful admiration the
achievements of their heroic menfolk'. But surprisingly, perhaps,
none of the women at Mürren seemed that interested in his plans.
'So I marshalled three or four rather bewildered women into Room
4 at the Palace Hotel,' says Lunn, 'and told them they were the
founder members of the Ladies' Ski Club.' The club thrived, and to
this day organises popular schoolgirl races each year.

But the battle for sexual equality continued to rage. At the 1927
International Ski Congress in St Moritz, the possibility of rules for
ladies' races was debated. The idea was rejected, although the
concept of points for 'elegance' was discussed.

Meanwhile, there was some debate about whether the word 'ski'
should continue, rather like a ship, to be treated – or at least sound

113

– is if it was female. Was it ski? Or shee? That was the question. Is
shee – still used today by a few skiers – an affectation? Or is it more
correct than *ski*? The question was addressed as long ago as 1926,
when F.F. Roget wrote to the Ski Club from the Reform Club.

> Sir – The word ski is now in common enough use in
> the English language for a review of its position in the
> dictionary and its pronunciation in the spoken tongue.
> Both should be at last unified. The status of the word
> and its derivation should be recognised. It is not a
> modern British acquisition. It is the recovery of an
> ancient possession. Its homeliness has been obscured
> by re-importation from abroad.
>
> From the hard k sound, modern Norwegian and
> Swedish have departed, and we have substituted for it
> a quash sound which is neither a clear vowel nor a
> clean consonant. Should we, then, pronounce to shid
> for to skid; a shiff for a skiff; confuse shirt and skirt;
> give up scudding for shudding; mix up shipper and a
> skipper; say to shate for to skate?
>
> The spurious, soft pronunciation came in as an
> adventitious trick of fashion. It has veiled the identity
> of the ski. They belong to an ancient family of footgear
> adapted to faring on water, snow or ice: the skate, the
> ski, the skiff.

In 1929, the Ski Club sent a mixed British team to take part in an
international downhill race in Zakopane, Poland. The Poles didn't
expect 'ladies' to race downhill, but had to accept them because
they'd innocently confirmed with Lunn that the races were 'open
to all'. So the women raced against the men.

Doreen Elliott and Audrey Sale-Barker caused a sensation by
finished 13th and 14th (beating 45 men in the process) and were
cheered by everyone at dinner in a Warsaw restaurant that
night. Their fame spread throughout Poland. 'The Poles were
thrilled by the courage they showed in one villainous icy glade,
strewn with tree stumps,' said Lunn. 'Both ladies took this glade
straight.'

Tributes even came from America. Writing in *Ski-ing, the*

International Sport, Alice Kiaer, the creator of the American ladies' team, said,

> It was the English girls in the 1929 races at Zakopane ... who first put racing for women on the map. What a flutter they caused in central Europe! Incidentally, they were the first girl skiers in the world to be well-dressed. Their long straight legs, encased in even longer beautifully-tailored flopping dark blue trousers, caused the most open-mouthed wonder and astonishment in Mittel-Europa. And when these slim creatures could also ski it was really too much! Up till then, women skiers had been baggily clad, khaki figures with cold cream streaked across their sunburned noses, and rucksacks on their strong backs ... Austrian girls who knew they could ski well shied away from the red flags and sat down between them in a way to wreak havoc and disaster ... There were plenty of good women skiers who were terrible cowards when it came to a race. The English girls were the first to do or die on any slope.

The faster the women went down, the more they were going up in the eyes of the skiing world. Their champion, Arnold Lunn, proclaimed, 'The day will come when lady ski-runners will be taken at least as seriously as lady tennis players or lady golfers. At present there seems to be a tendency on the Continent to regard ladies' races as something in the nature of a joke.' But in an early example of male anxiety about female supremacy, he worried that women racers 'impertinently display a callous disregard for the *amour propre* of the men competitors'.

Not everyone shared Lunn's enthusiasm for women racers. Lunn quoted the following extract from *Sport*:

> The development of ski-racing among ladies has its dangers. Are ladies capable of taking part without damage to their health in short langlaufs?
> This question will be raised by all those who have had the opportunity of seeing ladies at the finish of a

three kilometre race which includes flat racing and a certain amount of climbing, and who have watched their exhausted condition on passing the finishing posts. The organisers of the ladies' langlauf which was held at Zakopane, and who were present in the medical examination of the competitors, declared that this particular race was too long for ladies.

The Polish ladies who competed in this event declared after the race that, as a result of their training for such races, they were unfitted for competing in slalom and downhill races, but that in future they would prefer to take part in the latter races, which were far more suitable for women.

In other words, they preferred downhill to cross-country. Another blow had been struck in the campaign to bring Alpine skiing to the Winter Olympics.

Chapter 15

END OF THE
GOTHIC AGE

*Suddenly something shoots through the bushes and
hurtles into a tree trunk ... a black object is seen to
heave itself out of the deep snow. It is Captain Jibberer
covered with blood and perspiration. With a last angry
contortion, he hurls himself down the slope straight at
me. With a crash he disappears face downwards in the
snow between my feet. 'Am I through?' he gasps.*

January 1924 was 'the most revolutionary month in the history of
skiing', says Arnold Lunn in his book *The Story of Skiing*.

The Kandahar Ski Club, which was to revolutionise
competitive skiing, was founded in Mürren on January
30. The first Parsenn–Derby was held at Davos on
January 13, and was won by Peter Gruer. The founder of
this great race was an Englishman, Fred Edlin of the Ski
Club of Great Britain. The first open international
meeting to be decided on the combined result of a
Downhill and Slalom was held on January 12 and 13.

In 1923, Christopher (C.E.W.) Mackintosh, one of the finest of the

117

Kandahar's early racers, had won his first Roberts of Kandahar race in bizarre style. Again, it is Lunn, although he missed it through illness, who has the details.

'Somebody remarked that as Arnold Lunn was ill, it was unlikely that anything had been done about the finishing posts,' he wrote later. 'Two Swiss guides ... were therefore instructed to run down to the Egertental and post themselves and their sticks near "Menin Gate".'

The finish would be between the guides, who were given ten minutes' start. Before the starter could get from 'three-two-one' to 'Go', 'a tall, sturdy young man had already dived down the slope,' said Lunn. 'He overtook the guides well above Egertental and, a few minutes later, an elderly skier with a grey beard was startled by the sudden appearance of a human meteor.'

'Don't move,' shouted the meteor. 'You're a finishing post. Put your stick in the snow, and I'll stick mine here.' Needless to say, it was Mackintosh.

The Fédération Internationale de Ski (FIS – assumed by one Ski Club member of the day to be a soft drink), which today runs the sport's blue riband World Cup races, was founded in Chamonix in 1924. Its role was to co-ordinate various national ski federations and lay down rules for ski racing. The Ski Club of Great Britain was a founder member. Arnold Lunn, in contemplative mood, was asking readers of the 1924 *Review of the Year* 'Do we really enjoy skiing?'

Answering his own question, and later returning to the subject of the dreaded Ski Club 'tests', he continues,

I fancy not, for we are either skiing too fast and frightened, or skiing too slow and ashamed. It is not a characteristic of the Englishman to enjoy anything which he takes seriously. Now that the happy-go-lucky days are passed when skiing was an amusement, and now that skiing has become a religion, we have lost something of the simple, artless joys of the happily incompetent.

Unofficially I have every sympathy with those who detest and abominate Tests, and who speak evil of the centres from which this strange infection has spread. Before the Test plague had spread over Switzerland, the standard was so comfortably low that we could all keep pace with it, our failings were not shown up, and a very modest performer could be accepted at his own valuation, so very different from the very unpleasant valuation of a Test judge.

The club had been rather obsessed with tests in the early decades, but now *Ski Notes and Queries* carried the following announcement:

> We do not mean to infer that a skier's only business in life is to pass Tests – very far from it – but the Tests are, nevertheless, an excellent means of attracting the keenest novices to the Club, and in raising the standard of skiing within the Club and of British skiing generally.

The 1925 *Year Book* saw the funny side when reviewing Alan d'Egville's new book, *Sno Fun*, which included the following description of one of the dreaded tests:

> Suddenly something shoots through the bushes and hurtles into a tree trunk. After a long pause, during which a male voice can be heard saying something, a black object is seen to heave itself out of the deep snow. It is Captain Jibberer covered with blood and perspiration. With a last angry contortion, he hurls himself down the slope straight at me. But his feet seem to be going in different directions, and with a crash he disappears face downwards in the snow between my feet. 'Am I through?' he gasps, with his life-blood ebbing.

Getting fit, of course, was half the battle. E.O.W. had the right idea. He wrote to *Notes and Queries* about it:

> I beg to tender novices the following advice: 'Get fit before your holiday.'
> It sounds axiomatic, but the post-war office worker gets about one seventh part of the exercise he ought, and by midwinter, when the effect of lawn tennis and other summer games has worn off, he is often a trifle soft.

Last year, I tried the following, with excellent results. I rose 20 minutes earlier, slipped into old flannels and some mufflers and things, and went for a run. I live in the heart of London, and apparently caused some amusement to Bill and his mate on their way to work, but, like the taker of patent medicine, I persevered.

I started in early October, and in January, when I went to Switzerland, I was fit for long distances almost at once. On the second day I did a longish run, and on the fourth and fifth I skied for 10 hours. This may sound an unimportant matter to our university and soldier runners, but elderly office workers will know that I am talking sense.

I enclose my card, and sign myself, dear sir
E.O.W.

There was a reply: 'Some two years ago, my doctor suggested my giving up "running" with beagles,' wrote H.M.,

I did not see myself 'walking' so gave up beagling and took to pedal cycling ... in some degree akin to skiing, because in both a power of balance and quick decision is called for. I ran down yesterday from Saanenmöser to Lake Thun. The road-making season is in full swing out here now; but the Swiss, as a rule, leave a narrow passage on both sides on the road clear of metal. The effort involved, whilst keeping up a good pace, to steer along one or other of these two passages was good training for this winter's downhill skiing. Perhaps someone else, who is relegated to foot's pace on Shank's mare, will tell us his prescription for keeping 'middle-aged spread' at bay.

Advice of a different kind came to members from Switzerland. It was to be found under this heading: 'Important Notice to Ski-Runners in the Gemmi District', and read as follows:

We are reminded that the new overhead electric power main from Chippis via Leaukerbad–Gemmi –

Schwarenbach–Kandersteg–Kandergrund is now in use. The current is 45,000 volts, and owing to the big span, the wires may – especially under the influence of snow – hang very low. Ski-runners are warned against the extreme danger of touching the wires or even the masts, especially between the Gemmi Pass and Kandersteg.

Ski bindings were becoming a big issue. So much so that in 1924 the editor of *Ski Notes and Queries* asked his writing team to tell readers what their favourite bindings were. They were asked to keep it brief – a maximum of 35 words. Some writers made hay with this idea.

'Oh, my dear Sir!' wrote the Hon. E.C. Pery, the future Earl of Limerick (the sixth earl, a passionate mountaineer and an outstanding skier, who died in 2003, was President of the club between 1974 and 1981). Pery, the instigator of the club's Pery Medal, was about to become Club President. 'Only 35 words to epitomise years of pain and striving?' he protested. 'It's like the swift passage of his past.' This only left him 13 words to complete his task, which, inevitably, overran.

Captain B.J. Marden was rather more ingenious in his description of the B.B. binding:

B.B.
(1) Quickly on
(2) Quickly taken off
(3) Lateral rigidity for turns
(4) Safety in forward fall
But –
(1) Dangerous in side-twist fall
(2) I am not yet satisfied with any binding.

A. Price managed exactly 35 words – and even gave each word a number: 'Ericssen (1) because: (2) Ski (3) unpierced (4) by (5) toe-irons (6). Heel-straps (7) are (8) not (9) cut (10) by (11) mortice (12). Length (13) of (14) toe-irons (15) prevent (16) lateral (17) play (18). Less (19) friction (20). Irons (21) being (22) on (23) top (24) of (25) ski (26). Low (27) toe-irons (28) release (29) foot (30) in (31) serious (32) crashes (33). A (34). Price (35).'

Mrs J. Hollingsworth wrote,

> I think most bindings when they are good are very, very good, and when they are bad are horrid! I have recently used a binding made by *Bächtold* of Davos, which I find suits me best. It is a variation of the *Wray* binding, which is a variation of the *B.B.* I am exceeding the word limit!

The ever-inventive editor of *Ski Notes* even found himself encouraging members to renew their subscriptions with a bizarre parable, entitled 'A Sad Story':

> One day, a Man went out skiing. He went All Alone. Which is never a Good Thing to do, and this case, also, had Disastrous Results.
>
> As he journeyed on his Way the Clouds lowered and he was presently overtaken by a Fierce Snowstorm. Indomitable, he pressed on, and after a time came to a Large Forest, where, exhausted, he sat on a big Fallen Tree. But it snowed harder and harder, and, looking round for somewhere to shelter, he discovered the Tree to be hollow. So he crept inside it to shield himself from the Biting Blast. And it was a very, very tight fit. And, quite worn out, he fell asleep.
>
> The Blizzard then unfortunately turned to Rain and everything thawed. The Sides of the Hollow Tree and the Clothes of our Hero swelled, and when he awoke he found he was stuck tight within the Tree and could not move. After waiting in that position for some Hours and finding himself still stuck he knew that he was a Doomed Man. And his whole life flashed before him. He remembered the things he ought not to have done and the things he ought to have done; among the latter he recollected that he had not paid his 10s Subscription to the SCGB due on October 1st. And he felt So Small that he had No Difficulty in extricating himself from his Uncomfortable Position. Which he did, and went Home and wrote a Cheque – or a Banker's Order.

The parable concluded, *'Kindly note.'*

There had been much discussion in the 1920s about the *foehn*, the warm, dry wind blowing down the northern slopes of the Alps. Arnold Lunn recounts an amusing story in the 1923 *British Ski Year Book*:

> I was travelling down from the Little Scheidegg on a warm day in July, and I got into conversation with the only other occupant of the carriage. I remarked on the heat. 'Yes,' he said, ' I think there is a touch of the *foehn* in the air.'

'Ah!' I remarked, with a knowing air. 'And what precisely do you mean by *foehn*?'

I then leant back with the complacent expression of a chess player who has forked his opponent's king and queen, but my *vis-à-vis* did not seem in the least embarrassed, and launched into a most interesting explanation of the *foehn*.

> I was rather piqued, and remarked: 'You know a lot about the subject – perhaps you are a meteorologist.'
>
> 'I am,' he replied. 'I happen to be head of the Swiss Meteorological Department.'

Later, in the correspondence columns of the *Year Book*, Lunn would add this postscript, 'I take this opportunity of thanking the 43 correspondents who have written to me to point out the misprints in my last, my very last, attempt to describe the *foehn* in print.'

Skiing fashions continued to grip members. In 1924, J.A. Joannides wrote amusingly about 'An August Ski Tour', with sartorial subjects to the fore.

> Dr Hermann Gurtner, Mrs Gurtner and I lay stretched out on the tables of the Jungfraujoch Hotel – not slept, mark you, for it was not a good night. The apartment was filled to overflowing.
>
> The Germans put on white night-shirts, much to the irritation of the Swiss and the disgust and annoyance of

everybody else. When at length a majority judgement had been obtained in the leading case of excusability v. inexcusability of white night-shirts at high altitudes, a Spaniard began vigorously to snore, and continued to do so until we arose at 2.30 a.m. However, the League of Nations functioned so successfully, for perhaps the first and last time in history, that Señor Dabrage was left weeping bitterly in a corner, as we set forth, wildly waving a *lanthorn* [lantern] in the darkness, to climb the Jungfrau.

Having dealt with white night-shirts, the next controversial item was a hat. Again, the subject arose in the night.

That night, we slept in the Finsteraarhorn Hut in company with an English medical student, his sister and their guide.

Now comes the tale of the hat.

The medical student and his sister were extremely cheerful but their guide was not. He was worried, morose, preoccupied, and in fact he was thoroughly upset. We tried to find out the cause of his vexation. No ostensible reason was discoverable ... At last, in a torrent of Swiss that well-nigh choked him, he confided to Hermann, as a fellow-countryman, the secret of his trouble. It was A's hat. It was, I will admit, a dreadful hat. A large white straw hat with a small black ribbon round it. Such a hat, he said, had never appeared in the mountains before. It was an insult to the *Hochgebirge*, an insult to Switzerland, even to Central Europe, he added. Disaster was bound to overtake a party which contained a member who wore such a hat. And so, full of foreboding, he set forth next day up the Finsteraarhorn, complete with Miss A.A. and hat.

That night we met him at the Concordia Hut. He was a new man. The mountains had not suffered themselves to be outraged by a large white Panama hat. They had taken their revenge. Retribution had followed swiftly and surely upon the affront. They had called in the wind as their ally, and the wind had blown the hat away from the top of the Finsteraarhorn.

The story has an unexpected ending, however.

> Hardly had the Swiss guide had the chance of enjoying his newfound relief and happiness than another guide, complete with his guests, tramped into the hut, and started to unpack his rucksack. Suddenly we saw him blanch, his hand trembled, then with a harsh, despairing cry, he pulled out the hat! I believe he is a concierge in a Basle hotel now. His nerve has gone, never to return.

Technique, as ever, was an even bigger talking point than fashion, and arguments continued endlessly. It even emerges that some racers had discovered that it was possible to get round slalom gates more quickly by falling over!

In the 1923 Championship Meeting at Mürren, 'one of the competitors, instead of attempting the orthodox turn, fell deliberately at each flag. On deep, hard snow, a carefully-engineered fall seems to save time.' The race was won handsomely by Commodore Dowding (who would later mastermind the RAF victory by 'the few' during the Battle of Britain) – a full 47 seconds ahead of the field.

'Dowding's suggestion that falls should be penalised is obviously sound,' wrote Alan 'Deggers' D'Egville, 'and was adopted with success both in the Alpine Ski Challenge Cup and in the Schotton Cup. It is clear that on certain types of ground and snow, a candidate who falls, deliberately or accidentally, and who has the luck and intelligence to fall in the right way, may score.'

The following year, at Adelboden, the Ladies' Race caused considerable excitement:

> Mrs Elliott was first into the last field, and looked an easy winner. She sustained an awkward fall, however ... she could not get up again for some little time, and the delay enabled Mrs K. Dobbs to be first past the post ...
>
> In the afternoon ... a slight mistake was made, in that

the competitors did not get an opportunity of examining the course before they ran down. There were a few trees about, and the supply of flags had to be eked out with ski sticks. The result was that most of the competitors failed to see one of more of the turning points, and some confusion ensued.

On Tuesday the Handicap Race was run on the Old Test Hill course. This is always an amusing event, but in this instance, excitement was discounted by the fact that two competitors had finished before the scratch man started!

Members were still concerned about preserving the environment in which they skied, as a letter from N.G. confirms:

> Sir – It is becoming a common practice to bury paper bags, orange peel and suchlike in the snow, or even, in some cases, to leave them unburied. Has it ever occurred to these thoughtless lunchers what a favourite lunch haunt looks like later on, or what people say about them? Do their ears ever tingle in the spring? Litter of this kind weighs very little if put back in the rucksack.

Not all correspondents could be guaranteed publication by a busy editor, who requested the sympathy of members because of his need to produce this journal 'when he feels more like lawn tennis'. One such letter, signed *vieux skier*, was told that his letter had 'more to do with *skieuses*' than with the 'pure-white wastes' – and that, 'while appreciating the nom-de-plume of the contributor, we decline to publish his letter!'

Meanwhile there was grim news (rather belatedly) from Rickmers about his guru Matthias Zdarsky, the Austrian army officer who gave us linked 'stem-Christiania' turns and taught Hannes Schneider, who went on to pioneer the Arlberg ski technique. Serving as a ski-instructor to the Austrian Army during the war, he had, Rickmers informed members,

> in the course of his duties, met with the most fearful avalanche accident that any man has survived. He was

literally smashed, crunched, kneaded and compressed
by the snow, and almost every part of his body
subjected to enormous strain. Yet he survived, but as a
medical curiosity. He had about 80 fractures and
dislocations, among which half a dozen were
dislocations of the spine. With characteristic patience
he set about curing himself and inventing apparatus for
his limbs, suffering agonies all the while. He is quite
crooked and his legs twisted. But he wrote to me the
other day that he has managed to ski again.

An extraordinary phenomenon was reported by P. Neame, whose
eyesight and state of mind can hardly have been suspect, as the
gentleman in question was a lieutenant-colonel. And he had a
witness. He wrote a letter to *The Times* – later reproduced in the
Year Book – as soon as he got home to Faversham, Kent, in the May
of 1923. It was headed 'An Alpine Mirage':

Mr F.S. Smythe and I were climbing the Finsteraarhorn
in the Bernese Oberland on May 2nd, a day of perfect
weather and extremely good visibility ... at an altitude
of about 13,800 feet, we paused to admire the very fine
panorama. We could clearly identify the Black Forest
150 miles to the north. All the giants of the Alps, Mont
Blanc, Weisshorn, Matterhorn, Monte Rosa, etc. ...
stood out as if across the next valley.

So clear was the air that the visible horizon to the
north appeared to be certainly twice as far off as the
Black Forest.

Suddenly, at 11.55 a.m. the image of a ship appeared
in the sky just to the east of the Eiger peak, floating in a
blue shimmer just beyond the visible horizon. This
lasted for a minute or so, and then vanished. Very soon
after, a line of five ships appeared further east, funnels
and masts clearly distinguishable. This image lasted for
some fifteen minutes. The ships appeared of course
greatly exaggerated in size, and were right way up, not
inverted. The direction of the five ships was in a line
from Finsteraarhorn through Grindelwald. On reference

to an atlas, this brings their position on the nearest sea to approximately the eastern exit of the English Channel into the North Sea, a distance of some 400 miles.

This would appear a most extraordinary distance for a mirage, if such it was. Both Mr Smythe and myself saw the ships so clearly that we could not have mistaken any cloud effect for ships.

Whether F.S. Smythe, the Colonel's companion was related to F.E. Smythe – or, perhaps, was one and the same – is unknown, but the latter was also fortunate, it seems, in experiencing the mystique of the mountains. In a feature entitled 'A Solitary Run Through the Silvretta', he enthused with Lunn-like eloquence,

> Only those who have skied by moonlight in the mountains can appreciate to the full the magic of the slender wooden runners which bear one so lightly through the forest – where the moonbeams struggle down through the tall pines in vain attempt to master the dark shadows – until one emerges from the last straggling outposts of the forest full into the dominion of the Queen of Night, where silver snowslope and dim shadowy peak end mysteriously in the stars.

In conclusion, he relates,

> Next morning I shouldered ski, and tramped to Wiesberg, a distance of some fourteen miles, where a train to St Anton was caught. In the short week in which I had been on the heights, spring had come; but who can describe an Alpine spring when, after six long months of winter's icy hand, Nature is released from her captivity?

Spring in the Canadian Rockies brings the added risk of meeting a recently hibernating bear, and there is a poignant tale about such a meeting in the *Year Book*, which originated in a cutting from the 'Sunday Pictorial' concerning the respective merits of skis and snowshoes.

Ralph, the hero of our story, was the son of a trapper who lived on a mountainside in sunny Canada and generally wore Indian snow-shoes when he went out hunting.

Uncle Rueben, however, a man of wide vision, presented Ralph with a pair of ski. Ralph gave a whoop of joy as he unpacked them, and picking up his gun, he sallied forth. He was obviously a promising beginner as most novices would probably leave their gun behind on their first attempt on ski. Not so Ralph.

How nice and easy it was sliding over the snow on his new ski! 'They are much better than snow-shoes,' thought Ralph, as he went leaping gaily down the mountain side.

Clearly the boy had the right stuff in him. He had never heard of Tests, still less of 'Lifted Stems' and all those other new-fangled terms which are invented to plague the beginner. Left to himself, the boy did what every other beginner would naturally do. 'He leapt gaily', realising instantly that leaping gaily and not boggling is the road to Holmenkollen.

Suddenly Ralph discovered that he was being followed by a bear.

He picked up his rifle and fired, but alas! He had forgotten to load his gun. There was nothing for it but to run, and Ralph immediately darted away at full speed.

Then Ralph suddenly halted in horror. Straight in front of him was a yawning chasm – a cleft in the mountain side – forty feet deep! The gap was terribly wide: but in a moment the boy had made up his mind. He would leap for it – trust to luck that he would reach the other side of the chasm. If he failed – well, all would be over.

He did not fail. His gay leaping stood him in good stead. He cleared the chasm with a bound in the best Norwegian style. The miserable bear, however, was not so fortunate. Like too many modern ski-runners, he had neglected jumping, and consequently failed to make the chasm. And as Ralph observed the corpse he remarked sagely, 'Yes, decidedly, ski are better than snowshoes'.

Bears are one thing on the slopes, but how about Yaks? Viscount Knebworth took himself off to the Himalayas where he and the fellow members of his expedition abandoned skiing for *ski-kjöring* (which normally involved being towed on skis behind a horse). 'A magnificent yak was accordingly chartered for this purpose,' he wrote. 'The maximum speed of the yak is two miles an hour, but owing to bad snow conditions and the rarefied air, it was found impossible to maintain more than one and a half miles an hour.'

On Saturday, January 11, 1925, 'a new chapter in the history of British skiing opened,' trumpeted *Ski Notes and Queries*.

> For the first time a British team chosen by the governing body of British ski-runners was pitted against a foreign team ... the Federal Council of British Ski Clubs decided to challenge the Swiss Universities to a race ...
> The race started at 2.30 p.m. under a cloudless sky. The teams started together, and Mackintosh, an expert 100 yards racer, got off with a wonderful flying start. For the first 1,000 feet Mackintosh and Knebworth led comfortably, and then came a series of disasters.
> Mackintosh fell into a stream, collided with a tree, and a few minutes later fell a sheer 20 feet into another river. This gave Walter Amstutz, the Swiss captain, the lead – a lead which he never lost ... Amstutz was born and bred among the mountains. His home is Mürren; he is a first-class mountaineer and a brilliant ski-runner ... I was at the finishing post. Divided between admiration and disappointment, I watched Walter flash past in perfect style. The seconds passed – were we in for a debacle? Had Mackintosh broken a leg? Would the Swiss walk away with the first six places? ... And then suddenly I saw Lord Knebworth appear over the brow of the hill, sailing down with a cheery smile, and I knew that though we might be beaten we would not be disgraced.

Although Mackintosh came up trumps in the Slalom, the Swiss won this historic first match by 33 points to 17. 'To race against

Swiss born and bred among the mountains and acclimatised to the Swiss air will always be a severe test,' wrote the editor of *Ski Notes*. 'Had our tail been stronger, had the team been better trained, we should have done far better.'

There was another major development in 1925 – the Ski Club of Great Britain finally merged with its great rival, the Lunn-inspired British Ski Association. This also brought the end of the Federal Council, whose powers passed to the SCGB's committee. The amalgamated club would have its headquarters in London's Berkeley Square.

In 1927, Arnold Lunn, accompanied by Alan d'Egville, was persuaded to visit St Anton to meet the great Hannes Schneider. Almost as an afterthought, Lunn popped into a local shop to buy a trophy. It would acquire the mystique of a silver chalice.

'Before I left St Anton,' says Lunn, 'I bought a small cup in the village, and set a Slalom on the nursery slopes for the small boys of the village ... At the time I did not realise the outstanding importance of the Arlberg–Kandahar.' The A–K would evolve into the most important downhill races in the world, and survive as such until the innovation of today's World Cup races.

The following year came the first of the now legendary Inferno races – said to be the longest downhill in the world. Field Marshall Montgomery (a cousin of Arnold Lunn's wife, Mabel) was so impressed that he wrote a letter to *The Times* praising it, and later arranged for NATO's top skiers to compete. The year after the inaugural race, the Inferno was won by another hugely talented winter-sports enthusiast, Jimmy Riddell (who, in spite of the well-known cockney rhyming slang phrase 'going for a Jimmy Riddle', insisted his name should be pronounced Riddle as in piddle and not the more affected RiddELL). This delightful skier, a celebrated author (who would be vice-captain of the British team at the 1936 Winter Olympics in Garmisch-Partenkirchen, a Pery medallist, President of the Ski Club of Great Britain and Chairman of the Kandahar Ski Club), won by such a huge margin (half an hour faster than the previous year) that he didn't get quite the reception he expected:

> When I got to the finish – a line across the road from the
> entrance doors of the bottom station of the funicular, to

the railings opposite – there was absolutely no one in sight! No timekeepers, no judges no spectators – not even a flag or two to mark the Ziel! Nothing!

I was covered from head to foot in wet snow from a fall or two and from trees I had bumped into, exhausted and completely bewildered by this lack of any kind of reception. I came to a stop and looked in vain all round the little square. Save for one or two elderly people with shopping bags, it was quite empty. I made a quick sortie into the Grutchalp funicular station and another over towards the main Lauterbrunnen station ... no joy anywhere!

Then it suddenly dawned on me that there could only be one answer to this absurd situation. I poled myself frantically across the square towards the pub – 'The Drei Sternen' – pushed the front door open with my sticks, and, wet and dripping, looking like some very abominable snowman, clattered my way on ski right through the Gaststube, between tables of astonished people having various forms of sustenance, right on out into the back room. And there, glasses of *Dunkles Bier* in their hands, they all were, timekeepers, judges and all. All four of them! 'My God!' came the cry, as they leaped to their feet, 'It can't be! No one is due down here for another half hour!'

'I can't help that,' I puffed, 'I am here, and all I need is some of that beer.'

Famously, Riddell went on to teach skiing in the Lebanon where, on occasions, 'the snow was so deep that skiers were starting out of the second floor windows of their hotel!'

I first met Riddell at Mürren in 1988, during the memorable celebrations to mark the centenary of Arnold Lunn's birth. He regaled me with many sparkling stories and I become a Riddell devotee (a word which sounds more dignified than 'fan'!).

One was about the time he and some fellow racers staying at the Hotel Alpina were dismayed to find that blizzard conditions would prevent them skiing that day. Improvising in a very British way, Riddell and company ripped open their duvets, scattered the feathers on the hotel staircase, and held an impromptu slalom down the stairs. Imagine such a thing today – they would surely have been dismissed as louts and vandals!

On one famous occasion Riddell, in a group of skiers being led by two guides, was caught in a major avalanche in late April on the slopes of Castor, a peak high above Zermatt. Two German tourers were just ahead of them. A powerful account of it – 'Six Minutes Too Soon' – would appear in the *Ski Club Year Book* of 1952:

> It is not very often, fortunately, that one is permitted to stand directly in the path of a major icefall avalanche in the High Alps, to have it envelop one, and to live to write about the experience afterwards ...
>
> With the Col less than an hour's climb ahead, there came the terrible crack and thunder of an avalanche ... The party came to an abrupt standstill as 1,000 feet of ice and snow broke away from the west wall of the Lyskamm high up above and began its downward plunge.
>
> It is, I think, legitimate to record one's thoughts and reactions when faced by a situation of so sudden and so terrible a nature ... My first reaction, after the missed heartbeat that the sound of an avalanche always brings, was to stare in astonishment at the majesty of the spectacle ... the sight of this vast white turbulence was so breathtakingly beautiful that for a moment one stood in a condition of amazement and admiration.
>
> Although the impetus of this tremendous downrush of huge quantities of ice and snow was very considerable, things seemed to be happening very slowly ... From the slow, rhythmic, almost metronomic tread of climbing on ski, when one's mind is in a pleasant, semi-trancelike state, the brain seems to spring, at the approach of danger, into a state of abnormally high receptivity ... Then, quite suddenly, came the realisation that there was nothing to prevent this beautiful but terribly lethal instrument from sweeping down on top of us and engulfing our entire party ... I remember thinking that if this great roaring onrush of billowing white were bringing death with it –

133

then death was approaching in appalling splendour.
This thought brought still not fear, but rather a strange
elation and considerable excitement … I saw the two
Germans, roped together a little above us, in a state of
frozen indecision … As we stood, all of us, roped, with
climbing skins or our ski, and with deep breakable crust
for snow conditions, there was no kind of evasive action
possible. There was nothing to do but await whatever
was going to happen and hope that some unseen
obstacle above us on the terrace would somehow stop
the onrush. Meanwhile the great white cloud came on
down the mountainside and crashed to the bottom of the
cliff. A vast white wave of snow, which must have been
well over 100 feet high, came rolling down the terrace –
came on and on, until it became all too apparent that
nothing was going to stop it enveloping us.

Silhouetted against this huge and brilliant wave, I
saw the two Germans above us turn and try to run. I was
conscious then for the first time of fear – of fear of this
beautiful white wave, that was approaching at between
30 and 40 mph, churning and billowing in the blinding
sunlight … The next moment, the waves came over us
… the surprising thing was the sudden transition from
blinding sunlight to darkness … Presently there was a
great silence.

Astonishingly, not a single member of the group – or the two
Germans above – had been injured. 'Around the whole party,' wrote
Riddell,

sprinkled like huge pieces of shrapnel, and lying
innocently motionless in the snow, were large chunks
of ice – any one of which would have been sufficient to
kill one or all of each little group. It is difficult now to
understand how nobody was hit … I found that I was in
considerable danger of bursting into tears.

The two Germans climbed up a little higher, and
their discovery answered the question that had been
worrying us – namely, why we had not been hit by the

obvious full weight of the avalanche. Upon the sloping terrace above us there was, concealed by a snow bridge, a very large *bergschrund* – or crevasse. This snow bridge had naturally collapsed beneath the immense weight of ice and snow from above, and the major portion of the icefall had been swallowed in a gaping crack four to five metres wide and many metres in length. Beyond this fortunate obstacle only the debris and the snow had been able to reach us ... had that crevasse not been there, then the entire avalanche would have hit us ... Had we been so little as six minutes quicker on our climb, we would have been standing on, or crossing, that crevasse – and that, of course, would have meant a very quick and very efficient burial at a depth of some 60–90 feet.

It is only afterwards that one remembers the little unimportant fact that on the way up, at the beginning of the climb, one of my skins came off, and it took me four or five minutes to re-adjust it so that the climb could continue ...

Once back in the hut, after some undistinguished skiing, we had two bottles of wine. We drank a health to Castor for having defended himself so efficiently – and then I rather suspect that each one of us (I know I did) silently drank a toast to the Great Hand that had released that tottering mass of ice and snow from the rock wall above us just *six minutes too soon* ...

In the words of Lieutenant-Colonel C.H. Hordern, who survived an earlier avalanche near Davos, 'snow and its ways must be studied as a sailor studies the sea, or a wise man the woman he loves; and that even in places like the Parsenn, there are the makings of sudden, unsuspecting, overmastering trouble.'

There were other dangers – such as spiking yourself with errant tips. The Ski Cub received a letter from L. Crawshay Williams, a patient at the Central London Ophthalmic Hospital. It read:

Dear Sir – I shall be greatly interested to know if you know of many accidents from ski points hitting wearers in the face with toe bindings (without a heel strap). I never remember doing this with a heel strap, but bruised my left eye two years ago with a B.B. binding. I have this year dislodged the retina of my right eye with a similar toe binding (the one with the spiral spring in front).

There was clearly a problem here. Another victim, Captain B.J. Marden, having had the misfortune to spike himself in both ear and eye, proposed the wearing of aluminium goggles with eye-slits to prevent such accidents.

In 1929 the Ski Club announced its highest accolade, the Pery medal. It would be awarded annually for the most notable contribution to skiing. E.C. Pery had been described thus in *Ski Notes* in 1926: 'There is no man who allows his friends to exploit him more ruthlessly, and no man whom one would rather have at the other end of the rope in a tight corner.'

Observing that Samuel Butler had once remarked that 'he hadn't got much conscience, and what there was, was guilty,' the writer continues,

> Pery's conscience has never done him any good. It keeps him in London doing other people's work when he ought to be skiing. It fills up his sack when he is touring with spare kit for other folk. It freezes his fingers mending other people's frozen bindings.
>
> Here is a man whom the kindly gods intended for an open-air life ... and he spends most of his life in London and seems to average about five days skiing in the year.

Talking of sacks, it was Pery who famously discovered 'one extremely dead mouse' among the coils of a rope in his equipment box before a climb at Mürren. 'The equipment had been packed away in copies of *The Times*,' he wrote in 'The Oberland Traverse in May', 'and the mouse's inability to digest Lord Northcliffe or Mr Lloyd George in the leaders had been fatal to its equable Swiss constitution.'

Pery also provides us with some interesting snapshots of Arnold Lunn, whom we rarely meet in the third person. During their Oberland traverse, he describes how Lunn inadvertently takes a risky route too close to a crevasse on the Weissnollen.

> Some of the crevasses showed wonderful colours under the strong sun, and Lunn (with a large scarf keeping the light off his snow goggles), plodding mechanically ahead, insisted on cutting his tracks alongside a particularly nice one (to the admiration of the rest) until he looked up from his curtain of scarf. He then changed direction.

Spending a night in the Oberaar hut during a violent storm, the party found a large notice inside. 'It warned us in four languages,' wrote Pery, 'that it was prohibited to pluck wild-growing Alpine plants in large quantities. As the wind was some 70 mph, the thermometer showed between 30 and 40 degrees of frost, and the nearest wild flower was some miles away, we obeyed this order without hesitation.'

There follows an amusing exchange between Lunn and his old friend Hugh Dowding, which, thanks to Pery (who, endearingly, talks about himself in the third person), again throws a little more light on Lunn's personality. And, indeed, Dowding's.

> Somewhere about 7.30, Lunn, who was watching through the window the regulation mixture of clouds and snow streamers, suddenly gave a sharp cry and returned to the bunk where Pery and Dowding were still endeavouring to sleep. 'I say,' he explained, 'you can see the Matterhorn!' Dowding grunted. 'The *Matterhorn*!' repeated Lunn in tones of anguish. 'You can have it,' murmured Dowding. Lunn snorted and called Dowding a 'prosaic Philistine'. A minute later he was back again. 'I say, Dowding, you must get up. You can see the …' 'I know,' said Dowding sleepily. 'But I'll be damned if I'll be called a prosaic Philistine *and* get out of bed to see the Matterhorn.'

Pery continues to amuse. He writes,

> There is something infinitely delightful in the
> repressed bursting into flower of every tree and plant
> freed from its snow in the spring. It is a spontaneous
> and instantaneous creation of beauty, which needs the
> pen of a poet and the knowledge of a mountaineer and
> botanist. To attempt it is none of my business here; for
> mountains are (for the purposes of this *Year Book*)
> slippery places more or less covered with snow, and
> their interest varies with their ski-ableness.

Fittingly, the Pery medal's first recipient, in 1930, was Lunn himself.
(He celebrated that year with a *Year Book* running to 374 pages!)

Other distinguished recipients include E.C. Richardson (the Ski
Club's principal founder – 1934), ski pioneers like Hannes
Schneider (1953), André Roch (1963) and Walter Amstutz (1973),
great ski racers like Peter Lunn (1937), Jimmy Palmer-Tomkinson
(1947), Gretchen Fraser (1948), Evie Pinching (1949), Bill Bracken
(1950), Stein Eriksen (1954), Toni Sailer (1956), Jimmy Riddell
(1962), Divina Galica and Gina Hathorn (1972), Konrad Bartelski
(1982) and Martin Bell (1995).

Also honoured are Sylvain Saudan, the extreme ski pioneer
(1979), Lord Hunt, of Everest fame (1981), Marc Hodler, President
of FIS (1988), and the polar explorers Robert Swann (1991), Sir
Ranulph Fiennes and Dr Mike Stroud (1993).

In 1929, Peter Lunn had some useful advice for racers
confronted with one of their worst fears: a skier trespassing on to
the course:

> The moment he sees a casual skier on the course, the
> racer gives a piercing shriek and makes a bee-line for the
> skier in question. This is not quite so brutal as it sounds.
> The skier hears his yell and at once starts shifting. If the
> racer tried to decide on the skier's probable line of flight,
> he would probably guess wrong and collide with him.
> One thing, however, is certain. The skier will not be on
> the precise spot where he first heard the racer's shriek of
> rage, and consequently if the racer aims at that precise
> spot he is certain to avoid a collision.

Poignantly, Peter became friendly with Andrew Irvine, who was lost with Mallory on Everest in 1924.

> I remember sitting next to him at dinner and my father getting worried because he thought I was boring him with endless questions about oxygen. But he always answered me, never talked down to me. He always treated me as though I was on the Committee. And, in fact, as I now know, he had younger brothers of exactly my age so was very good at talking to young people like me.
>
> He learnt to ski faster than anybody before. He was a rowing blue and, of course, rowing blues do have very good muscles. He had done some climbing, but not very much. And when he was asked to do his elementary test, which used to start off at the top of the practice slope, he took the whole ruddy thing straight, and had the most appalling fall. He used to be called 'the human avalanche'! When he left, he wrote a wonderful letter to my father saying, 'I will always look back on Christmas Day, 1923 as the day when, to all intents and purposes, I was born. I don't think anybody has *lived* [and he underlined the word lived] ... I don't think anybody has lived until they have been on ski.'
>
> This was a fantastic tribute from somebody who was no stranger to adventure. He wrote three long letters to me from Everest. I wasn't allowed to keep them because when we knew that he wasn't going to survive, my father sent the letters across with a letter of condolence to his parents. And his biographer describes how somebody was going through some papers and said, 'I have got three letters here beginning, My dear Peter,' and I nearly jumped out of my skin. Because here were these wonderful letters that he wrote to me. And, in fact, the author did quote from the letters.
>
> But of course it's the biggest mystery in the history of mountaineering. When those two were killed, were they coming down to announce to the world they stood

together on the summit of Mount Everest? It's
something we shall ever know.

My favourite story of the 1920s comes from a letter sent from
Grisons to *Ski Notes and Queries* concerning a missing pair of
socks. It begins promisingly: 'Sir – have you space for a complaint?'
('Always. We thrive on them – Ed.')

And then, almost like a Monty Python sketch, it unfolds with
surreal hilarity. Can this correspondent be serious or is this some
kind of joke?

> The Club does not advertise itself sufficiently. I say so
> because I have just lost a pair of socks in Switzerland
> under rather distressing circumstances. I spent the
> night in a hut and my socks froze to the stove which
> was supposed to be warming it. I got up early and
> went outside to thaw. It took rather longer than I
> expected and I forgot all about my socks when I came
> in. In fact I never thought of them again until the time
> came to put them on the stove at night when I found
> they were missing.

At this point the editor gently interrupts: 'What were you doing
all day? – Ed.' Our unnamed sockless hero continues,

> On return to my hotel, I wrote to the man in charge of
> the hut on Club paper, enclosing postage, and asking for
> the return of my socks. I received no reply.
>
> During a warm spell, I took the opportunity to revisit
> the hut. The keeper was affability itself. He had sent my
> socks to Brighton. The money I had enclosed was
> insufficient to cover postage and would I pay him the
> difference. On being asked why he had sent them to
> Brighton he replied: 'You had on your paper Ski Club of
> Great Britain' [confusing Britain with Brighton].
>
> If anyone should see my socks in Brighton perhaps
> he would let me know. In the meanwhile can nothing
> be done to make England, and this Club, a little more
> widely known?

Chapter 16

DOWNHILL WITH HITLER

*The British contingent were carefully briefed that, as
they came before Hitler, they must make it quite clear
that they were giving the Olympic salute (arm to the
side) and not the Nazi salute (arm to the front). One
member of the team did this with such vigour that she
hit the nose of the young woman beside her.*

What Arnold Lunn liked to call the Gothic Age of skiing – and
indeed its Golden Age – ended when Downhill racing was
formally recognised by the FIS. 'Skiing in the Gothic Age,' he
wrote in *The Story of Skiing*, 'may be compared to cathedral fronts
in the Middle Ages.' He quotes Ruskin to explain what he means:

> Go forth and gaze on the old cathedral fronts, where
> you have smiled so often at the fantastic ignorance of
> the old sculptors; examine once more those ugly
> goblins, and formless monsters, and stern statues,
> anatomyless and rigid; but do not mock at them, for
> they are signs of the life and liberty of every workman
> who struck a stone.

141

'Modern ski racing,' says Lunn, 'no longer resembles a cathedral front, but reminds me of modern government buildings erected to house a host of unnecessary officials.' The Gothic Age was followed by the 'Silver Age' – 'like the Silver Age in Roman literature, an age of fading inspiration,' said Lunn, 'but with its own charm and its own appeal. I recall it with nostalgia, though with less nostalgia than the Golden Age.'

Racing was enjoying a renaissance in America too. Arnold Lunn mentions that one of the most active pioneers of skiing in California was Dr J.H. Hilderbrand, of the University of California. 'In 1930–31,' says Lunn, 'he took his family to Europe for skiing with the result that the first Slalom ever held in California (Badger Pass) was almost a family affair. (1st, Alexander Hildebrand; 4th, Milton Hildebrand; 5th, Roger Hildebrand, aged 10. Louise Hildebrand won the ladies' slalom.)'

By the 1930s, the influence of the legendary Kandahar had spread to North America. Although the recession of 1931 was seriously affecting the British love affair with the Alps, ten 'strong young men' had turned up on April 6 to compete in the Quebec version of the race. 'That was the occasion,' *Year Book* readers were told,

> when Harry Pangman and Bob Marcou, having missed the train, skied all the way up from St Sauveur to Tremblant. They were delayed by Harry going through the ice on Lac Ouimet, and having to stop and dry out, then they also had to wade across the Devil's River, at the base of the mountain. Sad to say, they arrived only in time to see the finish of the race, *but men were men in those days.*

Out of curiosity, Arnold Lunn once asked two people if they knew how the race had acquired this strange name. 'The first,' he noted, 'said the race was founded by a very distinguished Englishman called "Mr Kandahar", and the second that Lord Roberts of Kandahar was so interested in downhill ski racing that he had left a lot of money in his will to start races all over the world.'

Although the Kandahar races were now globally popular, Arnold Lunn was still working hard to promote downhill skiing.

'Luther, a German, had been asked to take over the General Secretaryship of the International Ski Federation,' wrote Lunn.

He was a great obstructionist in the days when I was trying to secure the recognition of downhill racing. He resented the introduction of a new skiing criterion, for he was a poor downhill skier. He never forgave the British for taking the lead in this sport, and he made himself a nuisance to me at the first FIS at Mürren in 1931. He was particularly obstreperous about the Grütsch-Lauterbrunnen course, which he declared to be far too steep for men, let alone ladies.

On the day before the race, I overtook him in a steep and narrow wood glade. He was at a standstill and unhappy. As I passed Herr Luther, I quoted the dictum of a still more famous Luther: '*Hier stehe ich und kann nicht anders*' – (Here I stand and can no other). Stung by this taunt, Luther moved forward, and fell heavily on his nose.

Could this possibly be the same Luther whose death Arnold Lunn 'deeply regrets' in the 1968 *Year Book* as a 'great pioneer of skiing in Germany' whose 'contributions to the history of skiing' in *Der Winter*, the magazine he edited for a quarter of a century, were 'notable for their scholarship'?

Probably not. But, if so, Lunn has certainly changed his tune. Perhaps, as the years rolled by, he forgave his 'obstreperousness' and the two men became friends. Carl Luther became a regular contributor to the *Year Book*.

Arnold Lunn, acting on behalf of the Ski Club of Great Britain, organised world championships in Mürren in 1931 and in 1935. What he did was unique. 'Those were the only occasions in history,' said his son Peter, 'that one country has organised world championships of any sport of any sort on the territory of another country.'

At Mürren, the British women's team triumphed by taking five of the first six places on the first day, and four out of the first five places the following day. In the men's events, Peter Lunn, aged 16, was the second-best British racer in both the slalom and downhill.

In late July 2003, just as I was reading through the proofs of this book, I had lunch with Elisabeth Hussey to tie up any loose ends. It turned out there was a veritble flapping rope-end about which I had absolutely no knowledge: an Englishman, Gordon Neil Spencer Cleaver (apparently known as Mouse – though why, in the circumstances, I cannot imagine) had won (overall) the very first Hahnenkamm. At first I thought she was pulling my leg. This was like discovering that Tim Henman had won Wimbledon, without anyone noticing. 'What!' I exploded over my spinach, bacon and avocado salad. 'How could we have all missed that?' But it was true. In 1931, at the first of the Hahnenkamm races, Cleaver, a member of the Kandahar Club, had famously (albeit now apparently forgotten, except of course by Kandahar Club members) come second in the slalom and sixth in the downhill, giving him a combined and overall victory. What's more, another British skier, Harold Mitchell, came fifth overall. Two out of the top five – who said the British have never won anything on the ski slopes?

In 1932, H.P. Douglas recorded an amusing and graphic account of a downhill race in Canada which appeared first in the *Canadian Ski Year Book* and was reprinted in the 1942 *British Ski Year Book*.

> One by one the frozen racers disappeared into the thick trees below. They looked as though they were falling down a green elevator shaft, and every now and then floated up a rattling crash followed by faint curses. About half way down ... I passed someone with his feet in a tree and his head hanging down the hill. He had given up the unequal struggle, and was resting quietly. Farther down, everyone began to pile up, and I passed two wrestling together in a heap of rocks. Someone in front fell down, and I ran over him, then he got up and fell over me.
>
> By this time there were bits of equipment strewn all over the place, mitts, caps, broken poles, and pieces of skis. One by one we finished. Everyone had lost something. Tam Fyshe arrived with both ears frozen and a large egg on the top of his head where he had landed on a stump half way down. Gratz Joseph finally

appeared, every few yards he fell flat on his face, on one foot a ski, on the other a sliver two feet long, the rest of his ski stuck between two trees somewhere up the mountain. But we all agreed it had been a wonderful race now that it was over.

In the Alps, hotels were getting ready to welcome the now perennial influx of British skiers. 'The orchestra is excellent,' trumpeted one Austrian hotel, 'and a resident English Hostess welcome guests and arranges introductions for bridge, dancing and excursions.'

In 1924, advertisements had been (reluctantly at the time) admitted in *Ski Notes and Queries* as a way of generating revenue, and had very soon been accepted and even welcomed by members.

'Members will notice with some surprise the striking of a new note,' readers were told.

It has taken some trouble to convince advertisers that a journal reaching only 700 people could pay them, but the point is that every one of its readers is a potential customer. Not only that, but SCGB members, being experts, are often consulted about the best place to obtain equipment, so that the advertisements will penetrate a long way beyond the actual membership of the Club.

Members are courteously requested to buy from advertisers and to mention *Ski Notes and Queries*, so that when the time comes for the advertisement to be renewed, advertisers will realise that this is a useful medium for their publicity.

Almost immediately, the editor had devoted a whimsical page to some spoof advertisements. 'CAULFEILD'S CRISTIANIAS – 57 VARIETIES' was a gentle dig at Vivian Caulfeild's obsession with technique. Ditto 'THE "RICHARDSON" SKIPOLE – Prevents that Sinking Feeling'.

Others included 'MELTO Ski Wax – Melts in the Rucksack', 'THE AROSA SHOEHORN – Used last year by over 9,000 feet above sea level' and the somewhat unkind 'Buy the "Visitor's"

Rooksack – will hold everything – except the bill – As supplied at all the Swiss Resorts'.

Then, at last, in 1936, came the event that must have vindicated all the work of Arnold Lunn and his colleagues in trying to get Alpine skiing recognised once and for all. Although it was unfortunate that the Olympics of 1936, in Garmisch-Partenkirchen were presided over by Hitler, Alpine skiing was – at last – part of the Winter Games. There were 755 competitors from 28 nations, with half a million spectators overall. The British team was led by Arnold's son Peter (his vice-captain was Jimmy Riddell), who later wrote in his *Guinness Book of Skiing*,

> Before the opening ceremony, the British contingent were carefully briefed that, as they came before Hitler, they must make it quite clear that they were giving the Olympic salute (arm to the side) and not the Nazi salute (arm to the front). One member of the team did this with such vigour that she hit the nose of the young woman beside her. (The victim walked past Hitler rubbing her injured nose.) But all this was lost on the commentator. He announced over the loudspeakers that the British were greeting the German Führer with the German salute ...

(Peter Lunn later told me in Mürren: 'I didn't go to the march past, for which I got a great deal of credit – but I don't happen to like marching about!')

> The special jumping attracted the greatest crowd, and after that the slalom, making its Olympic debut. There were 70,000 spectators, and it was only fitting that my father, who had invented the slalom 14 years before, should be the referee.

Curiously, Lunn now chastises himself for trying so hard not to fall in the downhill that his result was a great disappointment. 'I was very ashamed of my performance,' he said, 'because it was the only race in which I didn't fall. I was overawed by the importance of the event. I thought I mustn't do badly and as a result it was my most

shameful performance – and it was the most important race of my
career.' But surely, I asked, racers who fall are never going to win
any medals? Not so, apparently in those early days. 'In the world
championships,' said Peter, 'which were held in the same year, I
fell three times and finished ninth. At every big race people fell. If
you went fast enough you fell. You had to take risks and [in those
days] your ski didn't come off, you see!'

After the Games, Arnold Lunn was invited to take part in a
radio broadcast. He was expected to pay compliments to the
organisation, he said, but all he could bring himself to say was,
'Germans, may I let you into a little secret. There are still some
people who ski for fun.'

Writing about it later in the *Year Book*, Lunn said,

> The atmosphere of the Olympic stadium during the
> march past was electric ... The teams that were most
> warmly welcomed by the crowd were the Austrians,
> some of whom gave the Nazi salute, turning towards
> Hitler as they passed him, and the French, British and
> Americans, who gave the Olympic salute.
>
> The most tense moment in the parade was when the
> Swiss marched in front of Herr Hitler. First came the
> competitors for the Military Ski Race in uniform and
> these, of course, saluted, and a few individuals in the
> Swiss contingent followed their example. A
> momentary hesitation, and then suddenly the Swiss
> ranks seemed to stiffen, and the descendants of the
> men who had fought for democracy at Sempach and
> Morgarten walked past Hitler, eyes to the front, arms
> stiffly to the side.
>
> No cheers from the crowd. No comments from the
> broadcaster.

A week after the Olympics, Lunn arrived in Innsbruck to prepare
for the Alpine World Championships. In *Arnold Lunn – Ski
Pioneer*, Elisabeth Hussey says,

> On race day a heavy thaw had melted most of the
> snow, then a sharp frost turned what was left into sheet

ice. The worst part was about 150 metres above the finish, where a very steep slope led to a long glade, a narrow ribbon of snow about four metres wide. This glade contained a succession of bumps, jerking the skier onto the tree stumps which lined each side. The race was postponed for an hour and Lunn said afterwards that not postponing it altogether was the worst blunder of his skiing career. Out of 54 starters there were 17 casualties. Racers and spectators became hysterical, women fainted, men swore at the organisers. A row of men were posted towards the finish to catch women as they hit the bumps with a resounding whack and hurtled across a mixture of snow and earth towards the trees.

Arnold Lunn himself provides a wonderfully colourful description of the mayhem:

The Ladies' Race provided nothing so sensational as Steuri's crash, as none of the women tried to take the ribbon straight in the Devil's Glade, and there was only one serious casualty, a member of the Italian team, but it was a nerve-wracking race for the women, for their friends and for the spectators. Only one competitor succeeded in stopping beyond the finishing post without a pretty severe toss [fall], and those who fell continued to slide helplessly down the ice, sometimes feet first, sometimes head first, while gallant volunteers leapt on to the ice and interposed themselves between the flying *damen* and the tree stumps. I contented myself with placing the field, appointed Kessler wicket-keeper, Bracken longstop, and so on. The ground work was good, and few catches were dropped. On one occasion I counted the wicket-keeper and three fieldsmen all lovingly wrapped round the same tree stump.

Afterwards, Lunn was approached by an unhappy spectator. 'I hope you'll raise a stink about this,' he said. 'There was no lack of expert stink-raisers,' recalls Lunn, 'without any assistance from one who was himself in the dock!'

Lunn continued, 'In spite of such nightmarish conditions, the British team rose to the occasion. Evie Pinching skied magnificently to win the Ladies' Championship. Peter Lunn nicely judged a mixture of bravery and control to come ninth in the Men's Downhill.'

Peter would spend much of the war in Malta. He hated it. When I asked him whether that was because it was a frightening place to be he said, 'Good heavens, no. It was because I wasn't able to ski. I had not seen so much as a snowflake for four years!' He had last skied on his honeymoon in 1939. For him, as he would write later, 'a Lunn who does not ski is rather like the Great Auk, now extinct, a bird that does not fly.'

Finally, he was thrilled to be able to grab a week's leave and steal away to Sicily and the snowfields of Mount Etna, a mere 150 miles away.

In 'Through a Glass Darkly', in the 1944 *British Ski Year Book*, he said,

> I was glad to be alone. A man does not want companions when he meets his beloved after a long separation. I wanted no one to watch my tentative advances. I started down the best slope I could find. The snow was bad and scanty; my bindings were so loose that twice my ski came off; I fell repeatedly. I did not find here the glory of fast schussing, or the delight of high-speed turning. But I was wonderfully happy, because I was once again face to face with my beloved. The features might be dirty, the teeth a little crooked, but it was still the same adorable face that had bewitched me long ago.

In spite of all this excitement, the editor of *Notes and Queries* was, as usual, appealing for contributions under the banner of: 'Adventures – Have you had one?' He continued,

> If so, we shall be very pleased to hear about it. It should be as short as possible, and completely side-splitting if feasible. The odder the better. Curious falls, unless

monumental, completely shattering and stupendous, are ruled out.

Arnold Lunn quoted two falls which qualified:

> My oddest was when I skied nearly half a mile in the Silver Ski with someone else's ski sticking in my foot without my realising it till it tripped me up. I felt nothing till I noticed it, then it at once began to hurt. Perhaps I can add the occasion in the Scaramanga roped race when with Joannides as my partner, I was in sight of the winning post, when we both went opposites sides of a tree. I got up hastily and ran round to free the rope, but ran the wrong way! This we didn't notice, and hurled ourselves down the slope again only to be completely and irrevocably jerked off our feet. Joann, for once, was speechless.

At the annual dinner in 1936, the Club President, the Right Hon. L.S. Amery, claimed that skiing had started long before Hannibal. 'He [Amery] then passed the microphone to Mr Brian Meredith of Canada, who invited us all to Banff,' members were told. 'Owing to the length of Mr Meredith and the shortness of the microphone, Mr Meredith was compelled to bend like a collapsible table, but finally got down to it.'

1936 was also the year Gerald Seligman's *Snow Structures and Snow Fields* was published. Seligman had become fascinated with the structure of snow crystals after being asked by Arnold Lunn to review a German study for an article in the *British Ski Year Book*. In his *Skier's Encyclopaedia*, Mark Heller says, 'Until his magnificent study, little serious research had been done on either snow or avalanches.'

But Seligman, whose brother Richard was one of the original Ski Club of Great Britain members, was no dry-as-dust academic. He could write beautifully, and so his subject became as spiritual as it was scientific.

Ironically, it was Seligman, for many years editor of *Ski Notes and Queries*, who, in a feature entitled 'An Editor on Editors', wrote,

The aged are inclined to become reminiscent. This tendency should be firmly checked, especially by aged skiers. Otherwise most dreary documents emerge. If you used to be a racer, you will write: 'Joannides, having lost his stick, caught me up at Bishop's Curse and was himself soon lost to sight' ... or if a tourer, 'much heartened by the relief of Ladysmith, we caught the 8.30 to Wolfgang' ...

The thrill of recounting these ancient histories may cheer the writer a little, but the answering echo is remote and dim. As Club Editors for long years, Arnold Lunn and I know better than most people how many of these reminiscences have been turned gently away.

However, his letter to Lunn, 'The Treasures of the Snow', published in the 1943 *British Ski Year Book*, is certainly not dreary:

'My dear Arnold,' he begins, 'you have asked me whether my researches into the natural history of snow and ice have stimulated or dulled my appreciation of the beautiful in mountain scenery. You and I can call to mind many occasions on which we have skied by moonlight.'

Seligman recalls the day when he and Lunn set out 'at four o'clock on a late winter morning (no need to wait for the lifts to open – there weren't any!) to see the sunrise from the Weissfluh'. He continued,

> No flicker of wind stirred. No cloud could be seen. No track broke the surface of the snow. But it was not the purity of the snowfields which thrilled us most; it was the myriad gems with which they were studded, some showing pin-points of white light, others the many-coloured fires of diamonds, constantly changing as we moved so that the snow seemed alive with the scintillations.

'This, as you know,' said Seligman, allowing the tiniest hint of science to wander into his silvery prose,

> was due to the shapes in which snow crystals form

themselves. They had grown to unusual size, shielded from the sun's destructive rays by the extreme cold of the past few days. They had become sharp-cornered magnifications of their former selves, some tiny prisms, breaking up the moonlight into tiny spectra, others little mirrors and reflecting it. I think you will agree that this rather obvious explanation of a very simple phenomenon can only have the effect of enhancing its beauty.

I shall never forget my first apparatus for watching and photographing snowflakes as they fell – a crude, artificially-cooled plate in the field of an old microscope. I had read of their countless permutations, and had studied some two thousand photographs of their symmetrical shapes, but to collect them myself and to see them in actuality in their dozens was unforgettable ...

Not the least fascinating part of this microscope work was the tracing of the transformation of the fragile snowflake, stage by stage, into solid glacier ice. Is it possible to imagine that these microcosms, magnified many millionfold in the wild scenery of the Alpine highlands, do not add to its beauty for those who are lucky enough to be able to look beneath the surface?

Seligman describes a solitary exploration of the 'tongues' of the Gorner Glacier above Furri (Zermatt) on a cloudless spring morning: 'The absolute silence stimulated my thoughts. The sun provided my comfort. Good substitutes these, for the venerable architecture, the peaceful atmosphere and the sense of well-being in some ancient university.'

Seligman also talks of an excursion to the Upper Mönchjoch and digging a tunnel deep into the ice frozen to the ridge of the Sphinx. He writes,

In some places we reached the living rock; the ice frozen to that rock must have been there unaltered for tens of thousands of years. In that winding gallery some fifty or more yards in length, you could study both glaciology and geology, and in the deathly silence, save for the occasional groan of the overweighted ice, there was a snug feeling of remoteness from the jarring, warring world outside ...

In this sanctuary we could study and calculate and theorise uninterrupted by the howl of storms outside, even though on some days, in order to reach its shelter, we had literally to cleave our way through the blizzard tearing through the narrow joch.

I think that even in the study of avalanches there was something beautiful. In one sense there are few things more hideous or grating than to see masses of snow lying untidily strewn on the hillside; perhaps there is the added discordance of human tragedy. Yet there is also something sublime – some awe-inspired beauty, the great masses of snow, the evidence of gigantic power.

Seligman did much of his work in the fearful but awe-inspiring world of crevasses. He wrote,

Some are wide and brilliantly sunlit, others are so narrow that your body can scarcely squeeze between the two cold hard walls, and there is twilight or even complete darkness in the depths. Especially when the crevasse is part of an icefall – a mass of snow or ice with little design – there is practically no end to the weird shapes of corridors, chambers, trenches and shelves which spread in wild disorder in all directions. Here you could wander for hours or days without retracing your steps. Throughout our crevasse wanderings, I often felt as if I were reliving a Jules Verne or Ballantyne novel. Wherever we went there was wild, unbelievable beauty.

From the moment you lower yourself over the crevasse lip you become conscious of the most fantastic decoration nature can fashion. Here there are rows upon rows of icicles; there part of the crevasse side has peeled off, like a vast strip of neglected wallpaper, to form a curtain perhaps 20 yards in vertical and horizontal extent, but only a few inches thick, convoluted into the most graceful folds and bends, and imprisoning between it and the crevasse wall a sea-green half-light.

On another occasion, Seligman describes a triumphant night-time visit to a platform overlooking the Aletsch Glacier – the longest in Europe. 'The lower crags of the Drieeckhorn opposite glowered black and threatening,' he wrote,

> but everything else was brilliantly lit by a full moon ... there was a creaking and groaning, a rubbing and scraping, below us, but ever varying. And suddenly I realised that I *knew* what these noises were, exactly what caused them, and exactly how the ice grains were shifting and adjusting themselves to the sweeps and bends as the great frozen stream flowed over its rocky bed. Who can doubt that this knowledge added the splendour of completeness to that already impressive scene?

Seligman and Lunn, as respective editors of *Ski Notes and Queries* and the *British Ski Year Book*, enjoyed a playful rivalry that sometimes spilled over into something which could, perhaps, be described as good-natured tetchiness.

Seligman wrote,

> My first contact with Lunn was both physical and unfortunate. We were in the same football game at school, and he was distinctly the heavier, both in body and boot. *I well remember those flail-like arms but cannot find a suitable epithet for the legs.* From the early days our ways lay apart until after the last war when we met again as members of the Federal Council ...
>
> I was asked to take on the editorship of *Ski Notes and Queries* ... I do not say that we always saw eye to eye, nor that there was no competition. Nor, indeed,

did the editor of the one allow himself lightly to become the recipient of the chaff from the threshing floor of the other. There may even have been a little guile, in passing, or refusing, the buck. There was certainly much leg pulling.

On one occasion, after Seligman had accused Lunn (in print) of 'an absence of moral rectitude', Lunn countered with, 'Mr Seligman ... has done the dirty on his colleague on more than one occasion.'

Like a newspaperman triumphing over a rival, Lunn once admitted, 'I am glad to say that I have just intercepted a fine batch of photographs which were intended for *Ski Notes*, some of which will appear in the next issue of the *BSYB*.'

There was more. Lunn wrote,

> *SN & Q* was originally intended to be nothing more than a news bulletin. It was never intended to compete with, much less surpass, the *BSYB* in the matter of illustrations. My disapproval when the first photographs began to appear was severe but silent. It has never ceased to be severe, but it has ceased to be silent.
>
> On November 18, 1933, I wrote to the Council a letter from which the following is an extract: 'Something must be done to regain for the *BSYB* the proud position of our leading Club periodical, a position which has been seriously menaced by the tactics of Mr Seligman.'

A competition was duly announced – in *Ski Notes and Queries* – for 'the best skiing photographs submitted by an amateur for subsequent publication in the *British Ski Year Book*'. Lunn chuckled to himself as he thought of Seligman including such an announcement in his publication – designed, as Lunn deemed it, 'to put *Ski Notes and Queries* firmly in its proper place'.
Lunn recalls,

> Photographs poured in ... and the first prize was won by Mr W.A. Ragge for a beautiful study of ski tracks

near the Mönchjoch. Mr Ragge wrote such a nice letter
... A few weeks later, I had another letter from Mr
Ragge, in the course of which he asked me for a
contribution to a 'journal which I edit'.

I noticed that this time he signed the letter 'Watt A.
Ragge'. 'PS,' he added, 'the journal is called *Ski Notes
and Queries.*'

Sometimes the badinage was gentler. Back in December 1923,
Seligman described a critique by Lunn of an article entitled 'Ski-
Running and Mountaincraft' as 'kindly and moderate'. In fact, he
suggests, 'I think he praises my words with faint damnation.'

Chapter 17

A LAST HURRAH

The editor knows of no better escape than on ski!
Consequently ... we were studiously deaf to the
thunder on the left, and full of announcements about
the things that really matter – annual dinners, tests,
races, and ski-mountaineering ... and then the
balloon went up.

The storm clouds of war – or at least the first serious wisps – were gathering, but the routine day-to-day concerns of skiers continued. Under the heading of 'You Have Not Been Warned', readers of *Ski Notes and Queries*, in October 1937, were greeted with: 'The following notices which should have appeared in the May issue arrived too late for publication. One was late owing to Miss Holt-Needham's illness; the other owing to the mental anguish of Mr Peter Lunn on finding himself engaged to be married.'

Things were not looking good in the Alps. In 1938, Hannes Schneider, a strong opponent of the Nazis had been arrested, but the Germans tried to persuade Lunn to run the Arlberg–Kandahar in the great man's absence. (Lunn, in Rome, had been contacted by telegram. Since no one knew where he was staying, they sent the message to Arnold Lunn, 'care of the Pope, Rome'. It duly reached him. And he left immediately for St Anton.)

'Schneider, though not a Jew himself, had always been anti-Nazi,' says Elisabeth Hussey. Lunn hinted that the race would go ahead if Schneider were released and allowed to go to America. 'Your only reason for cancelling it is political,' he was told. Lunn responded by asking if they had interned Schneider for telemarking. The new pro-Nazi Burgermeister told Lunn, 'You can't stop us calling it the Arlberg–Kandahar.'

Lunn agreed: 'And the Jockey Club couldn't prevent you racing the Nazi leaders on donkeys round a field in St Anton and calling the donkey race the Derby,' he retorted.

Back in England, 1938 saw the retirement as editor of *Ski Notes and Queries* of Alan d'Egville, the celebrated *Punch* cartoonist (and skier). 'Deggers' had enjoyed a huge influence on the Ski Club, where his vibrantly coloured paintings of skiers were hung on the walls, and still are. They complemented his personality. He would turn up at Ski Club balls and parties dressed in the most colourful way – once as a Swiss admiral, another time as a Chinese mandarin, or even as a waiter, yodelling or playing the concertina.

At the time, the *Year Book* observed, 'His emphasis on light-heartedness, combined with light-footedness is perhaps unique in the instructional nature of the sport,' adding, 'perhaps on the snows we shall get a chance of laughing at him and in London we always laugh with him.'

Peter Lunn recalled d'Egville's 'enormous sense of humour and incredible ability to think of the right answer at the right time'.

'He was incredibly funny,' he said. 'He'd pretend to be a waiter in the dining room and everyone would roar with laughter.'

As Elisabeth Hussey, who for almost two decades edited *Ski survey* (the magazine which finally combined the *Year Book* and *Ski Notes and Queries* in 1972), recalls,

> He learnt to ski in the Black Forest in 1908, using one vast pole to turn around. He began the First World War as a despatch rider, and ended it as a Chief Intelligence Officer. His pictures were published in *Punch*, *The Bystander*, *Tatler*, the *Sketch*, and many other papers. He had a great gift for showing skiers struggling with the

elements, with the different techniques being tried out in the 20s, and the many rules laid down by the judges. Deggers wrote a book called *Modern Skiing* ... showing all the impossible contortions that skiers got up to – as well as the clothes they wore. As a clown himself, he knew how to make a clown out of a skier. He took part in hundreds of races, usually just missing out on winning. For years, Arnold Lunn printed a running joke in the *Year Book* about a cup d'Egville offered for a langlauf (cross-country) race because the cup was never actually seen ... Finally, after fire destroyed half the Palace Hotel, Deggers announced: 'Isn't it tragic that my beautiful cup has been destroyed in the fire?'

By December 1938, with war just around the corner, insouciant skiers were still forging ahead with their winter arrangements. Or was it a conscious 'last hurrah'? Lillywhites were still in optimistic mood, promoting their 17th Winter Sports Catalogue with the caption: 'As Essential As Your Passport'. Not many people would be using their passports the following winter.

Meanwhile, the new editor of *Ski Notes and Queries* was anxiously asking what the readers thought of the change in the cover picture. He obviously wanted to give the magazine a more modern feel. In 'Editorial Notes', readers were told, 'If you do not like what he has done to our beloved magazine, then he will dutifully commit hari-kari.'

By May 1939, the prospect of war was unmistakable. Reviewing the 1938–39 season, readers were told, 'Several matters have distinguished the past season. It began in doubt and is ending in doubt. Alpine frontiers grew tense. You could no longer ski in Austria, in the sense that Austria as Austria no longer existed.'

By October, in a feature entitled 'Mice and Men', the war had well and truly arrived. 'This issue of *Ski Notes & Queries* is produced as a kind of counter-irritant,' members were told.

When it was written, set-up, and put together during July and August, one still dared to plan optimistically. It's difficult to recapture the mood, but it was there. Another Great War was unthinkable: no man, no government, could deliberately precipitate one. The best way to discourage it was to ignore it. With such matters as skiing the only thing to do was to go ahead as usual. Consequently this issue took shape in its present form, studiously deaf to the thunder on the left, and full of announcements about the things that really matter – annual dinners, tests, races, and ski-mountaineering. It awaited the usual advertisements to enable it to go to press in ample time ... and then the balloon went up.

As a result *Ski Notes* might have been suspended, but having got so far it seemed a pity to go back. The alternative was to go ahead, and at the same time to annotate most items 'in abeyance'. And this has been done – just to give you something else to think about. *The editor at least knows no better escape than that on ski.*

One such function now 'in abeyance' was 'the coming Annual Dinner on November 14th, in the old ice rink of Grosvenor House;

This huge and beautiful room accommodates something like 1,000 persons, and seven or eight hundred can fill it comfortably and leave space for dancing without the floor getting as crowded and as dangerous as a nursery slope on a sunny day. Consequently it is a case of come one, come all, and come early with your reservations.

But it was not to be.

Yet, a still-optimistic Lillywhites were thus far refusing to buckle in the shadow of war. By December 1939, they had come up with a new slogan: 'Winter Sports In War-Time', and a 'sherry party' for members went ahead on December 19th. An embryonic 'spirit of the blitz' was obviously already at large in the land as members were told, 'This time there may not be much skiing to anticipate; but it should serve to lighten the black-out, if nothing else.'

The Second World War would, effectively, bring to an end the second – and, arguably, the last – Golden Age of skiing, which Arnold Lunn thought of as more of a Silver Age.

Chapter 18

WAR AGAIN – BUT THE SHOW GOES ON

I remember being gratified by my wife's choice of war-time reading when I found her staggering downstairs with an armful of bound volumes of the British Ski Year Book, but I was soon undeceived. She proceeded to barricade our windows with them as a protection against blast and anti-aircraft shrapnel.

As the delightful halcyon days of the 1930s came to an end – never to be repeated – and the long shadow of war descended, the editor of *Ski Notes and Queries* wrote a moving editorial which he called 'Variations':

History repeats itself. The SCGB editor in December, 1914, was writing: 'The European War, which is having such far-reaching effects all over the world is, of course, not going to leave this sport or this club untouched. About 63 members are known to be serving with the forces, and it is likely that many others have joined in addition'. And later were recorded the names of several members killed, wounded or missing, and one, who died of wounds as a prisoner, had been awarded the Victoria Cross.

For December, 1939, we might write the same: Alpine skiing is of course out. The club has had to suspend many activities. And innumerable members are in uniform. But history repeats itself with striking variations. If continental skiing proves impracticable, skiing in the British Isles may be possible. And the number of ways in which our members have joined the forces, offensive and defensive, make the classifications of 1914 seem as rudimentary as those of *1066 And All That*. Members are of course flying and putting vorlage (forward lean!) into the joy stick.

They are soldiering and sailoring in a score of strange ways. They are auxiliaries of many breeds and both sexes; and they have disappeared into the glamorous black-out of hush-hush occupations. They serve in all ranks from the very top to the very bottom; and only the inhibitions of war time forbid us from proudly naming names.

As to casualties, little is known, except that one well-known member was accorded the additional distinction of being mentioned in an unconfirmed report as assassinated. With things continuing as they are in Poland, however, this may become commonplace.

It was suggested by a member of the Alpine Club that 'Commando training is based largely on principles evolved by mountain-climbers for the past 50 years.' D.B. Wyndham Lewis treated this suggestion with a touch of cynicism. He wrote in the 1942 'Review of the Year' that

The rugged virtues claimed by Alpinists, openly or obliquely, in their writings are courage, perseverance in right, strength of mind and body, purity, chivalry, altruism, fortitude, beauty of spirit, prudence, modesty, and a few more we forget. Stout fellows, their books invariably make them out to be dear chaps, dear persons. In our view there is something possibly evil in their masochistic pleasures. His peaks are notoriously haunted by demons, and that Alpine fondness for looking down on people from immense heights is presumptuous folly, if nothing worse. The Offensive Spirit is certainly essential in Commando training, but we think Alpinists, while boasting, should take the public more in to their confidence.

Unlike what happened during World War I, both the *Year Book* and *Ski Notes and Queries* continued to publish on a limited basis, with special war issues each year. The publications carry reviews of skiing in Scotland, Wales and England but, not surprisingly, few, if any, from abroad.

Arnold Lunn wrote most of the *Year Book* himself – Miriam Underhill, a celebrated American mountaineer, wrote a letter saying, 'Congratulations on the *Year Book*. It's true most of the articles seem to be by the same author, but as he happens to be one of my favourite authors, I don't mind.'

Immediately after the war, it was even worse. 'The first issue,' said Lunn, 'was produced immediately after five years of war in which the only British who had skied had been the British officers interned in Switzerland. There was practically no copy, with the result that I had to write 120 pages of the 166 pages of literary matter.' A friend, C. Myles Matthews of the Climbers' Club, wrote to Lunn saying, 'The most marked effect of amalgamating the various *Year Books* appears to be that, whereas before the war there were many *Year Books* to all of which you contributed, now there is one *Year Book* written entirely by yourself.' It wasn't until after the war that an assistant editor was officially appointed.

The continuing publication of the *Year Book* prompted an intriguing sequence of events. The volumes found their way to Field Marshal Montgomery in the desert. He said, 'In the desert campaign, I used to look forward to getting the *Year Book* with its pictures of snow and ice.' It also reached prisoners-of-war in Singapore's dreaded Changi jail. In the 1943 'Review of the Year', members were told,

The last issue of the *British Ski Year Book* was not

passed by the censor for prisoners-of-war because it contained some remarks which sensitive Nazis might have considered faintly uncomplimentary. In these days the poor scribe has to consider so many susceptibilities, that it is a little trying to be forced to measure one's words lest the finer feelings of the Nazis should be ruffled.

It has therefore been decided to remove from the *Year Book* any paragraphs which might conceivably irritate our beloved enemies and to continue the 'Review of the Year' in *Ski Notes and Queries*.

There is a delicious moment in the *Year Book* when a Mrs Otley, the Club Secretary, recalls a wartime meeting of the Council during the 'Flying Bomb' period. 'My spirits soared,' she said, 'at the thought that for many hours not two, but several people stood the chance of being buried beneath the ancient [Clubhouse] brickwork.' What could she mean? 'Surely 20 buried people,' she explained, 'must make more noise than two, and have more chance of attracting the attention of a rescue party, if the worst happens, and – who knows? – one "wise virgin" may carry a whistle.

'How delighted I was to see them all!' Mrs Otley continues.

I could have embraced every single one, but I hid my ardour beneath a cloak of seemly servility. We sat round the Council table and the meeting started; the siren sounded and we heard the flying bomb, far away at first, and then gradually nearer and nearer. I was quite happy. On one side a DSO, on the other an MC. Facing me generals and 'high-ups' in all the Services. I gazed at them all in turn; how would they react? Suddenly the Editor of the *Year Book* [Lunn] looked dreamily out of the window and said: 'I think I hear a Gentleman overhead; our illustrious President is sitting in a position which is extremely dangerous, and I suggest that we open the window just behind him.'

At least eight pairs of hands pushed open the window, at which moment I remembered that the sash cord was broken. 'Sash cords! Sash cords!' I stammered desperately. Nearer and nearer roared the Doodle-bug. The Editor of the *Year Book* disappeared beneath the heavy Council table, and emerged triumphant, like a diver from the sea, with a suitcase – but what a suitcase! Not a brown utilitarian suitcase, but a beautiful blue one with white bound edges and a white pinstripe, three inches apart. The kind of suitcase that is used to Continental travel, is at home in sophisticated surroundings, and has a festive look. 'What will he do with it?' I wondered. The Editor rushed to the window and jammed the bag between the window and the sill, thereby reducing the area of splinterable glass behind the illustrious President, Admiral of the Fleet Sir Roger Keyes. Eight pairs of hands relaxed slowly, and the Council resumed its dignified progress through the agenda. As the Doodle-bug roared over the Clubhouse, I gazed at a label which fluttered gaily from the case with the words 'Lady Mabel Lunn' inscribed on it. I often wonder if it would be nicer to be decapitated by a blue and white striped suitcase labelled Lady Mabel, or by a piece of glass. It is a debatable point. Anyway, it was a nice meeting.

In 1940, the Captain of the destroyer HMS *Kandahar*, Commander W.G.A. Robson, wrote to Arnold Lunn to thank the Kandahar Ski Club for sending Christmas presents to the crew. He said,

> I hardly dare to ask this, but more than anything else we would like the honour of being made an honorary member of the Club, and that the ship's name should be on the list of members. And perhaps we might be allowed to use the 'K' above our crest when we have qualified for it by 'running' far enough. I think we have almost qualified now as we have just done 29 days at sea with two nights in harbour.

Lunn regarded this letter as 'the greatest compliment ever paid to the Club'.

At the 35th Annual General Meeting in July 1942, the Club's President told members,

> In spite of the continued suspension of all its normal activities, the Club has continued to flourish, and the Council feels that its decision to keep going as far as possible within the present limits has been justified ... The continued support of a large proportion of our members during times when there is little to offer in return for their subscriptions justifies our confidence that when better times return, we shall be able to look forward to a speedy revival of the sport.
>
> Many of our members have continued to distinguish themselves in the Royal Navy, the Army and the Royal Air Force, and a number have received awards for gallantry on active service. There are others of whom we are no less proud who have given their lives for their country and whose names will appear on the Club's Roll of Honour.

This must have been a particularly poignant moment for all concerned, because the roll call of honour would include the President's own son, Lieutenant-Colonel Geoffrey Keyes, who, at 24, had been posthumously awarded the Victoria Cross. He had been killed at Beda Littoria, in Libya, during an attempt on the life of Rommel, the so-called 'Desert Fox'. The young Royal Scots Grays officer, commanding a detachment of a force which had landed 250 miles behind enemy lines, led his men, without guides, in dangerous and precipitous country to attack the house which was believed to be General Rommel's headquarters. When they reached their objective, Colonel Keyes took only one officer and one NCO with him and, having evaded the guards and dealt with the sentry, he dashed into the first room he encountered and shot the occupants. He then rushed into the second room where the occupants were the first to fire and Colonel Keyes was mortally wounded. As well as his VC, he was also awarded the Military Cross and the French Croix de Guerre.

Sir Roger reminded members that the *British Ski Year Book* 'remains as almost the sole remaining contact with our members ... within the limits of the "Paper Controller" it is our hope that the publication of the *Year Book* will be continued as long as possible.'

Without the *Year Book*, how could we have ever know about such amusing trivia as was brought to readers in a 'Letter from Lebanon' by Edward Coles?

> The Libanese [sic] call all British soldiers George – 'Hello George, how are you?' It is supposed to have come from the Aussies after they arrived last summer – they call everybody George. The Libanese, I think, regarded it not as a name, but as a respectful address, such as 'gentlemen' or even 'Sahib'.

Arnold Lunn debated the decline of cross-country and jumping among Canadian skiers. 'A pity,' he wrote.

> Though I campaigned in the past for the recognition of downhill races in downhill-racing country, I agree that the resources of the typical langlauf country round Montreal should be made use of, and that it is ridiculous for skiers to spend all day sliding down a slope of about 200 metres in height and re-ascending on a rope tow.

There was always skiing in dear old England, of course, though not everyone was encouraging about the prospect, including R.C.K. Renshaw, who was in playful mood in his 1942 essay on 'Skiing in Swaldedale'. He wrote,

> Serious skiing is not advisable in England. One has to approach the season with a spirit of fun and adventure. Fair-weather skiers will rarely enjoy skiing in this country. We decided that we would enjoy ourselves whatever happened. There is a thrill about setting off in a snowstorm in a £5 open Austin 7 tied up with string, never certain of the snow conditions, or if the car will return! The car always did return, however, though it had to be pushed in heavy snow on one or

two occasions, and there were others when the tyres developed punctures at the end of tiring days.

My warmest memory is of a long day in mid-February, spent alone on execrable snow in the Gunnerside area until in despair, I begged for shelter to eat my sandwiches in a shepherd's cottage. There, in the cosy kitchens with hams of bacon strung from the ceiling, and with a singing kettle hung over the fire, I ate my lunch ... Truly a major part of the enjoyment of a skiing holiday comes from its associations. The honey and rolls and butter and coffee in the morning on the Continent; the jingling of sledge bells and the winking lights of the Tirolese twilight and the sweet chocolate and cakes earned after a sunlit day near Chamonix – these have their part, and why should not with them be associated the northern comfort of a Yorkshire kitchen?

Meanwhile, war or no war, a Mrs Fairclough was enjoying skiing in Derbyshire's Peak District. 'My particular job is driving a mobile canteen,' she disclosed.

The day following the first snowfall, I stowed my ski in the van, hoping to find an opportunity to use them. This duly came when we arrived at a steep, snow-blocked lane up which it was impossible to drive. So I and my 'mate' filled rucksacks with stores and walked up to the camps on the moor-top, I carrying ski in anticipation of the return trip downhill to the parked van. We covered five miles altogether on foot, but two and a half of these I was able to ski, while my envious and ski-less companion had to walk it.

We earned a certain amount of notoriety when one of the daily papers heard of our exploits long after that particular snowfall had thawed and sent out a photographer. We had considerable difficulty in finding sufficient snow for the pictures to give credence to the vivid write-up they gave us to the effect that 'valiant ski-woman braved colossal snowdrifts on ski to get through with cigarettes, chocolates, etc. to marooned and snowbound troops.'

Mrs Fairclough skied whenever she could. 'It has been a great source of joy and satisfaction,' she wrote, 'to have been able each winter of the war to have spent so many of my leisure hours on ski,' while awaiting the dawning of that 'happy day when once more we can spend our holidays in the Alps'.

The *Year Book* continued to publish letters 'from the field' which included one to Arnold Lunn from Captain Ian Munro in North Africa, who wrote, 'Well, Arny, all is quiet for the moment, and I can shut my eyes and picture how Mürren will look that first winter after all this. I'll be there and I've no doubt you'll be there before me!'

Lunn, too, in contemplative mood, was missing Mürren. He later wrote,

> I was in Florence when the Germans invaded Holland. I had said goodbye to the Alps from the terrace of Berne, while the Panzers were breaking through at Sedan, and the next mountains which I saw were the Rockies from Denver. Beautiful in their way, but I missed the dead, the Roman, the Burgundian, and the Hapsburg. For there are moments when the tramp of dead legions can still be heard on the roads which the Romans built.

Lunn would not return to England until the Easter of 1942. 'I have crossed the Atlantic, since the beginning of the war,' he wrote, 'in a passenger ship, in a man-of-war, and in a clipper. And I am looking forward with great interest to a bomber passage.' He would be finally flown home from Newfoundland by one Squadron Leader G. McDougal. He wrote,

> As an old mountaineer, I was technically interested in the effects of altitude, but my removal of the oxygen mask at the height of Everest's North Col, 24,000 feet (7315 m) did not long escape his eagle eye or stern remonstrance. We flew at night. It is desirable to keep

awake, as the oxygen requires attention, and I was glad to discover in my travelling companion, Mr Blair, a chess player. I had no mittens, and as one cannot handle chess men with ski gloves, there were times when my fingers looked a little blue, for the temperature in our cabin sank to some 60 degrees below zero, Fahrenheit.

I have visited 25 countries, and travelled 80,000 miles since Hitler invaded Poland, and I should not be sorry if I were kept at home for the rest of the war. It is certainly good to be in England 'now that April's here'.

Lunn had undoubtedly missed his home country almost as much as his spiritual home in Switzerland ('the only European country which has never fought either as our ally or as our enemy') and the mountains in general. Lunn liked to make a distinction between the attitudes of climbers and skiers to the mountains which gave them so much pleasure. 'There are mountaineers,' he wrote, 'for whom a mountain is only a problem in technique, and there are skiers for whom mountains are nothing more than things down which to slide. But there are others, and it is for them that I write.'

And write he did – even at night!

Night among the mountains blots out the visible evidence of Man's presence in the hills, the campanile [bell tower] and timber-stained chalet no less than the ugly scar of funicular and mammoth hotel, and throws into strong relief the basic mountain form which has changed so little since Man first followed the retreating glaciers into the Alpine valleys. Night breaks down the bridge of associations which Man builds between himself and the mountains; the Matterhorn is no longer Whymper's mountain, but that same nameless obelisk which towered above the uncharted glaciers when mammoths were still lumbering across the Piedmont plain. Night re-establishes the autonomy of the hills and restores their memories of a life which is infinitely older than Man.

Lunn was equally eloquent about the differences he felt between the Alps and the Andes, which he had recently visited:

> The Alps is little more than a geographical expression, for one does not think of the range as a range. One thinks of individual peaks, each with its own name, personality and tradition. But the Andes have a group soul. The individual personalities of the mountains are subordinated, as in a Communist film, to the mass personality of the range as a whole.
>
> The Alps have been humanised rather than vulgarised by human contacts. Their austere majesty has, perhaps, been diminished, but there has been gain as well as loss, for even trippers and picture postcards contribute something to the personality which the Alps have acquired by long association with Man. Man is at home in the Alps, an intruder in the Andes.

In 1942, Lunn warned readers that the next *Year Book* might be late as he might have to edit it abroad – possibly from South America. He revealed,

> When I was in Chile, I was told that the German Chileans had managed to persuade themselves that the British had played no part either in mountaineering or in skiing. I hope that the *British Ski Year Book*, copies of which are being sent to Santiago and to our various British Institutes in foreign countries, may help to remove this impression.

The Americans, on the other hand, needed no such convincing. The *Oregon Journal* wrote,

> After two years of war, during which the Club's London headquarters have been damaged with bombs, and hostile armies have separated Britishers from their ski grounds in the Alps, the Ski Club of Great Britain lives on and makes plans for its annual *Year Book*. It is an example and a challenge.

171

Harold A. Grindon, the historian of the National Ski Association of America, sent this message to his English colleagues: 'This is Christmas Eve, and our thoughts within our home are running across the great pond, and we thank God that we are in this battle together, and we further pray that Hitler and his kind may soon be driven from the face of the earth.'

By 1944, casualties among Ski Club members had reached a disturbingly high level. 'The war has taken further toll of our numbers,' said Mr I.G. Aitchison, on behalf of the retiring president, Sir Roger (now Lord) Keyes, who was busy on active service. 'Thirty-six members are known to have been killed in action or died on active service.' The presidential address concluded with these words: 'This is the fifth Annual General Meeting held during war-time. On the next occasion ... I express the hope that we may meet again in more peaceful circumstances and closer anticipation of returning to our ski and the Alps.'

On a less sombre note, Arnold Lunn, who by this time had edited the *British Ski Year Book* for a quarter of a century, recalled that his wife Mabel and their daughter Jacqueta had been putting the good book to good use at their Victoria Street flat in London:

> I remember being gratified by my wife's choice of war-time reading when I found her staggering downstairs with an armful of bound volumes of the *British Ski Year Book*. But I was soon undeceived. My wife proceeded to barricade our windows with the *Year Books* as a protection against blast and anti-aircraft shrapnel.

UNBOMBED –
AS YET

Since you have persevered, dear reader, to this point in our book of skiing memories, you can now enjoy a special treat. The feature below really belongs in Chapter 18, along with all the other tales from World War II. But I have plucked it like a pearl from its 1941 shell because I feel it deserves to be savoured. Like so many features that have lain relatively, or in some cases completely, undisturbed for years in the Ski Club of Great Britain's Arnold Lunn Library in Wimbledon, South West London, it is poignant, funny and steeped not only in the indomitable spirit of the blitz, but also in that of the Ski Club of Great Britain itself.

Miss Quick, who has not only worked but slept at the Club headquarters since the War began, undismayed by the bombing, has been prevailed upon by the Editor to describe her experiences on one of the hottest nights of the Blitz. This chapter in the history of the Club will be of interest not only to our members today but to those in happier years to come, when the Club headquarters will resume its peaceful character as the place where we meet to revive memories of adventures abroad, rather than as the central point of perils more dramatic than those of avalanches and racing blitzes. – Arnold Lunn.

Oooh, nice to have a free evening ... Shall I finish that 'Penguin' or write to Uncle Harry? It's high time I did ... What's on the wireless? ... Oh good ... well perhaps I'd better do some mending ... Blow it, the wireless is off; wonder how soon they'll be here ... Can't possibly mend without the wireless ... Oh, well ... *Dear Uncle Harry, it's ages since I wrote to you ...* (there go the sirens – bit early to-night) ... *but life is rather hectic these days. Am all that's left of the Ski Club staff now; the housekeeper and I prop the establishment up by day, and I keep a wardenly eye on it at night, except when I'm on the W.V.S. job; what a joy it is when the canteen has to go out, for to be needed is such a satisfying feeling, and the gratitude of cold, wet and exhausted firemen, wardens, rescue and ambulance squads for a cup of hot tea, something to eat and somewhere to eat it repays a thousandfold any puny sacrifices of one's own. It's a privilege to be in that atmosphere of imperturbable good humour and incredible endurance in such a world of wanton wickedness; to know that the area of the dimmed canteen hurricane lamp provides them with a momentary haven – a withdrawing room – from the ruins upon which they have been working and to which they must return. There's something sinister and evil about that mass of debris, lit by the fiercely flaming house next door – a sort of panting, gasping pulsation as though bricks had not yet died – as the people underneath them have not yet died ...*

Gosh, what a racket there is to-night! ... You all right, Mrs Newman? Noisy, isn't it? Just going upstairs to shut the shutters ... Ummm, bit eerie up here, torch seems a bit low ... Ow! That table was hard; shan't be sorry to get downstairs again ... My hat, they *are* letting fly – and no wonder, there seem millions of planes. PHEEEEEEEEE ... CRASH! Umm, that was close ... where's my stomach? Get back, you silly thing; that was miles away; you know you can't hear your own bomb coming ... I say, look at that fire ... What a target ... poor devils ... And a flare – gosh, it's like daylight; what a marvellous view from up here ... pheeeeeeEEEEEEE ... Crash, CRASH ... Go on downstairs; it's silly to stay here ... Ow, that fire-extinguisher hurt; hope it never has to be used, haven't the faintest idea how. Bump the bottom, I think ... Are the buckets full of water? ... CRASH, CRASH. Oh, go downstairs, this is giving me the creeps ...

So I'm sometimes a bit sleepy in the daytime, but luckily the few faithful members who use the Club are very nice, if they catch me before I've washed and brushed up. I wish that more members could really make use of the Club; it is so interesting to put a face and a personality to a hitherto impersonal record card, or to a usually quite misleading handwriting. It was always this thought which encouraged us to go bumping breathlessly down the stairs from the office to open the front door – and to climb up again afterwards! During my years here, I've grown rather Mother Carey-ish, from watching the progress of my chickens, keeping their records, answering their letters, and, sometimes, making their acquaintance. It's enormously strange how deeply this sport sinks into them and lives in their memories and their anticipation; it must be mountain-magic or something. Even now they seem determined to keep the Club alive; this is manifest from day to day in letters from men in the services, women in the services, members in far Dominions and members at home, paying subscriptions that they can perhaps ill afford, resigning with unfailing regret, but all expressing good wishes for the Club's future. Escapism, if you like, but of the stuff which will win the war.

PHEEEEEEEE crash, crash, CRASH … ummm, wish I was on duty to-night, hate sitting around here like a rabbit waiting for doom … Horrible word, doom … hope I'm not trapped and have to lie and think about doom … what's the name of that ghastly buried-alive music? … I believe I'd go mad … but that would be awfully feeble … try and imagine it now so that it won't be so bad if it comes … It'll be pitch dark and filthy dirty and you won't be able to move … (Perhaps I'll put the torch a bit closer, or hold on to it) … and you mustn't think about going mad or that bit of music or anything silly … the wardens will be around … I say, they must be having a bit of a night … I've never heard so many bombs; wonder if they'd like an extra pair of legs? … Well, let's get this letter done …

Excuse interruptions and slight incoherence of letter now, but I can't concentrate. Honestly, London hasn't had quite such a pounding before. The bombs are fairly whizzing down, far outdoing the shells which are whizzing up. Our bombardment is terrific; one of our guns blew open the office shutters just now, which was a bit hair-raising. The noise is almost too big to hear; its intensity makes it incredible, and its incredibility makes it interesting. But I don't think

I'm interested enough to stay here any longer; waiting for something to happen dents my aura of nothing-can-happen-to-me. Mrs Newman has gone to bed, faute de mieux, *as she is in the basement anyway, so I'm off to see if there's something I can do ... There are so many bombs and they all come down with such fearful screams and whistles, followed by the most unholy explosions, that ...*

Gosh, that's close ... Gosh, that ... Gosh, DUCK ...

Well, Uncle Harry, we're all right. I had just decided to offer my legs to the wardens, when with a whiz and a sort of PUFF, things blew about, soot blew around, and one's main feeling when the four floors above stood firm in the second was, 'Hooray, we're all right, so SUCKS,' addressing thus the bomber in the vulgar but expressive manner of one's childhood. What a mess, though; everything open to the sky, and tinkling twinkling glass all over the place. Mrs Newman's clothes had almost to be dug out before she could dress, drink some hot tea and go over to the crypt for the rest of the night. We had to climb over the bomb crater to get there ... life's funny, isn't it? ... but hadn't time to appreciate it as we quite thought another one was coming. So now I've come back to the Club and am going to prowl round to see how it is feeling.

Wish my torch wasn't so low ... Oh yes, this is the landing window, blown frame and all into the hall ... Oh, those poor shutters, torn to bits; suppose it would have been better to have left them open ... Thank goodness the glass hasn't hurt the members' room; glad the bookcases are all right and the lovely arm chairs too; it's a gracious room ... Ow, whatever ... oh, it's the office door blown right off and into the passage ... my, what a mess; half the ceiling's down ... oh my, WHAT a mess. Let's go higher ... snf snf ... gas? ... snf snf ... there, look, that gas fire is flat on its face. Where in heaven's name is the main gas tap? ... cellar, isn't it? ... well, down you go, sister, and do something about it ... golly, WHAT a racket there is; it hasn't slackened since it started ... How I loathe stairs; I swear I'll have a bungalow in heaven ... Bother the torch, it's almost gone ... oh well, maybe dawn will come soon ... Suppose I'd better prowl back to the Club ... might as well begin to get some of this glass out of the way; how lovely it looks – like stardust ... What a fantastic night ... 'Hobgoblins hop and witches ride the moon' ... 'drunk with a monstrous and inhuman glee' ... I'll bet they are ... gee, It's cold ... well, sweep you ass ... it'll soon be dawn.

Chapter 19

MEANWHILE, BACK IN SWITZERLAND

A long roll call – and many who will never answer
again. Shaw Stuart has worn his last disguise; Squire
will never again stump through the door with his
skates on, his legs bandaged like racehorses', telling
an Irish story in an accent only he imagined was
Irish; Tony Knebworth's voice is rollicking through the
corridors of another world.

Oh, to be in Mürren, now that winter was here – even if there
was a war on. How they all missed their spiritual home! But the
Swiss, it seems, were prepared for the worst. Arnold Lunn set
out their position thus:

> In the event of an invasion, they would begin by
> blowing up the Simplon and Gotthard tunnels,
> essential for the German communications, not only
> with Italy, but also with Libya. They would abandon
> the plains, and concentrate their stores of food and
> munitions in the Rhône Valley. Defeat would be only a
> matter of months, perhaps weeks, but the Swiss

believed that they could kill 200,000 Nazis before surrendering, and thus contribute a noble service to the cause of all free men.

It was a close-run thing. Arnold Lunn reported an overheard conversation at Interlaken in 1940, when two senior German figures were discussing just such an invasion. The German Minister to Berne was telling a senior Nazi, 'You do not know these people. Every man has his rifle and we shall have endless trouble even after we have conquered the country.'

The Nazi, later the German Ambassador to Madrid, replied, 'It is very bad for our prestige that Switzerland is still free. Their press is not at all respectful. The Swiss are really a very impertinent people.'

A little-known fact is that Switzerland, neutral or not, was not immune to German bombing. One example was reported in the London *Evening Standard* of August 9th, 1944:

> Morgins, a Swiss winter-sports station in the Canton of Valais, was bombed and machine-gunned by three German planes which came from the direction of France yesterday afternoon. Flying low, a German bomber, accompanied by two fighters, dropped two bombs, one of which pulverised a soldiers' rest chalet and damaged a number of dwellings. Then the fighters dived, firing their machine guns along the village street. Half a chalet where a number of young girls were on holiday fell into a torrent. Three girls were injured and the rest fled panic-stricken into an adjoining forest. Among 20 people injured were two Swiss soldiers.

But such attacks, presumably aimed at French resistance forces, and in this case probably the result of geographical error, were extremely rare. By and large, Switzerland remained a peaceful oasis in the fierce theatre of the European war.

Perhaps the most resplendent bouquet Mürren has received before or since was sent by letter to Arnold Lunn by his cousin Kingsmill Moore in Dublin, on Christmas Eve 1941:

Mürren, geologically a narrow shelf above a glacier valley, became in turn a cow alp, a hamlet, a climbing village, a tourist centre, and finally, in the 20 years of peace between the two world wars, reached to European fame as the Mecca of skiing. Here the technique of downhill racing was evolved, the Kandahar founded, the racing rules of the world drawn up, and a new standard of ski-running created.

Mürren was a home, and each new visit a homecoming. The indiscriminate welcome of the concierges at the station, the tour of the shops after tea and finally the great hour of the day, the Palace lounge with the old familiar pictures and notice boards and trophies and all my friends, grown almost to brothers and sisters from long acquaintance, seated at the tables, or drifting to and fro … a long roll call and many who will never answer again. Shaw Stuart has worn his last disguise; Squire will never again stump through the door with his skates on, his legs bandaged like racehorses', telling an Irish story in an accent only he imagined was Irish; Tony Knebworth's voice is rollicking through the corridors of another world. Before this war is over there will be other absentees.

Mürren, the real Mürren of those who returned with the snows of every year, was a microcosm. Not so cosmopolitan as some other centres, not so full of fashionable notorieties, it seemed to attract men of real eminence from every walk of life. I come from a people and a city famed for good conversation, but the best and the best-informed talk I have ever listened to was at Mürren.

In the Palace lounge I first heard of the *Anschluss* from a British minister, the intricacies of modern banking from Jakobsen, the extent of modern diabolism from Allinson, and the philosophic basis of Catholicism from you. And the arguments, the never-ending arguments, starting between a couple of people (of whom you were usually one) and collecting a gradually growing circle of auditors and intervenients!

Where but in Mürren could you have found a group of anything up to 20 young men and women listening with deference and attention to a debate on Thomist [followers of Thomas Aquinas, the 13th century philosopher] fundamentals? Where but in Mürren could you get first-hand information on any subject by walking a few yards across a room? Artists, lawyers, doctors, diplomats, businessmen, schoolmasters, generals, admirals, every branch of human activity, and everyone in an expansive holiday mood which produced the best that was in them ...

Mürren was selective. Brains, athletic powers, social position came not amiss, and served at least for an introduction ... Mürren had many detractors. It was, said one young gentleman, in a Wengen train, 'lousy with Royals'. It is an age of easy superciliousness towards those who come from ancient and royal blood, but when I think of courage in adversity, of devotion to duty, or reckless gallantry, of humour, of sane, tolerant judgement, and of acts of rare courtesy, I find my exemplars of those virtues among the 'Royals' I got to know at Mürren.

Another stock jibe was that Mürren was an overgrown public school, with the public schoolboy's attitude to athletics, and their insignia in the form of badges, carried on into adult life. There is just sufficient truth in this to make it worth while to confute ... Before you condemn these things, it is worth considering why they are fostered at public schools, and if you find that the athletic cult produces courage, endurance, decision and initiative ... there seems no valid reason why even adults should not receive a refresher course in those virtues ...

The spirit of the Kandahar was the spirit that was the Battle of Britain, and the man that directed that battle [Dowding] and many of those who fought in it were members of the Kandahar.

Memories of the great skiers are pursuing me tonight. Bracken rippling down a slope like a snake, Joannides who attacked the snow almost as if he hated it, Mackintosh superb in his strength and recklessness, Peter [Lunn] strung up to a very fury of tenseness, Durel who 'moving seemed asleep' and Doreen, in Telemark position, leaving her faultless furrow straight down the steepest course ...

Meet me on the Schiltgrat after the war is over, and I will race you to Kandahar Finish for a bottle of champagne.

There was a continuing appeal for skis to be provided for Mürren's internees. *Year Book* readers were told,

Mrs Clifford Norton, the wife of the British Minister in Berne, has appealed for 100 pairs of skis for Allied internees. Any member who has ski stored in Switzerland and who is willing to lend them can obtain details of the scheme and a form of authority for their release, from the Ski Club of Great Britain.

Meanwhile, skiing was developing apace. Walter Amstutz, missing his old English friend, wrote to Lunn,

Since you left this country, international tourism has practically come to a standstill – but this cannot be said about skiing. In fact it has gone ahead in leaps and bounds. Skiing in Switzerland has become more than a national sport – it has almost become a national vice.

Running down Parsenn on a Sunday last winter stands out particularly in my mind. It was just an ordinary Sunday, and conditions were not especially good, but I felt over half the course that I was running in a convoy of fellow ski-runners.

There were hundreds of them, and they were all good and fast runners. At Schwendi I asked my friend Peter Juon, the advertising manager of the Grisons Tourist Office: 'What are you going to do when all the visitors come back again after the war? You will have to issue tickets not only for the railways, but also for

the Parsenn runs!' Othmar Gurtner suggested to me
the other day that we will be forced to rent an Alp
before our skiing days are over for fear of collision!

Readers of the 1943 *Review of the Year* were informed that
there was

> an increasing tendency for famous aces to retire from
> races in which, through a heavy fall or other causes,
> they had lost all hope of doing justice to their
> reputation. It is unfair to deprive other competitors of
> the credit of beating them, and it is bad luck on
> competitors who have the courage to finish after doing
> badly that their names should appear low down on a
> list which does not mention the competitor who failed
> to finish.

A new rule required that

> a Result List shall contain not only the names of those
> who have finished but also the names of those who
> shall have started and failed to finish. The names of
> those who have failed to finish shall be classified as
> follows:
> a) Competitors who have fractured a limb
> b) Competitors who have retired injured without
> fractures
> c) Competitors who have retired because of broken ski
> or equipment
> d) Competitors who have retired because they were
> dissatisfied with their performance.

The war would drag on for a while yet – but everyone was just
itching to return to the slopes.

Chapter 20

THE ROCKET AGE?

The Kick Turn is indeed secure. I couldn't move
an inch, in any direction, including the required one.
I have been there all the summer. I am still there.
And I would be grateful if you would kindly ask your
correspondent to contribute a further letter to
illustrate how to proceed in the required direction.

The 1950s were a great turning point in Britain. They ushered in a sea-change – and something of a ski-change – following a decade dominated by the dark years of despair of the early 1940s. And prepared us for the superficial, skittish and seductive 1960s. Life was beginning to be fun again. Serious fun. But one aspect of skiing remained unchanged, as Guy Wilson pointed out in a letter from Newdigate, Surrey, to the Golden-Jubilee issue of *Ski Notes and Queries*: 'Sir – I have read the following quotation from Confucius: "And greatest glory is not in never falling, but in rising every time we fall." I suggest that this is very sound advice to all incipient skiers.'

There were moves afoot to beautify Arnold Lunn. Or should that possibly read *beatify*? Let Lunn tell the story himself:

On my return to New York I found an article on last year's Arlberg–Kandahar from the gifted pen of Ethel Van Degrift, who is rapidly becoming one of the leading ski journalists on the American continent. In the course of her article she referred to 'the beautification of Arnold Lunn.' The beatification of Arnold Lunn is not inconceivable in the remote future if skiers start the appropriate cult after my death. Two miracles would, of course, be necessary. A couple of Gold Medals for British competitors at the Olympic Games might satisfy the most exacting *advocatus diaboli*, but the beautification of Arnold Lunn is a much tougher proposition. Many enthusiasts have taken on that job only to abandon it in despair.

Lunn had become rather indignant that people were now asking whether he still skied. 'I still ski because I still walk,' he would say. 'It is less tiring to slide slowly downhill on ski than to walk along the level.' He would later suffer the further indignity of being roped down from the platform after a speech in St Anton following the 1958 A–K in St Anton. 'This was too much,' he protested. 'To be roped for the descent of a ladder! After all, I was a mountaineer – once!'

During the winter of 1951–52, skiers from the British Army enjoyed a visit to Bad Gastein. A report of the proceedings concluded:

> Bad Gastein is an interesting town, almost a museum-piece through which one suspects the ghosts of King Edward VII, the Emperor Franz Joseph and Kaiser Wilhelm still take leisurely drives: it would be hard to find another place – even in Austria – so permeated with the atmosphere of the age which came to its sudden end in the first week of August, 1914.

The *Year Book* carried a letter from the newly appointed editor of the *Scottish Ski Club Journal*, Philip Rankin, asking for a contribution. 'As you can see,' Mr Rankin wrote, 'I am only barely literate and a sample of your work at first hand would be very good for my Editorship, which I trust may not be as long-lasting as yours

– meaning no offence. Yours very sincerely, Philip Rankin. PS – If you don't I'll tear your rotten rag to shreds.'

Meanwhile Owen Lawrence-Jones was amusing readers with a delightfully illustrated letter concerning the notorious kick-turn and the difficulties he had encountered attempting it after reading instructions in *Ski Notes and Queries*. The concept which had finally caused his undoing concerned the additional 'refinement' of an axe! Lawrence-Jones quoted from the original instructions: 'I believe this turn to be of value in a situation where a slip may be dangerous. For extra security the axe or inverted ski-stick may be driven in between the first and second movements.' Not having an axe about his person, he tried the ski-stick option. He wrote,

> I went back, inverted my ski-stick, and drove it in between my first and second movements. An axe would have been better really. Now I would like to confirm that the instructions were perfectly correct. The turn is indeed secure. I couldn't move an inch, in any direction, including the required one. I have been there all the summer. I am still there. And I would be grateful if you would kindly post me the next number of *Ski Notes and Queries* and ask your correspondent to contribute a further letter to illustrate how to proceed in the required direction.

The Ski Club's sense of humour was certainly well established, as the following notes on 'Lesser known types of alpine fauna' by Professor Robert Eden illustrate. Eden starts with a word of caution:

> Note – As this is possibly the first time that these very elusive animals have been mentioned in print, the author would like to point out that a great deal of energy, lubricant and alcohol, etc., was required to obtain the details given here. The author would be very interested if any readers have further information on these animals.

The good professor – if indeed he really was one – begins with an animal notorious for causing undignified wipe-outs.

1. The Snowsnake – An irritating little animal which lives under the surface of hard or packed snow. It therefore appears mainly on nursery slopes. The Snowsnake is white in colour and almost invisible. Its chief habit is to pop up suddenly out of the snow, making a hissing sound, between the ski-points of beginners practising snow-ploughs, causing them to fall over backwards. This is the reason why beginners have so much trouble with *rücklage*.

2. The Sidehill Gouger – This is a four-legged doglike animal found on steep slopes, always moving on the same level. In order to stand upright its two right legs are longer than its two left legs, therefore it always walks round a mountain in an anti-clockwise direction. Sidehill Gougers are frequently employed by map-makers and surveyors for tracing contours. Very occasionally this animal is found in towns, where it may be seen walking with its two short legs on the pavement and the longer legs in the gutter.

3. The Keewee Bird – A small white bird which resembles a cockatoo. It should not be confused with a similarly-named bird which is a native of New Zealand. The Keewee Bird makes its nest on the very top of a steep snow slope, just under the cornice. When disturbed by approaching skiers it swoops down, crying out: 'Crrripes, what a slope!'

4. The Mish-mish Bird – A very rare animal which has seldom been seen. It feeds on apricots, hence its name (*mish-mish*: Arabic for apricot). It lives at great heights, following behind ski-mountaineers, tourists, porters and members of Alpine expeditions. It shows a marked preference for persons with bulky rucksacks. It carries around a supply of large stones which it drops into rucksacks, hence these always appear heavier than they are. Most perplexing and irritating phenomena connected with ski-mountaineering are caused by the Mish-mish Bird, such as the habit huts have of receding constantly when approached over long, tedious glaciers.

Ski Notes and Queries readers were also able to take advantage of some valuable information and advice about equipment. In a preamble to a 1951 skiing glossary, they were reminded that 'In any sport, to know the proper words is more than half the art; to use the implements – the lesser part.' Naturally, the glossary begins with the central plank, if you will, of the skiing world:

> **1. SKI.** A narrow piece of wood, longer than the user. Ski, like grouse, live together in pairs; though, unlike grouse, they have a permanent tendency to part company. A single ski is a tragic sight, but has a surprising turn of speed. The points of ski are turned upward; this is so that skiers will have to buy goggles to protect the eyes. It is impossible to ski without ski, though most people would prefer to.
>
> **2. WAX.** Is applied to ski to make them run faster. The novice will not require this, and should urge the instructor to apply glue instead.
>
> **3. BINDING.** A contrivance affixed to the ski to ensure that, after falling into deep snow, the skier must remove his boots before rising. This always causes amusement.
>
> **4. SKI BOOT.** A converted canal barge, made waterproof, so that snow which gets into it cannot get out again.
>
> **5. SKI STICK.** A kind of inverted steering wheel, useful for fending off experts who exceed the speed limit.
>
> **6. SKI HOSEN.** Ski-ing trousers. If these are cut properly, the knees cannot be bent, and thus excessive *vorlage* (*q.v.*) is prevented.
>
> **7. SKI-LIFT.** A device for transporting the unsuspecting skier to the top of a hill down which it is impossible to ski. There are several kinds of ski-lifts; but all are uncomfortable.

Having itemised the basic equipment, the writer then moves on to methods of skiing:

> **8. VORLAGE.** An imaginary excellence to which no one attains. It was invented by ski instructors so as to be

able to say 'more *vorlage*' when unable to think of anything else to say.

9. RÜCKLAGE. The opposite of *vorlage*; one always has too much of it.

10. STEM. Alleged by ski instructors to be an easy method of stopping. The true stem position is obtained by forcing the ski apart until you are about to split; and then forcing them further. At this point a complete stop is suddenly achieved.

11. TURNS. These are a necessary part of ski-ing, as our friends in the Alps have not yet been able to invent a mountain with straight sides.

12. LANGLAUF. Badly named. It is always very long, but does not run.

13. SKATING STEP. In this the weight is shifted rapidly from one ski to the other – the wrong one.

Next on the list – more fauna:

14. MURMELI. The murmuring noise made by the class when the instructor says '*nun steigen wir dort oben*' (now we're going up *there*).

15. GEMS. Chamois. The dark spot on the snow a long way behind you is not a chamois, but your sack which has fallen off.

Children in 1950 were obviously still struggling with excessively long skis, as the following advertisement in *Ski Notes and Queries* confirms: 'For Sale – Two pairs of children's ski. Pre-war. One with bindings, both with edges. About 6ft 6 ins length. 45s the lot.'

But there was good advice in 'Hints on the Storage of Ski Equipment' by Isobel 'Soss' Roe, which included:

Ski
- Scrape and lacquer.
- Varnish uppers, or, if in bad condition, strip, stain and varnish.
- Grease edges with Vaseline and metal bindings with 'thin' oil to prevent rusting.

Boots
- Clean and polish with a good boot polish.
- Fit boot trees or stuff with newspaper.

Sticks
- Apply saddle soap or leather dressing to the leather parts. The metal part should be treated with Vaseline.

Skins
- Take precautions against moth.

Touring kit was also a talking point. 'Mr Allinson's article in our September issue has drawn a short comment from another keen tourer,' readers were told. Mr B.W. Richards says, 'The article will be of great help to prospective tourers ... In the list of kit, I think the waxing iron superfluous and I prefer to have a shirt in preference to the pyjama jacket. For next season my friends and I plan to do the Saas–Fee–Chamonix Tour (Uncle Joe Stalin permitting).'

And, by way of jovial final touch, the editor of the day wrote, 'In typing out Mr Richards' letter for the printers, the word "shirt" above was typed "skirt": I was very tempted to let this go uncorrected.'

Like all editors before him, the redoubtable Colonel C.A. de Linde was pleading for more articles to be sent to his Chelsea home – and, in particular, better photographs. He wrote,

> In one department, at least, we are much below pre-war standards, *viz*, in the photographic. I get few, very, very few really striking photographs: I go green with envy when I look at the photos in the Swiss and Austrian ski periodicals – one scarcely ever sees one that is not lovely *or* dramatic *or* both – and (I don't think this is merely a display of my photographic ignorance) *technically* good. Until photos of this sort become available, it is hard to justify the extra cost of more than two pages of photos.

A quarter of a century on, there was still much debate about whether to let the plural of *ski* become *skis*. And whether it was skiing or ski-ing. Predictably, the good Colonel was still, quite reasonably, sticking to his guns. 'We prefer *ski-ing* to *skiing*,' he said, a touch haughtily, 'and still like *two ski* better than *two skis*.' This was *still* being debated more than a decade later, when R. Brock-Hollinshead wrote to the *Year Book* as follows: 'Dear Arnie, Our ridiculous habit of writing ski without an "s" ... is now ripe to be dropped ... I humbly claim a place on your pages for that most admirable of four-letter words, namely SKIS.'

Peggy Kaiser, describing the problems of limited funds caused by post-war currency restrictions for travellers, wrote,

> Over and over again I have been told that Austrian hotel proprietors would rather have the English guest with his very limited spending capacity, than the more wealthy of other nations. Reasons: we are more sporting, more appreciative, better behaved, and generally give less trouble. As long as we can live up to this reputation we will always be welcome, even if our visits do little for the financial profit and loss account.

Meanwhile, Captain Luttman-Johnson was complaining from the Western Oberland that snow reports did not always tally with reality:

> Sir – It's so interesting to discover what snow conditions really are here; we are marked daily in the official report as *poudreuse* [powder snow], but all I can find is a hard sheet of ice, except for a miserable thin, very thin, covering of powder and not always even a covering. We have had no [new] snow for the last eight weeks.

Skiing fashion was much debated. The *Year Book* noted that 'An article in the *Observer* mentioned that it appears that it is only the British who are unaware that there are such things as ski-ing fashions, and who consider that for ski-ing "any old thing will do".'

In her feature 'Socks Outside', Doreen Elliott noted, 'Novices sometimes remark that they are shy of wearing accepted ski-ing fashions, as they consider this to be the prerogative of the expert. Nothing could be further from the truth, for their mistakes in ski-ing are far less noticeable if they are correctly dressed.'

As in every new decade, the crystal-ball gazers were keen to guess at brave-new-world developments in technology ahead. One particularly daft idea was suggested in September 1952 – a tongue-in-cheek description of ski slopes with no lifts. Who would need them with their own 'personal ski-lifts'? Members were told,

> It is on the cards, it seems, that in the not very distant future all funiculars, chair-lifts, funi-luges, and meat-hooks will fall into disuse, gradually rotting and rusting away till they no longer disfigure the mountain side. Old gentlemen will lament that the romance has gone out of ski-ing, shareholders (who are slow off the mark to sell) will get shabbier and shabbier, and piste addicts will be much discouraged. For why? Well, because we are now in the rocket age!
>
> Herr Dipl. Ing. Tinkler of Vienna has invented a nine-jet personal rocket-pusher which (my information comes from the *Grosse Oesterreichische Illustrierte* through the kindness of a member, Miss P Davies), on one fill-up of fuel will discharge you to the top of the highest run as fast as you are likely to like. Or should you miss the 'Sport Zug' back to your hotel from the bottom of the run, you will avoid an hour's hard road-slogging by just hitching on your rocket, and allowing it to propel you home at anything between 30 and 70 mph according to taste.
>
> I understand there remain a few technical difficulties to overcome before the machine is put on the market, e.g. an effective braking device has still to be evolved, also the present asbestos sheet between you and the machine's heat is *not quite* proof against *all* contingencies. But the Dipl. Ing. from Vienna says he is satisfied that these little troubles can soon be banished.

There was a reply. In London's Upper Montagu Street, Mary Bulloch put pen to paper and dashed off a letter suggesting that the best way to ski a mountain was to reverse the normal procedure: to walk up on 'skins' and take a nice empty funicular down!

> Sir – The Swiss authorities may dub you a somewhat gloomy prophet. But Kurvereine [tourist offices] need

not despair – funiculars, chair-lifts, funi-luges, etc., will not fall into disuse if my Uphill Only Club flourishes. After an ambitious but sadly ill-advised Christie on the slopes of Alp Languard (Pontresina), I spent a long and painful year in a leather-and-steel collar contraption, only to find subsequent winter holidays overshadowed by the doctors' grim warnings not to plunge again nose-first into the snow. What next, then, when one is consumed with a passion for mountains, ski and snow?

In spite of the 'Pistiferus' clan, climbing with the aid of skins has a tremendous appeal – a sense of satisfaction, time to stand and stare, and no 'species P. downhillus' to upset the equilibrium. But even the genus uphillus must sometimes descend, and I look hopefully to fellow-members for bright suggestions. Failing inspiration, I aim to plod up a nearby trail and take the empty ski-lift down. The story is told of a like-minded skier at the bottom of Corviglia who retorted that the mad scramble for the *bahn* had become too much and he proposed climbing up to earn the unaccustomed bliss of an empty compartment down. If only I can trace him, he shall be my second founder member! Friends say, 'Keep away and don't risk your silly neck again.' But, as my boss resignedly wrote after the accident: 'Can't understand this craze you have for such a dangerous sport. Ah well, passion is what matters, not the object thereof!'

Chapter 21

FIFTY YEARS ON

My dear, have you heard that dear Colonel Brown
Had quite a bad accident on the way down?
Yes, the one with grey hair that Bill knew in Libya,
Such a nice fellow, he's broken his tibia.

Everest. The Coronation. Fifty years of the Ski Club of Great Britain, which had only recently moved into what would be its flagship HQ for almost half a century: 118 Eaton Square. What a year! No wonder the editor of *Ski Notes and Queries* was in jubilant mood. 'The triumphant end of a great crusade has coincided, to a day, with the opening of a new Elizabethan age,' he wrote. 'Not all members of the SCGB are mountaineers, but there is not one who will not have been thrilled at the news that came through on Coronation Day of the conquest, after more than 30 years of stern endeavour, of the highest point on the earth's surface.'

Lord Hunt, who had led the team which made the dramatic assault on Everest (news of which had burst upon the nation on the eve of the Coronation) was a climber and skier, and had some interesting views on the relationship between the two breeds. Were they, perhaps, one and the same? 'I have always regarded ski-ing and climbing,' he said, 'as twin facets of the relationship between a man and a mountain; as the dual make-up of the complete mountaineer; as complementary rather than separate.' Arnold Lunn tended to agree with Hunt: 'Skiing was for many years a *branch* of mountaineering,' he said.

Lord Hunt, an honorary member, would often visit the club for lunch: his office was round the corner in Hobart Place. Elisabeth Hussey, editor of the Ski Club's *Ski survey* magazine for 18 years, recalls a speech he made in the Council Room one day, saying, 'it would not be a long speech because he was asked to stand on the window seat and was rather scared of heights!'

It was intriguing to note how much ski racing had changed. In one of his many books, *The Story of Skiing*, published in 1952 to mark the club's Golden Jubilee, Arnold Lunn wrote, 'The young racer of today may find it difficult to believe that there was ever a time when the mere luck of the draw determined whether a potential world champion lost a race because a third-class racer fell in front of him in a narrow section of the course.'

The *Year Book* told its readers,

> The Club was born on May 6th, 1903. It was a healthy baby of somewhat over the usual weight – 11lbs ... I mean members. [*Fifty years on, and they were still vague about the numbers!*] It grew steadily, but not surprisingly fast, for the first ten years or so of its life. In those days ski-ing was a new thing. So, although those who had once put on ski never, as it were, took them off again, the number who put them on was necessarily small, and growth was rather slow.

A healthy vein of black humour was, as ever, percolating through contributions to *Ski Notes and Queries*, although poetry (and cartoons!) had, at one stage, been banned as both self-indulgent and a waste of space. However, a poem entitled 'Holiday in Switzerland' might have made some non-skiing or squeamish readers wonder why people took to the slopes at all, with such lines as ...

My dear, have you heard that dear Colonel Brown

Had quite a bad accident on the way down?
Yes, the one with grey hair that Bill knew in Libya,
Such a nice fellow, he's broken his tibia.

Or this:

My dear, have you heard? George can't come to tea:
He's fractured his pelvis and twisted his knee
Mr Jones says they're bringing him down in the train,
And he's screaming and screaming in terrible pain.

The verse, penned by P.F.N., ends thus:

In the winter there's always a general ovation
For ski-wounded sportsmen at Victoria Station,
Who, covered with plaster, are back from the fun
Of Switzerland, land of the snow and the sun.

Arnold Lunn was soon moving on to contemplate the next 50 years:

I wonder what my successor will have to report on
May 6th, 2003? Shall we during this period have a
second Golden Age of British ski-ing or racing?
Surely not, and I doubt whether we ought to hope for
it in the changed circumstances. As in cricket, golf
and many other sports, the grouping of ski-ing skill is
no longer Amateur and Professional, but rather the
Part-timer and the Whole-timer. In ski-ing we must
perforce be part-timers – praise be. With this in mind
let us do everything we can to improve the
performance and the skill of our members on the
snows. But part-timers can often set the tone,
administer the rules, and judge the events as well as,
or perhaps better than, the whole-timer. We do not
now win at Wimbledon, but we run it to the envy of
all. We are moving into our second half-century with
a record as administrators and judges second to none.
    I hope therefore that my successor can and will say
in 2003: 'We keep our end up in performance on ski

with all other part-timers. We are also recognised as second-to-none in our behaviour on and off the snows, and we not only judge all our own performances on the snows through our own part-timers, but those self-same people are even invited to judge those of others.' Ski-heil, ladies and gentlemen, for 50 more years and may they be as much fun as the first 50.

I suppose that as Sir Arnold's successor as Editor of *Ski and Board* in 2003, I should respond in some way. As one Arnold to another, therefore, I'd like to say what an inspiration you have been to us all. If only I could ask you to write a centenary feature for the magazine, or – better still – a foreword to this book.

Chapter 22

AMBUSHED BY MONTY

Just because you invented the slalom in the stone age, it does not mean that you have the right to pontificate, legislate and hold things the way they always have been. The old guard are suffering from a high degree of mental constipation. I'd like to administer a strong dose of weedkiller to whoever stopped full teams being entered for all the top races.

In 1958, to mark Arnold Lunn's 70th birthday, he was given a rare and poignant treat – a plane ride to the mountain tops of Switzerland, enabling him to be 'on ski' once again in the rarefied atmosphere of his beloved playground in the High Alps. (He had evidently had second thoughts about his remarks – almost 40 years earlier – about the intrusion into the silent glaciers of an 'arrogant aeroplane' and his sense of foreboding about a future invasion of 'Alpine solitudes by aerobusses'.)

In the *Year Book* of 1959, he wrote,

> From the first, I felt that this expedition was a return not only to the High Alps, but also to my mountain

past, and this indefinable conviction was reinforced when I learnt that my guides, Walter von Allmen of Mürren and Hans Furrer of Zermatt, were to meet me in the Hotel Terminus at Sierre, below Montana, for it was at Montana that my brother Hugh and I served our apprenticeship as mountaineers ... If we deserve and attain beatitude we may, perhaps, be allowed to re-live some of the happiest hours which we spent on earth, and if this be so, I shall rejoin my brother, who crossed his last pass some years ago, for a sunset hour outside the old Wildstrubel Hut.

Elsewhere, Lunn told an amusing story about Montana:

The first of the 50 books which I have written was a guide to Montana, Switzerland, which I published while I was still at Harrow. Some years ago the Chairman at a lecture which I was giving in a small town in Montana (USA) introduced me to the audience with these words: 'Our lecturer tonight has written a guide-book to our State, and probably knows it better than any of us.'

Lunn was 'faintly embarrassed by this unexpected tribute', his knowledge of the state being 'limited to the few hours which I had spent in it before my lecture'.

Back in the aeroplane, Lunn continued,

It was not until we were airborne that I would allow myself to believe that the flight to which I had looked forward with such passionate anticipation was an accomplished fact. Nothing in some 150,000 miles of airborne travel could compare with this flight. I have flown round the summit of the Matterhorn and across the Dome of Mont Blanc. I have watched the massive peak of Aconcagua rise above the lower ranges as the plane climbed from Santiago airport. I have seen the snows of Mount Hermon against the tenderness of the April sky in Palestine, and Olympus beyond the

Aegean, patterned by the isles of Greece, and Etna mirrored and reversed in the blue Mediterranean. I have flown over the majestic monotony of Malayan jungle and Australian desert, but nothing that I have ever seen from the air could rival either the beauty or majesty of the flight from Sion to the Tête de Valpelline.

It was as if our plane had liberated me not only from the bondage of the earth but also from the chain of time, as if time were indeed a fourth dimension of space through which I could retrace my steps at will, and return on airborne wings to the mountains of youth, to the Wildstrubel and Wildhorn, faintly showing through a gossamer veil of mist ... The effect ... was suggestive of an old man's memory, precise in recalling the exact details of some particular hour from the remote past, but otherwise confused by the mists of time.

The mountains of memory may be compared with a painting obscured by the grime of years, and the return to the mountains, as, for instance, after the long exile of the War, had an effect comparable to that of a skilful restorer.

We landed on a snow recess some 800 feet below the summit of the Tête de Valpelline (12,510 ft). I climbed out of the plane and Herman Geiger followed. 'Thank you,' I said, 'for piloting me on my last visit to the High Alps.' [In fact many years later, he would enjoy one more such outing.]

After climbing to the summit – 'the dividing line between my two beloved countries, Switzerland and Italy' (no mean feat at 70, though Lunn makes light of it) – they begin their descent.

We enjoyed about 5,000 feet of delightfully varied skiing. Walter skied just behind me. Once when I dropped a stick and apologised, he said: 'That is all right. I did not come along only as a guide, but to see you brought ski boots and not London boots, and do not lose too many things, and pick up the things you dropped.' Guide-valet, in fact. We sat down to a delicious lunch ... cold chicken washed down by *Fendant* and rounded off by strawberries.

Lunn's party continued down towards Zermatt.

Walter von Allmen suggested that I should wait for the cable-lift ... but I was interested to see whether I could walk down to Zermatt without undue fatigue. Lower down, however, we were picked up by a lorry, and drove down the last 1500 feet to Zermatt. 'I've been a bit anxious,' I said to Walter, 'how I'd stand this expedition. I was a bit nervous that I'd pack up.'
'I was not nervous,' said Walter. 'You did not pack up.'

Lunn celebrated his birthday at the Hotel du Lac in Interlaken, where he was half way through lunch with friends when he was called to the telephone. 'After an animated discussion on a skiing controversy,' says Elisabeth Hussey, 'he returned, forgetting the birthday party, to the solitary table at which he normally sat.' As the head waiter approached, he looked thoughtfully at the menu. 'You've had the first two courses,' said the waiter helpfully, 'at another table. Perhaps you would like to finish your meal there.'

More understandable, perhaps, was Lunn's confusion over which year he had founded the Oxford Mountaineering Club, of which no minute books had survived. Just before attending what he thought was the club's 50th anniversary, it occurred to him that he had probably got his dates wrong and was a year too late. (As Lunn got older, there would be many more examples of such absent-mindedness, as we shall recall in the following chapter.)

In the same year, the much-travelled Lunn had visited the Timberline Lodge at Mount Hood, Oregon, to help celebrate its Silver Jubilee. On the train, two girls 'helped enliven a tedious journey' when they discovered that he had skied. The exchange went like this: 'My friend,' said one of them, 'won a race on Mount Hood called the Arnold Lunn Cup.' 'Why is it called that?' asked Lunn. 'Oh, it's called after a prehistoric ski-ing guy. He's been dead a mighty long time, I guess.'

Seeing wildlife is one of the joys of ski-touring, but sometimes it can be a distressing experience, as Pauline Sitwell Stebbing found in 1961 while touring near the shores of Lake Derborence, not far from Villars. She wrote,

> We were woken up at about 5.30 to what sounded like someone crashing chairs together; it proved to be a couple of chamois fighting to the death on the edge of the lake. I have never seen anything so fierce in my life, and at the end, the younger, smaller animal pushed the older one into the lake, which was melting fast, and kept his head under until he nearly drowned, by which time the guardian [of the refuge] said the chamois would be as good as dead even though he climbed out, for once they have lost a certain level of body heat they get pneumonia very easily.

Spotting Chamois from back-country tours had usually been a rather less harrowing experience, as Colonel Luttman-Johnson had observed in a report from Canada's Laurentians some 20 years earlier:

> Game is never so much in evidence as in Switzerland; for example, it would be hard to match the 12 chamois, four white ptarmigan, and one hare met with on a single tour at Saanenmöser, or the 142 chamois counted in the Rhône Valley south of the Petit Moeveran on another occasion. As I have always been accompanied by a spaniel, I think we would have put up any game there was about. As there are no long descents and the snow is of Christiania lightness, a spaniel can in this terrain keep up with a skier.

It was Colonel Luttman-Johnson who gave his name to an intriguing race now held in Zermatt which has more emphasis on mountain restaurants than skiing. The Luttman-Johnson trophy was first organised at his beloved Saanenmöser in 1963. It was described thus:

> A new innovation [sic] and the next excitement in

Saanenmöser: a 'lift-assisted' point-to-point cross-country race run in pairs with a *geschmozzle* start and competitors taking any route they chose, providing they visited all the necessary 'control points'. These included the Horneggli Restaurant, the Kubeli and Kornfluh Huts and the Bears Restaurant at the Sporthotel. A great deal of interest was caused by this race and it is hoped that a large entry will be attracted for next year.

Says Elisabeth Hussey, 'I think today in Zermatt the same rules are followed and that it all depends on covering a big mileage and many lifts in a short time, while spending as long as possible in restaurants.'

Readers' letters still flowed in. Some were bizarre, some delightful, some hilarious, others extraordinary. Some all four.

Dear Sir

It may sound a little bit odd to say that I broke my legs instead of my ankles thanks to my excellent Kandahar boots. Anyone who has ever broken an ankle will, I am sure, realise the difference. If the ankle joint escapes dislocation or damage one's recovery is simplified enormously. Both my breaks finish two inches above the ankle joint.

One of my first remarks when I bought them was, 'Well, if I break anything with these boots on it will be above the ankle.'

I was right.

Yours, etc., Lesley S.A. Thomson

(*British Ski Year Book*, 1955)

Dear Sir

Many and frequent are the remarks made by foreign friends on the subject of high touring skiers who, in the eyes of the local inhabitants, degrade the snow and rock they tread and the huts they use, with their drab, dreadful, tasteless and often dirty garments.

No one looks smarter on his home ground than an Englishman, but are we up against something fundamental in him when he travels abroad? Is he showing off in an inverted form, not with the bright feathers and dazzling plumage of his foreign counterpart, but by dreary and dirty contrast, making himself doubly conspicuous? Poverty cannot be the reason, for the shops now contain good stuff, reasonably priced, sensible in usefulness and cut, *and* pleasant to the eye. But it would seem that the eternal 'Gov. Surplus' is searched for and clung to till every outworn thread screams to be thrown into the garbage bin.

On Basle station I was oppressed by the number of oily old raincoats and old respirator haversacks ... wartime 'make-do and mend' carried to extremes. In the words of the local dignitaries: 'These people make the village look as though we have a local prison camp.'

An Austrian friend tells me of trousers patched and still in being there this winter which several years ago needed a ritual funeral pyre ... We live in a sombre climate; let us therefore wear colour on the few occasions when it is both glorious and right to do so. Perhaps in the rain of our beloved Lake District, garments ingrained with grime do not show much, but in the bright and sizzling light above three thousand metres, beware!

From Switzerland comes the plea: 'Can nothing be done?' We are liked in the mountains, but we do look awful! To a Swiss his mountains are hallowed ground. We should not desecrate what others respect.

Yours sincerely, Pauline Sitwell Stebbing

(*British Ski Year Book*, 1957)

Dear Sir

While reading the *British Ski Year Book* I have noticed that on page 265 in the illustration showing the 'Houghton' ski sling, the owner of the ski illustrated must have either deformed feet, or he enjoys the unusual sport of skiing backwards, as the toe irons and cable levers are facing toward the heel of his ski*.

Yours wondering, Alexander Sykes, Aiglon College, Villars Sur Ollon

*Congratulations. I am flattered to discover how attentively BSYB is read by our junior members. I was tempted to adapt the ingenious defence of error which I here quote from that lively paper *Nachrichten, the Journal of the Grindelwald Ski Club of Los Angeles*: 'If you find a mistake in this paper, please consider it was put there for a purpose. We publish something for everyone, and some people are always looking for mistakes.'

(*British Ski Year Book*, 1958)

From the HRH *The Infanta Beatrice de Orleans-Bourbon*:

My dear Arnold

All this is very long ago and I am a very old woman. In the early 90s, about 1892 or 1893, I received as a Christmas present from some Russian cousins three or four pairs of wooden objects which they called ski.

It now astonishes me that they looked like any other ski, but they had a sort of slipper made of leather fixed permanently into which one slipped ones feet, and also had skins permanently fixed underneath which allowed one to climb uphill and also slide downhill owing to the way the fur ran.

I and my friends in Coburg started this noble sport, to the astonishment and delight of the local population.

It will horrify our present-day fine sportswomen to know that we wore long skirts and some of us red flannel petticoats which undoubtedly contributed greatly to the spectacular effect of our falls.

I would like to add that each pair of ski had a perfectly good pair of ski-sticks very much like the present ones.

We found it safer to ride down very steep hills on the sticks like a company of witches on their brooms.

Though I never became an expert skier, as you know, I adhered to this witch-like habit until I was severely told it was dangerous and indecorous. I then gave up ski-ing and took to figure skating.

Skiheil and best love.
> Your old friend, Beatriz
> (*British Ski Year Book*, 1960)

Dear Sir Arnold

I should like to draw your attention to the poor presentation of material intended for publication in the 'Racing Section' of the *British Ski Year Book* ... It is surely not too much to ask that reports should be accurately and legibly written. Such phrases as (I quote but a few examples) 'I am sorry, the results are from memory' *or* 'I have left gaps for you to fill in the names of the finishers' *or* 'I couldn't remember how you spelt their names' *or* 'I always find place names so difficult' cannot be described as helpful.

After wasting many hours checking and re-writing the material that has to be begged to be sent in, one comes to the conclusion that, as the majority of contributors appear to have so little interest in what they send in, it would be better to abolish the 'Racing Section' as it is now, and just record the results at the back of the book.

It is not unreasonable to expect some kind of standard for a book which, after all, is a book of reference on skiing. It is surely lacking in consideration to expect the Assistant Editor to pick up the pieces.
> Yours sincerely, Christobel Haward
> Assistant Editor
> (*British Ski Year Book*, 1961)

In 1961, Arnold Lunn, whose beloved wife Mabel had died, remarried. His new wife was his faithful former secretary and helpmeet, Phyllis Holt-Needham. By co-incidence, it was also the year he would fall out in spectacular fashion with his first wife's cousin, the waspish Field Marshal Montgomery, with a spectacular exchange of venom. The row was all about whether British skiers should compete in the top races of the day, in which they had virtually no chance, or concentrate, as Lunn wanted, on lesser races which they might actually win. First blood to Monty, when he was quoted in the *Observer*:

> Just because you invented the slalom in the stone age, it does not mean that you have the right to pontificate, legislate and hold things the way they always have been. The old guard are against change and progress and are suffering from a high degree of mental constipation. I'd like to administer a strong dose of weedkiller to whoever stopped full teams being entered for all the top races.

Lunn waited until he'd been made patron of the Curling Club in Mürren until hitting back, but by comparison it was a relatively mild counter-attack: 'Knowing nothing about curling, I was diffident about taking this on, but consoled myself with the reflection that Field Marshal Montgomery accepted presidency of the Kandahar Ski Club. One thing you can be sure of. I shall not recommend concentrated doses of weedkiller for the committee.'

Chapter 23

UNKILLED AND UNDECORATIVE

There was a feeling that the Ski Club was, in a way,
finished. We were determined that it was not finished.
People came from the Alps, from all over the world,
to the building in Eaton Square where they were
looked after and entertained. So – boo to the generals!

Bond leapt for the ski room. Unlocked! He ... found the
ski he had marked out for himself in the morning.
There were sticks beside them. Opening the main door,
he laid the ski and sticks softly down in the snow.

The three-quarter moon burned down with an
almost dazzling fire, and the snow crystals scintillated
back at it like a carpet of diamond dust. Bond spent
several minutes getting the binding absolutely right.
He pulled the goggles down over his eyes, and now the
vast snow-scape was a silvery green as if he was
swimming under sunny water. The ski hissed
smoothly through the powder snow.

He punted himself forward as fast as he could with
his sticks. What a trail he must be leaving – like a tram-

line! ... There was the staring point of the Gloria Run ... Bond didn't pause. He went straight for it and over the edge. Bond got down into his old Arlberg crouch, his hands forward of his boots, and just let himself go. His speed was now frightening. Like a black bullet on the giant slope, he zoomed down the 45-degree drop ...

Something was nagging at him mind ... something unpleasant. Yes, by God! The last flag! It had been black. He was on the Black Run, the one closed because of avalanche danger! From high up above him, he heard that most dreaded of all sounds in the High Alps, that rending, booming crack!

Bond hurtled in to a right-hand Christie just as, to his left, he heard the first trees come crashing down with the noise of a hundred monster crackers being pulled ... Bond flung himself straight down the wide, white glade between the trees ...

On Her Majesty's Secret Service, by Ian Fleming, was published by Jonathan Cape in 1963. Bond's moonlit, headlong dash, accompanied, had we space to remind you, by grenade attacks and attempts to shoot him, ends with him jumping clean over an express train. Following the publication of Fleming's book, the following points, some perhaps a trifle churlish, were made to Ski Club readers as part of a review in *Ski Notes and Queries*:

All members of the SCGB must agree that the above is one of the finest ski descents ever to have been made. Consider:

1: Its length. The height of the Gloria Club is given as 3,605 metres (11,828 ft). Samaden is about 5,000 feet, which means Bond's vertical descent was not far short of 7,000 ft.

2: He did it *non-stop* and virtually *flat-out*.

3: It was by *moonlight*, itself dimmed by the use of dark goggles.

4: It was in *deep new snow*, which avalanched.

5: He was being *shot at* or *grenaded* most of the way.

Consider also:

Bond's lack of training. He had just arrived unexpectedly in Switzerland after two months in England. As his descent took place on Christmas Eve, he cannot have skied previously in the season. And not having expected to ski now, it is unlikely that he did any pre-skiing exercises.

His inadequate equipment. Gloves, goggles, ski and sticks all had to be 'borrowed' and though there is a bit of a mystery about his actual clothes, there is no mention at all of boots. (The picture shows him in quite low *bootees.*) If he did borrow boots too, he clearly had no time to fit them properly to the ski.

Bond's age. At the start of the run he 'got down into his old Arlberg crouch'. Now the Arlberg crouch went out in the early 30s, with the advent of fixed-heel bindings, and the implication that Bond was already skiing then makes him considerably older than Mr Fleming has previously admitted – and his performance the more remarkable ... And finally there is the crowning achievement of his *Geländesprung* over the railway. What other members of the Club would like to attempt this, even if young and fit, at the end of a 7,000 foot descent?

Recommendation: That James Bond be elected an Honorary Gold Racing Lion of the Ski Club of Great Britain.

The Ski Club later returns to the subject in saying,

It is difficult to believe in the *Geländesprung* across the railway near Samaden, by means of which Bond escapes the assassins hot on his heels, and if ever Mr Fleming had found himself, as I have, in the pathway of an avalanche he would not have written that 'the ground shook violently under Bond's ski.' It is interesting to learn that Bond had won his 'Golden K' [a much-coveted Kandahar award] at St Anton [instead of Mürren]. It is, however, captious to pick out a few technical flaws in a thriller which provides all the entertainment which Bond fans have learned to expect.

A subsequent reader's letter from Kenneth Todd (unaware that Ian Fleming was, sadly, close to death) added extra spice:

Dear Sir

A short stay at Pontresina gave me the opportunity to trace the scene of James Bond's awe-perspiring exploit, so vividly described in your spring issue ... A minute inspection of the mountainside led to the discovery of a stray bullet, and, in a laboratory test, this bullet was found to have been in contact with a metal ski, painted black.

An equally minute inspection of the rest of the Languard range, however, failed to discover a mountain on which the Gloria Klub, at 3,605 metres, could conveniently be placed. This was at least partly due to the fact that the Piz Languard, the highest peak of this range, does not exceed 3,261 metres.

I should be obliged if you would ask Mr Fleming to explain this mystery, and to produce the missing piece of mountainside. In return, I shall let him have the said bullet as a souvenir.

Six years later, of course, the film of the book would present George Lazenby with a one-off chance of playing Bond, following Sean Connery's temporary retirement from the role.

Curiously, when the film was being made, some of the production team were involved in a real-life drama. While a scene was being rehearsed in which Lazenby and his girlfriend Tracy (Diana Rigg) are trapped by an avalanche, two skiers on the opposite side of the valley were buried by an avalanche, and a radio call for help was made. A senior cameraman, John Jordan, who had been filming while suspended from a rope beneath a helicopter (he was killed soon afterwards while filming in Mexico) helped to transport shovels, dogs and other lifesaving equipment to the scene by helicopter. Both skiers survived.

The Lanzenby and Rigg show wasn't the only attraction in

Mürren that year. Sherpa Tenzing of Everest fame turned up. After his historic climb with Edmund Hillary, he had been appointed head of the Himalayan Mountaineering Institute, and he'd brought six sherpas to Switzerland for a three-month course for Swiss guide apprentices.

In 1963, Arnold Lunn – still managing to ski occasionally – also achieved one of his greatest ambitions: to set foot on the summit of Mont Blanc. He had rather hoped to accomplish this years ago on foot, but in the end achieved it in a helicopter.

Back in 1956, he had organised a cunning and elaborate plan to try to get to the top while pretending to Lady Mabel that he was taking things easy in Mürren. Elisabeth Hussey tells the story in her biography of Lunn:

> He knew Mabel would worry. In July, Mabel was in England for the wedding of a nephew. Lunn went to Mürren for a week and composed five reasonably convincing letters to be posted to her while he went off to Chamonix. They were carefully worded to convince her that he was writing a book in Mürren. With Camille Tournier, a famous guide, he climbed 1,500 metres to a hut on the Tête Rousse. He confessed that five hours of climbing was all he could manage. Then the weather broke and after a try the next day, the attempt had to be abandoned.
>
> The press, however, had learned about the failed attempt. On the same day that Mabel read in the papers that bad weather had prevented the climb, she received by post a letter complaining how dull life was in Mürren.

And now, seven years later, here he was, actually on the summit. It was time for another of his famous nostalgic moments. He wrote,

> I felt as if I were flying not only through space but through time, airborne back to the mountains of my youth. Shortly after taking off, the first slope down which I had slid and tumbled on ski appeared below, the Aiguille du Tour, my first peak, rose above a

shoulder of the Brévant and then in swift succession
the mountains of memory occupied the eastern sky; the
beloved Oberland, the Combin, the last mountain
which I had climbed with two legs of the same length,
the Dente Blanche; the first painful return to the High
Alps after my smash and then, as the helicopter turned
towards the east, the Gouter, the last peak I shall ever
climb on my legs.

All things seemed possible in the swinging 60s. Even ski-jumping,
at the end of May 1961, at Wembley Stadium – featuring some of
the world's greatest jumpers and sponsored by Cow & Gate! The
Ski Club had organised real snow to be brought to the stadium and
erected a ski-jump. They almost didn't need the snow – it was
bitterly cold on the opening evening and rained throughout the
next day.

A year later, the club held its first Reps' Course. It was held over
ten days, and Reps were taught safety in the mountains, how to
look after members in resorts, and how to co-operate with resort
staff – much the same as today. The organising team included Joan
Raynsford, Isobel 'Soss' Roe, Neil Hogg, Aubrey Lincoln and Mark
Heller, a prolific writer and author who would become the
unchallenged doyen of British ski writers.

Soss Roe, who was tragically killed at the age of 70 when she
was knocked off her bicycle by a lorry in 1987, was an exceptional
athlete, and became British ladies champion in 1938, 1939, 1948
and 1949, when she helped Bunty Stockwell organise the first
British Junior Championships. She also represented her county in
tennis and squash, and was ladies croquet champion in 1961.
Women at the Ski Club in the 1960s were now all the rage!

In February 1963, the *Year Book* published this intriguing letter,
under the heading 'Women Preferred':

Dear Sir,
I was particularly interested in your proposals in the
last *Year Book* on the Slalom. There is one thing,
however, which irritates me – no doubt I'm somewhat
over-sensitive! – this is the reference to races being for
'ladies' and 'men'. Surely it should be 'ladies' and

'gentlemen' (snobbish suburban expressions except on a limited number of special occasions), or else 'women' and 'men'? According to the *Year Book*, the men's races are open to all males whereas the women's races are restricted to females of the upper classes. If that is so, I'm glad that I'm a man, as the fact that I am not a member of the upper classes would otherwise bar me from entering – just supposing I could ski properly!

Yours truly, J.G. Pickwell.

In 1963, readers of *Ski Notes and Queries'* 120th issue said farewell to the editor, Colonel C.A. de Linde. Mervyn Kemmis-Betty was particularly sorry to see him go. He wrote,

Change is acceptable when progress demands it, but much of our pleasure derives from practically natural phenomena, for which progress has no meaning.

Would anyone, for instance, ever want a change in the feel of powder snow under his ski, in the sound of the Swiss Railways ding-dong in his ears, or in the taste of Wiener Schnitzel? Such things arouse very special sensations, and we look forward to them and want them to be exactly the same for all time.

I, for one, have come to count on 'the mixture as before' in my *Ski Notes*, which I find every bit as interesting, informative, entertaining and bracing as I could wish, and I shall sadly miss the familiar de Linde flavour. I am sure that in offering him my sincere gratitude for a masterly performance over the last 16 years, I am speaking not for one, but thousands of us.

The following year, the woman – or should I say lady – who would be, by far the longest-serving editor of the Ski Club's magazine, *Ski survey*, joined the club. Her name was Elisabeth (with an s!) Hussey. In 1964, *Year Book* readers had been informed, under the title 'Change of Assistant Editor', that 'all good wishes' were on their way to Miss Christobel Haward who had resigned. 'Miss Elisabeth Hussey, who is now the Assistant Editor of the *British Ski Year Book* and *Ski Notes & Queries*, is a keen skier and a member of the

Kandahar Ski Club. She is the sister of Miss Philippa Hussey, J.P., who is secretary of the Kandahar.' She would prove to be a tower of strength behind the Lunn throne – before being seated there herself. (Her story is eloquently told in her own words in Chapter 28.) Lunn was something of an eccentric, as the following extract makes clear. This was the kind of thing the newly appointed Miss Hussey was up against, but she bore up remarkably cheerfully.

Under the heading *'Yiut Ecolsbayipm'*, Sir Arnold, explaining that he often hit the wrong keys on his typewriter, wrote,

> The Chairman of the Winter Arrangements Committee was mildly annoyed when I began a letter 'My dear Hibby' but mollified when I pointed out that 'i' was next to 'o' on my typewriter. His reply began *'Yiut ecolsbayipm nalrs ebetytjimf clwar,'* which, as anybody who has a typewriter handy can easily see, means 'your explanation makes everything clear.'

Fortunately, over the years there were dedicated, diligent and resourceful assistants and proofreaders – such as the ever-patient Colonel Bowdler and both Philippa and Elisabeth Hussey – to put matters right.

Lunn's original 'speedwriting' typescript of *A Century of Mountaineering* was presented to the Dartmouth College Library where students found that trying to interpret some of the strange typography was almost as interesting as the subject matter (once discovered). 'The unwritten history of the Alpine Club is an invaluable source for the historian', for example, comes out as *'The unwritten h4 vv/èpa is an invaluable source for the h4n'*. And 'I am old enough to have met men like Whymper and Hereford George who made Alpine history in the Golden Age' was delivered as *'I am old nf to have met men like W1/ and Hereford George who made èpn h4 in the GA 1/'*.

One of Lunn's publishers had described Lunn as 'a tempestuous but ever-welcome intruder at the office ... who dished up books of theology and apologetics like fast food, often with the same ingredients ... He was an editor's despair: quotations unchecked, endless repetitions and misspellings in the untidiest of typescripts ever submitted.'

(Lunn had started his absent-mindedness early in life – famously when he put two letters into the wrong envelopes. One, in which he compared the qualities of his fiancée, Joan Plowden, with another *amour*, Mabel Northcote, went to Mabel by mistake. Suffused with guilt, he rushed round to apologise to her, and whatever he said did the trick – she forgave him. And, of course, married him.)

By now his eccentricity had branded him a real character. He even described himself as a 'helpless ass' (countering this occasionally with, 'when it comes to humility, I'm tops'). Phyllis, his new wife, had remarked, 'As a guest, you must be an acquired taste,' adding quickly, 'I don't deny that the taste could be acquired.' Lunn would say of her, 'From defects in my prose she passed by natural transition to defects in my character.'

Gina, Princess of Liechtenstein, once described Lunn as 'full of energy and curiosity like a schoolboy and at the same time a wise old owl'. Another famous quote from her was, 'When I tell the servants that Sir Arnold is coming, they give a tired smile.'

Elisabeth Hussey says,

> He was tremendously absentminded – which was to dog him throughout his life. Though more than capable of finding his way in the mountains and avoiding danger, he needed a guide for ordinary journeys. Many stories are told of his wearing two ties because he put on a second forgetting the first was already on.

There are numerous tie stories. In 1951, Arnold Lunn was telling his *Year Book* readers,

> I always dress for dinner before lecturing, because the Far-Westerner believes that all Englishmen dress even in the jungle. I was rather disconcerted to discover at the end of my lecture that I had forgotten to put on a tie. 'Why on earth didn't you tell me,' I grumbled to my host with whom I had dined, 'I could have gone upstairs and collected the tie before the lecture.'
>
> 'We thought,' he replied in all seriousness, 'that this was the latest English fashion.' And a lady who was

present added: 'We thought you must belong to a high
English order which doesn't wear ties.'

One night at the Palace Hotel, Lunn forgot his tie again, and
borrowed one. But it came off during his speech. The tie was
replaced with the help of safety pins.

There were many other stories. Hussey mentions the time he left
all his luggage on the train in Vienna, en route for Zakopane, Poland.
Then at breakfast he appeared with his trousers inside out. It was
easy to do, he reported in the *Year Book*, 'for with elastic round the
ankles, you pull them off – and climb in again the next morning.' On
another occasion, Lunn put on his evening trousers to go skiing, got
them soaking wet in heavy snow, and so had to wear his ski trousers
with his dinner jacket and tie at a formal dinner. In Lauterbrunnen
he was once discovered wearing one ski boot and one town boot.

Then there was the story about the legation bag. Just before the
outbreak of World War II, Lunn returned to Switzerland for a final
visit. On his way home, he collected the legation bag, insisting that
he would deliver it to its destination. His absentmindedness was
now well known, and Lunn reassured those concerned, 'I have a
very untidy outside but a very tidy inside. I classify things into
those I can lose, such as hats and overcoats, and things I can't, such
as passports, passes and legation bags.'

The friend who handed over the bag did not find this very
reassuring, says Hussey, and told Lunn, 'I was told in Budapest
that a Romanian attaché had a legation bag stolen on the way
through Bucharest. He shot himself. We should, of course, expect
you to shoot yourself if this bag goes astray.'

Lunn, never stuck for an answer, came back with, 'This is one
of those rare cases where ecclesiastical and diplomatic etiquette
seem to clash.'

After staying with the Royal Family during the Spanish Civil
War, he wrote a letter saying he had left his overcoat, his missal
(prayer book) and his false tooth at the palace. Would the *Infanta*
(with whom he had become great friends) kindly forward the
missal and the tooth – the coat could be used to help her relief
work. She duly handed the coat to a bank manager who had been
successfully hidden from the attentions of the communists – but
had had all his clothes stolen.

On May 1, the following letter appeared in *The Times*, and later reappeared in the *Year Book*.

> Sir – We read in travel folders of California and the Lebanon, where it is possible to ski on the mountains and swim in the sea on the same day. It may be of interest that this can also be done in Great Britain. On Easter Monday my family and an incredulous friend from the United States were swimming in the sea off Ardsheal in Argyll within an hour of taking off our ski above Glencoe. The sun and snow had been superb on Meall Buidhe, and the water of Loch Linnhe, warmed by the Gulf Stream, provided a fitting end to a day that surely could not be surpassed anywhere in the world.
>
> Yours faithfully, W.H. Harper.

Writing in his beloved *Ski Year Book* for 1967 (when Harold Wilson's devaluation of the pound added to the misery of the £50 foreign currency allowance, which readers were urged to consider avoiding by skiing in sterling areas such as Scotland or Cyprus), Sir Arnold Lunn told a curious story that sat well with the many he wrote about during a long career of *belles-lettres*. He recounted,

> I was walking along a street at Zurich with a very charming colleague and absent-mindedly stepped into the road just as a car was coming. I am not wholly unfamiliar with the subsequent sounds, the screech of brakes and the indignant protests of the driver who had pulled up in time. My charming Swiss colleague said, 'I wonder you've remained unkilled for so long,' and my wife unkindly commented that this had a far wider application than the Swiss lady who made the remark realised. In fact my wife suggested that her remark would provide a suitable title for my next book of memoirs to be published on my 80th birthday. My publishers adopted this unflattering suggestion.

When Lunn was re-elected President of the Kandahar and wrote to Walter Amstutz to tell him how flattered he was, since they could have found someone younger, he said the job was purely decorative. 'You have been undecorative for so long,' Amstutz replied, 'that to be decorative will be a pleasant change.'

The late 1960s produced two of the most powerful and successful British women skiers of modern times: Gina Hathorn and Divina Galica. Hathorn had memorably been second in the slalom at Grindelwald in 1967, and Galica third in the downhill at Badgastein in 1968. At the Grenoble Winter Olympics, Gina Hathorn (officially Georgina) missed a bronze medal in the slalom by the narrowest of margins – three-hundredths of a second – in an incredible tussle with three champions: Marielle Goitschel of France, who won gold, Canada's Nancy Greene (silver), and another French champion, Annie Famose, who took the bronze from under Hathorn's nose. In the Giant Slalom, Greene, the eventual women's Alpine champion, stormed to gold, but Galica, captain of the British women's team, managed an excellent eighth place.

In the Combined, Gina Hathorn (seventh) and another powerful British woman skier, Bunny Field (ninth), found themselves in the world's top ten. Great days for the British women's team. As Lunn wrote at the time, Hathorn's result was

> the finest achievement by a British racer since the early days of Alpine racing. It was tragic to miss this coveted medal by so narrow a margin. Divina Galica had the wrong wax but was later consoled ... by being the first British racer for many a long day to be placed in the first three of an Arlberg–Kandahar race (at Les Houches, Chamonix). Gina is a member of the Kandahar and Divina of the DHO and it is interesting that these, the best results in top class racing since the war, should have been divided between the Kandahar and the DHO.

In 1966, with ski-racing going through the doldrums, the French journalist Serge Lang had an inspirational thought: why not have a World Cup for skiing? That year, amidst great excitement, the World Championships were held in Chile. Far from the opposition forces they would undoubtedly have encountered had they been in the Alps, Lang carried off a brilliant coup. But the World Cup would mark the decline of the A–K.

The A–K, which had moved from St Anton to Mürren after the war, initially alternated between the two, but then started moving round the Alps. The circuit had gradually increased to include Chamonix, Sestrière and, thanks to Hannes Schneider's forgiving nature, eventually to Garmisch-Partenkirchen in Germany. Now each country would have a World Cup as their major international event and it was difficult for the countries to fit the A–K into their calendars as well.

The substantial difference between them was that, whereas the A–K, although competed for by the world's top racers, was essentially a race between clubs, the World Cup was really between countries. And, as Elisabeth Hussey says, 'Arnold Lunn deplored xenophobia and did not want racing to become nationalistic. He discouraged a lot of flag-waving and anthem-singing at prizegivings.'

But the World Cup was here to stay.

Chapter 24

A DIAMOND
JUBILEE

*There would seem to be little in common between
the vast majority of the crowds who hurtle with gay
abandon down the winter slopes without having
climbed them, and the sober circumspection of the
mountaineer or ski-tourer.*

In 1969, the *British Ski Year Book* recorded the 60th birthday party of the Alpine Ski Club. Sir Arnold Lunn, who had been knighted in 1952, told readers, 'It was a memorable occasion. I founded the club while I was still an Oxford undergraduate, and one has to found a club when one is very young, and to live a very long time, to enjoy the experience of taking part in its Diamond Jubilee celebrations.'

In an address entitled 'The Wings of Memory', Lord Hunt of Llanvair, better known as John Hunt of Everest fame, said, 'The aims and achievements of the Alpine Ski Club strike a special chord in my own affections. Ski-ing and climbing, and in particular a combination of these, have been my twin passions ever since childhood.'

Speaking at the 60th anniversary celebration Jubilee Dinner, 'in the impressive setting of the United Services Club', Lord Hunt continued,

> It is an ominous sign for oneself and one's friends when one begins to look back rather than forward. But the wings of memory grow with the years and I am in imminent danger of taking off 38 years into the past: to the Pir Panjal in 1931 and 1932, to the Karakorum and North-east Greenland, where we used skis to explore mountain ranges. I still experience a vestigial sense of grievance when I am hoisted up by lift or helicopter to the summit of, say, the Corvatsch or the Grande Motte, or a pass such as the Diavolezza or Dorftäli, up which I plodded hour after laborious hour on skins (I remember it was on rope up Corviglia) in by-gone times – though, mind you, I would not rate my sense of grievance as a notably strong one.
>
> I would simply say that I have always regarded ski-ing and climbing as twin facets of the relationship between a man and a mountain; as the dual make-up of the complete mountaineer; as complementary rather than separate sports. But of course I must qualify this; it is only a half-truth. For we have seen ski-ing and mountaineering develop into a number of very different kinds of activity which appeal to different tastes and attract, or shape, very different types of people. There would seem to be little in common between the vast majority of the crowds who hurtle with gay abandon down the winter slopes without having climbed them, and the sober circumspection of the mountaineer or ski-tourer. But different though they may often be, it is well to remember that the differences are sometimes differences of mood of the same person, i.e. of you and me. For myself, I am as much concerned about the mountaineer who takes himself and his mountains too seriously, as I am about the inconsequent piste-basher who is apt not to take the mountains seriously enough. It all goes to show what a many-splendoured thing is a mountain ...

The Toast to the Founder and the Original Members of the Club was proposed by the senior vice-president, Robin Fedden. 'It is a curious thought,' he said, 'that if A. Lunn of Balliol College had not summoned eleven friends to a meeting at the Devonshire Club on Saturday, March the 7th, 1908, none of us would be here this evening. At that meeting the Alpine Ski Club was founded and A. Lunn was elected Honorary Secretary.' Fedden continued,

> No single individual has done more than Arnold Lunn for ski mountaineering or has led more of us off the piste into our particular white paradise. He has done so no less by his writings than by his example. *Alpine Ski-ing*, first published in 1921, remains the best book of its sort. It is replete in wisdom. For me, when first read, it had the impact of sacred writ, and no doubt it has inspired many others besides myself.
>
> I am told that in certain circles our founder enjoys a considerable reputation as the father of downhill racing and the inventor of something called a 'slalom'. Here we prefer to pass over these achievements in discreet silence. We celebrate rather the first notable traverse of the Bernese Oberland in the year this Club was founded, and such things as his epic ascent of the Dom on skis in 1917 and of the Eiger in 1924. Perhaps above all we celebrate the fact that he enriched the lives of thousands over nearly three generations by bringing them to untracked snow.
>
> In 1909 the Swiss newspapers announced that Arnold Lunn was dead on some ski-ing expedition. How wrong they were. He is, of course, indestructible.

And so, it seemed, was his son. Peter Lunn was reporting on what sounded like a highly unusual event: the 1968 European Ski Championships. What was bizarre about the event was its location: London. This, he suggested, was something that readers of the first issue of the *Year Book* would have found most difficult to foresee. 'The championships,' he wrote, 'were organised by Princes, a club affiliated to the Ski Club of Great Britain. Nineteen nations competed. They were held at Bedfont in the Greater London area.

On water, of course.' Peter Lunn was no mean water-skier himself. In 1972, he would jump 66 feet at the Princes Water Ski Club Championships.

Meanwhile, Divina Galica wrote amusingly in 'The Lighter Side of Racing',

> For two years running I have flown to North America to take part in the World Cup races there. This year I flew from Frankfurt to Reno with all the teams – possibly the most dangerous thing I have ever done in my life!
>
> To coop 70 athletes up in any confined space for any length of time is asking for trouble. I must say that the air hostesses were magnificent in serving the endless trayloads of monotonous meals, as they had an obstacle course of restless skiers doing press-ups in the aisles, bodies swinging from the racks and several bright sparks who discovered that you could use your mineral water bottle as a water pistol, to dodge. The steward deserved a medal for not murdering the prankster who released all the oxygen masks, as it took him hours to fit them back into the panelling. I also reckoned we had had it when everyone rushed to the front of the aircraft to try and be the first into the cockpit. Luckily the pilots had the sense to lock themselves in so everyone filed back to their places and the plane righted itself.

Chapter 25

My Dear Fighter Boys

*Hugh Dowding, the first skier in the world to win a
national Slalom Championship, piloted England through
a storm far more terrible than any Alpine blizzard.*

In 1970, the *British Ski Year Book* paid tribute to Air Chief Marshal
Lord Dowding, architect of the Battle of Britain ('the only battle in
the history of the world to be fought entirely by aircraft'), who had
died at the age of 88. Dowding had joined the Ski Club of Great
Britain in 1921 and was President from 1924 to 1925. He was
elected an honorary member in 1947.

Only three years earlier, Lunn had written eloquently of his old
friend, 'We had skied and climbed together for many years before
the outbreak of the war. I spent many nights with him during the
Battle of Britain.' (They sat in Dowding's room at Fighter Command
– the Prime Minister usually rang up around midnight. Once Lunn
spent a night with a group of fighter pilots.)

The 'few' had won, said Lunn,

> because, against immense pressure to send more of our
> squadrons to take part in the battle in France, Dowding
> insisted on keeping sufficient squadrons in England to

resist invasion, and also because he had been equally insistent, against the weight of expert opinion, that the fighter planes should be armed with eight machine guns. We won the Battle of Britain because our fighter planes had superior fire power. Had the Germans possessed not only superior numbers, but superior fighter power, all the gallantry of our pilots would have been in vain ... and Hitler would have been installed in Buckingham Palace.

Hugh Dowding piloted England through a storm far more terrible than any Alpine blizzard ... I should not be editing this *Year Book* if an ex-President of our club ... had lost what was the most decisive battle in all history.

On June 6, Dowding was still stubbornly resisting the Prime Minister's chivalrous anxiety to throw as many squadrons as possible into France. He knew that France was beaten, and that we should need every squadron we possessed if our country was to be saved. As he drove me back to his home on that fateful night ... he said to me: 'Three times in my life I've been on the point of being bowler-hatted, but I've been kept for this job because, of the other candidates for this job, I am the only one who could say "No" to Churchill. But mark my words, once the battle has been won, I shall have fulfilled my purpose, and disappear from the Command like a cork from a bottle.' As indeed he did.

Dowding was 'a versatile skier, ski-racer and ski-jumper', although not such a keen mountaineer. 'I had never climbed anything that was not well within the powers of a reasonably athletic traction engine,' he once said, comparing himself with mountaineers who were 'veritable human chamois'.

He was perhaps happiest, members were told, when skiing in the High Alps.

In 1921 he won both the Downhill race and the Ski-jumping competition at the SCGB meet in Davos ... In 1923 the Slalom was introduced for the first time into

any national championship, the British Ski Championship held at Mürren, in January ... Dowding won the
Slalom and was therefore the first skier in the world to
win a national Slalom Championship. He was an
original member of the Kandahar Ski Club, which was
founded at Mürren in the following year.

Dowding, although something of an introvert, was up for anything
on the mountain, but would occasionally draw the line at the
stranger antics of those he climbed with. In 'A Winter Ascent of the
Finsteraahorn' (1925), he suggested with a hint of sarcasm that
readers might enjoy 'skiing down a glacier reasonably supplied
with crevasses, roped, and by candle', adding dryly, 'The practice
was, I believe, invented by an almost blind goods-train shunter,
after a visit to the Rodeo and a heavy lobster supper.'

After being disgracefully 'dumped' following his Battle of
Britain triumph – just as he had forecast – Dowding was sent to
America, where he was interviewed by a journalist. 'Most visiting
celebrities tried to say something which would please the
Americans,' reported Arnold Lunn. 'Dowding was just his natural
self. On being asked his impressions of the States he said, "Your
Sunday papers are too thick, and your lavatory paper is too thin."
The journalists were delighted. "Air Chief Marshal Dowding," said
one, "went over big with the boys. He sure is a great guy."'

As a young Air Commodore, Dowding, as we know, had become
a firm friend of Arnold Lunn, and in the halcyon days between the
wars, the two men often toured together. An elegant skier and an
eloquent writer, one of Dowding's most charming *oeuvres* was
called 'May in the Oberland'. It is reproduced below, virtually in
full, because to me it speaks of an enchanted age, now, sadly, long
gone – with some caustic asides which perhaps explain a little of
Dowding's determined Battle of Britain spirit.

Readers may reasonably ask themselves from what
institution I had escaped in order to subject myself
afresh to conditions which I appeared to find so
distasteful. I know, however, that I shall find many
sympathisers with my view that any form of
discomfort or inconvenience is preferable to work.

Hence the evening of May 20th found Robinson (a fellow 'inmate') and myself at Grindelwald, in company with Arnold Lunn, preparing for the expedition. The intelligent reader will assume that so experienced a party spent the evening in the methodical collection of food and in holding a kit inspection in the strict accordance with Chapter VI of *Alpine Ski-ing*. If so, the intelligent reader has another guess coming. The party effected a burglarious entry into the premises of the local grocer, and proceeded to organise the commissariat on the principle that the necessities of life might go hang, provided that its luxuries are forthcoming.

So far as my memory serves me the principle items were *pâté de fois gras* and caramels. About the kit inspection perhaps the less said the better; suffice to say that every member of the party forgot something, but nobody forgot everything, so we managed well enough between us. Next morning early we went to Interlaken instead of waiting five hours for a train at Lauterbrunnen, so as to get a comfortable breakfast. I had one or two things to buy. So my friends gave me some little commissions of their own; with the result that I got no breakfast at all (comfortable or otherwise), and had to run a mile, laden with parcels, in a hot sun, in order to catch the train. The railway was open all the way up to Jungfraujoch, so we had no climbing to do on the first day – a boon to men coming straight from an office stool.

Considerations of space (and an inartistic temperament) prevent my describing at length the Jungfraujoch Railway; but the marvellous glimpses which one gets from holes, punched in the middle of awesome precipices, first of the Grindelwald Valley in its spring suiting, and later of the tumbled seracs and crevasses of the Grindelwald Eismeer, must impress the most unimaginative.

We had now collected the remaining members of our party, who consisted of Schlunegger, the concierge of a Mürren hotel, a pleasant person attending in an amateur capacity. Then there was Bischoff the guide; a large blonde individual whose extreme good nature and capacity for work was shamelessly exploited by the brothers Amacher, porters to the expedition. The Amachers compensate for their laziness in the huts by their amazing energy as weight carriers. The ultimate straw which shall break the backs of Fritz and Adolph Amacher is yet to find, and they sauntered along with the utmost nonchalance under heavy burdens, grievous to be borne, which after all is the principal excuse for the existence of the porters.

Apart from this, Adolph's principal attribute was a superhuman clumsiness, while Fritz was the possessor of an imperfectly suppressed sense of humour, wasted on (and indeed misplaced in) a porter. His activities off the line of march approached to absolute zero, his ideal being to lie in bed till others had done the work, and then to arise and do his share in the absorption of sustenance.

From the Jungfraujoch we got no view to the northward owing to cloud, but the well-known view down to the Concordia was at its best. We left the Joch at 2.30 and arrived at Concordia Hut at 4.00 p.m. after an uneventful run. The snow at that time of day was naturally softish and slow, but the running was not bad. During the evening Lunn introduced Robinson to the delights of auction picquet and chice (a game in which a childishly simple game of chess is suitably complicated by the introduction of dice in an ingenious manner which now escapes my memory). In due course it was discovered that Lunn was the inventor of auction picquet, and he was roundly accused of inventing a new rule to cover each crisis unfavourable to himself. The chess game was still more one-sided, since neither Robinson nor I were quite sure how many paces a knight took to the front before side-stepping.

The next day (May 21st) was devoted to the ascent

of the Agassizjoch – a project of Lunn's, long cherished but hitherto unrealised. We started at 5.15 a.m. The sky was overcast and a little snow was falling, but it soon cleared up, and we had an almost cloudless day. We reached the Grunhornlucke at 7.45 when we ran down to, and crossed, the Fiescherfirm Glacier and made a depot of our rucksacks and impedimenta at 8.30.

We left the depot at 9.00 and reached the *bergschrund* below the Agassizhorn at 11.00. Here we made a halt and took off our ski, preparatory to the final steep ascent. We reached the top at 12.30. We got an excellent view to the south and east, but not to the north and west, owing to a large cornice which prevented our near approach to the edge. The final peak of the Finsteraahorn shows up well from this point, as the accompanying photograph will show. We roped for the descent, which I, cow-mountaineer and *jochbummeler* (ridge-wanderer) that I am, found sufficiently exciting, especially when I saw that a sinister hole occupied the site of our morning's path across the *bergschrund*. The replacement of my ski, however, restored my serenity.

The run down, which we started at 1.30, was not very good, since the snow was by now thoroughly thawed. Robinson struck the note of adventure by going through a crevasse up to his waist; but he was running downhill at the time, so he fell clear on to the lower edge of the crack without doing any damage. Adolph succeeded miraculously in breaking a ski while traversing a six-inch crack at right angles to its course. Then followed the loathsome grind up to the Finster hut, which we reached in various stages of ill humour at 3.15.

I had a splitting headache from the sun, and was feeling thoroughly peevish. I was reaching up to unhook a basket from the roof to put my belongings into, when the well-meaning but maladroit Adolph leapt forward to assist me. Instead of the basket he dislodged a fifty-pound bundle of firewood, which fell with a crash upon my already tortured cranium. 'A laughable incident,' as the reporter said when a cricket ball stunned the square-leg umpire. I cannot sully my lips by repeating the remarks which escaped me, though they seemed to meet the case at the time. I retired to my blankets like a bear with a sore head, filled myself up with aspirin, and awoke the next morning my usual, sunny self.

Lunn always takes it to heart if one criticises the siting or construction of Swiss huts, so I hasten to assure him that it is not his fault that they are all teed up on inaccessible pinnacles. I do think, however, that it ought to have occurred to Swiss architects to put them on glaciers. The matter is perfectly simple. You construct the hut like Noah's ark on a species of pontoon, which is broader than the largest crack which can open beneath it. You moor the pontoon to a convenient promontory, and let the glacier slide by beneath. The bows are constructed so that the motion of the glacier causes the pontoon to ride up continually to the surface of the snow and the gentle undulations of the passing ice-stream rock the weary *bergfarer* to a dreamless slumber.

Next day (22nd) we had designs on an inconsiderable pimple, just north of the Agassizhorn, named by Lunn *Frau Gassyhorn*. Its merit consisted in the fact that it gave us the view to the north and east which we had missed on the previous day, and gave us an improved run down on harder snow earlier in the day.

We found a delightful slab of rock on which we could lie in the sun, eat our lunch, and look right down on to the Grindelwald Glacier, across to the Schreckhorn Ridge, and out over the lakes and plains to the north. After lunch Robinson and I put in a little ski-ing practice, while the others plugged dutifully up the last little steep slope to the pimple top. We had a jolly run down over crust just too hard to be easy, and then descended the Fiescherfirm to the Rotloch, and climbed wearily up to the Oberaar Hut in a blazing sun. During the afternoon Adolph did his kind action for the day by upsetting a pot of scalding tea and splashing its contents over the unprotected ankles of his companions.

All the party were by now suffering more or less from sunburns on small patches which had inadvertently been left unanointed with face cream. It is more difficult than might be imagined to cover the whole exposed skin surface with antilux without looking glass; and a small mirror such as is carried in vanity bags is a useful item of equipment. Lunn, who has written a book on the subject, left his antilux behind in the sure and certain hope that we should be familiar with his works and have supplied ourselves with the necessary unguents. In this he was perfectly correct; his mistake lay in borrowing the wrong tube and in anointing himself with lanolin, which proved quite ineffective. The result was that his usually handsome countenance resembled nothing so much as a neglected round of raw beef, and he spent the night in considerable pain, accompanied by a high temperature.

The next day (24th) Lunn had to go down to the Rhône Valley, taking with him Schlunegger and Adolph of the mended ski. The plan was for them to cross the Bachilucke Pass, and then go down to Munster via the glacier of that name. Bischoff and I were to accompany them to the pass, climb the Galmihorn, and return to the Oberaar Hut about noon.

Robinson, who was far from well, elected to have an easy morning. The programme proceeded according to plan, and Lunn and his party reached Munster in safety, in spite of gathering clouds, and the difficulties inherent in reconnoitring a new route from above.

Above the Bachilucke the clouds hung in dense masses, and although Bischoff and I reached the top of the Galmihorn by the map and compass, and waited there an hour on the chance of a view, the clouds persisted, and we had to return gingerly to the hut.

Our food was now almost exhausted, and the next

day it was essential that we should reach the
Concordia Hut, where we had left about a third of our
original stock of provisions. The weather seemed to
have broken for good, so we spent the afternoon in a
short expedition to the Ober Studerioch in order to
practise navigation by compass and aneroid, and
running on a rope.

I started well by falling heavily and breaking my
aneroid, which remained out of action for the
remainder of the trip, in spite of first aid scientifically
administered with a hammer and a corkscrew.

The expedition proved educative though
uninteresting. The Studerjoch cannot be
recommended as a convenient means of access to
the northward; it presents a sheer drop into a
cauldron 1,500 feet deep. Fritz relieved the tedium
of the journey by describing with saturnine humour
a three-year-old expedition during which he, Lunn
and two other unfortunates subsisted for two days
on no other sustenance than toffee caramels, and a
chunk of weevilly bread found under the stove in
the Dollfuss Hut.

The next day (25th) fulfilled our gloomiest
expectations by snowing, and blowing, and surrounding
us with cloud with a visibility limit of fifty yards. The
really difficult part came first, since we had to descend
the open glacier to the Rotloch. The presence of a large
and dangerous icefall made it impossible to cross to the
right bank and descend by that, and the same icefall
prevented us from making a bee-line for our objective,
and made us take a curving course. Here the prismatic
compass justified its existence. One member of the party
went on ahead. And I steered him with the compass
from behind till he was lost from sight, when he was
halted and we followed up. The process was then
repeated indefinitely.

Our process was naturally slow, but our navigation
worked out to a yard; and after two hours of blind
stumbling we came plumb onto the rocks of the

Rotloch, which were our first objective. It was sad to think that the journey might have taken us ten minutes in happier circumstances. From the Rotloch we then had an easy journey up the left bank of the Fiescherfirn till we reached the bottom of the spur on which the Finster Hut is situated. This side of the glacier is much crevassed and as the snow was soft we roped for the climb.

From the spur, compass bearing took us into the broad mouth of the re-entrant leading up to the Grunhornlucke, which we reached without further incident except that it was ludicrously difficult to locate the pass itself even when we knew we were within a few yards of it. At this moment the clouds were at their densest, and as it never ceased to be possible to walk uphill, three persons were standing in different places, each asserting that he was standing on the pass itself. Fritz stood in the middle apathetically waiting for us to finish our argument.

We now had a great stroke of luck, for after we had descended towards the Concordia for about 200 feet, the clouds broke and we had a clear run down to the hut on newly fallen snow. We found our food all right at the Concordia and had a thoroughly satisfying feast. We took six and a half hours from the Oberaar to the Concordia Hut: probably about three hours longer than we should have taken in clear weather.

Directly we reached the hut the snow started again. It had now snowed almost continuously for twenty-four hours, and Robinson wanted to get back to England. I had intended to spend a night or two at the Egon von Steiger Hut, climb the Ebnefluh, and then go down to Goppenstein *via* the Lotschenlucke, but as matters turned out there was so much new snow that I abandoned my project. In any case I had proposed to convey Robinson to the Jungfraujoch, which was our next objective.

It snowed and blew all night and was bitterly cold. On emerging in the morning I remarked that I wished I had two pairs of trousers, for then would I put them both on. Quoth Robinson, 'I have and will' (and did). This poetical action brought forth the following:

Ours is an ice-house, ours is,
We who wears two pairs of trousis;
The fire's gone out in our little shack,
And there's no more wood in the pile at the back.
Ours is an ice-house, ours is.

Whereon we sallied forth into the snow. After our navigational exploits of the previous day we did not expect to have much difficulty in hitting the Jungfraujoch Station. A compass bearing took us up the left of the glacier. Thus we could check our progress and direction for about half our journey, while the remainder of our route lay across the open glacier. It was fairly clear at first with a visibility of about half a mile, but soon it came down again as thick as ever, and we plodded on into blackness strung out on the rope, with myself steering the party by compass from the rear end.

After leaving the last rocky promontory on the glacier bank we got into a maze of crevasses and ice walls, which prevented our keeping an absolutely direct course, and introduced an element of uncertainty into our calculations.

Strange fancies seize on one in a thick fog, when one can see neither sky nor skyline, and one seems to be plodding along inside a dense mass of wet cotton wool. One gets an obsession that one is walking in quite the wrong direction in spite of the evidence of the compass. To those who have not got the compass this suspicion of error amounts to a certainty, and about this time the other members of the party began to evince signs of uneasiness for which I could not blame them. Robinson exercised an admirable restraint, recognising that once we started to ignore the compass we should soon be completely lost. Bischoff, too, was very patient, though he was convinced that we were marching at right angles to our proper course, and we were now approaching the Mönchjoch. Since, however, he had omitted (like so many Swiss guides) to provide himself with any navigating instrument, or even a map, I felt bound to ignore his counsel until we struck some definite object, which even if immediately unidentifiable, might serve as a centre for 'casts'.

Shortly after this we came upon a steep rock face about forty yards away, which Bischoff thought he recognised. He announced his intention of unroping and going forward to the left edge of the rock, whence he hoped to identify our position. We were standing on a slope of about 25 degrees with the hill on our right, and were separated from the rock by a steeper slope of about 35 degrees. It looked a nasty place after so much new snow, and I made some such remark to Robinson, but Bischoff advanced confidently and I fell to studying the map.

A violent agitation of the rope on the part of Fritz caused me to look up, and I saw to my horror that Bischoff has disappeared. I felt a horrid clammy sensation in the pit of the stomach, for we had been marching for hours through a maze of crevasses lightly bridged by the new-fallen snow, and it seemed almost a certainty that our journey was to terminate in a tragedy. Our relief may therefore be imagined when we heard a faint shout out of the mist from far below. We hastily picked our way down through crevasses below us, and found Bischoff about 300 feet down, absolutely unhurt. He had started an avalanche and gone down with it just beyond the crevassed area, and had slid out on to the open glacier.

While we were congratulating him on his escape and beginning to wonder what our next move should be, the clouds blew apart for a moment and there was the Jungfraujoch Station 200 yards away to our left front. Our troubles were not yet over, because the station was situated on a slope nearly as steep as that down which our guide had just slid, and he had had quite enough of that amusement for one day, so he decided that we should climb up a rock chute made by workmen who were extending the railway tunnel. Our first difficulty was to attract the attention of the workmen, who were unable to see us for the mist or hear us of the wind and the falling rocks.

At last by united shouting we managed to attract their attention, when the foreman was understood to say, 'Go away; you can't come up here; don't you see we're busy?' Bischoff replied in suitable Billingsgate, which appeared to make the required impression. We started up the fan-shaped slope of jettisoned rock, only to be met by another truckload of leaping stone. More profanity ensued and we finally reached the foot of the solid rock, rendered smooth and greasy by the fall of countless tons of stone.

As already explained, I am no trapeze artist, and the prospect of scrambling up a smooth greasy gully, even with the aid of a stout rope let down by the workmen, left me strangely cold. However, there was no more attractive alternative, and I watched Robinson go up first, hand over hand, walking up the rock face lying right back with his body at right angles to the slope. I then imitated him to the best of my ability, and arrived at the mouth of the tunnel in a state of utter collapse.

Profound was the sensation caused by our arrival in the station restaurant. They could not believe that anyone had been abroad on the glaciers in such weather. At last they accepted the theory that it was unreasonable to be surprised at any lunacy on the part of Englanders, and set to work to satisfy our by no means inconsiderable requirements in the matter of food and drink. Thus ended an expedition to which I look back with mixed feelings; it had many pleasant, some painful, but very few dull moments.

In conclusion I should like to add a tribute to my friend Arnold Lunn. His acknowledged position as an expert, together with his enthusiasm and good humour, somehow make it inevitable that fun should be poked at him by the more frivolous members of any expedition which he may conduct into the High Alps. He is held personally responsible for the structure of the mountains, the position of the huts, and the behaviour of the elements. All the organisation of the expedition and the settlement of the accounts fell upon his capable shoulders, and my libellous remarks about him in this article would constitute the height of ingratitude if they were serious, which they are not.

If any proof of his good humour is needed it is to be found in the circumstance that this article appears as written, in spite of the fact that he wields the blue pencil of an editor of the Y*ear Book*.

Dowding is on form again in his article for the 1922 *Year Book*, 'Monte Leone in May' (May was obviously his month). He writes,

At about 4.30 p.m., we reached Refuge Five. It was a forbidding looking hovel, and my heart sank when Knubel announced that this was our destination. Our only means of communication was a mixture of Dumb Crambo and the French language, with which latter we were both imperfectly acquainted. The inhabitants (a man, his wife and boy, and his great grandmother) were kindly and civil, but the commissariat was limited in the extreme. It consisted of bread, tea, goats' milk and goats' cheese. I am not a connoisseur of the products of the goat, so I subsisted for the first day on the two former commodities. By superhuman efforts some eggs and black ham were later produced. I gathered that they had to send to Zurich for them. The small boy was extraordinarily well behaved, a phenomenon which was explained by a birch rod hung in a conspicuous position on the guest-room wall.

The goats' cheese was full of small holes containing poison gas, and was the nearest thing I saw during my tour to the 'Perforated Crust' with which students of Mr Lunn's works will be familiar.

Dowding goes in to record that his attempted visit to Monte Leone – hampered by disgusting weather – was not a success.

> My compass and Knubel had a difference of opinion as to the direction of Monte Leone, and as we were not really enjoying ourselves vastly, we decided to descend ... Merry peals of laughter arose when one or other of us (principally myself) fell with a resounding squelch beneath the surface; we were both strong swimmers, and had ample opportunity of testing Caulfeild's rudder action theory ... I have no idea what Monte Leone is like, or what the difficulties of the final ascent may be, because I never caught even a glimpse of it.

Finally, Dowding closes with, 'Well, my dear Lunn, that's that. Mind you print it all in the *Year Book*.' And, as far as we can tell, Lunn did.

When, after his triumph in the Battle of Britain, Dowding was relieved of his post, there was a much more mellow tone to his writing in a touching message to the young RAF pilots he regarded almost as his own sons:

> *My dear Fighter Boys*, In sending you this my last message, I wish I could say all that is in my heart. I cannot hope to surpass the simple eloquence of the Prime Minister's words, 'Never before has so much been owed by so many to so few.' The debt remains and will increase. In saying goodbye to you I want you to know how continually you have been in my thoughts, and that, though our direct connection may be severed, I may yet be able to help you in your gallant fight.
>
> Goodbye to you and God bless you all. Air Chief Marshall Hugh Dowding November 24, 1940.

Chapter 26

FAREWELL AND HAIL

*It is with inevitable sadness that I write this, the
last paragraph of the last of fifty-two British Ski Year
Books, but the sadness is tempered by gratitude to all
those who have conveyed their appreciation for the
Year Book, and in particular for the moving
valedictory tributes by eminent skiers.*

In 1972, a now frail and elderly Sir Arnold Lunn, who had edited
the *British Ski Year Book* for more than 50 years, reluctantly
accepted that it was, once again in his long and eventful life, time
for change. From now on, the role of the *Year Book* and its sister
publication *Ski Notes and Queries* would be fulfilled by a new
publication, *Ski survey* – a magazine in the true sense of the word.
Lunn wrote his piece with a rather heavy heart:

> In future, for financial reasons, the *British Ski Year
> Book* and *Ski Notes and Queries* are to be
> amalgamated. Two or three issues of *Ski survey* will be
> published annually, co-edited by the present editors. I
> am, of course, distressed that the *Year Book*, whose

241

annual appearance even the World War could not interrupt, should be a casualty of increasing costs, but it is a waste of time to bemoan the inevitable. I am confident that the best features of both publications will be retained in *Ski survey*. Let me therefore reverse the normal *Ave atque Vale*, and begin with 'Farewell' to the *Year Book* by way of preface to a confident 'Hail' to *Ski survey*.

In 1971, Lunn's life-long friend Walter Amstutz had remarked,

> While you busied yourself preparing these 52 issues, many things have happened in the world at large, and even beyond it. We are reminded that man has recently even visited the moon, and more than once ... But to visit the moon without, or even with skis, is one thing; to edit 52 *Ski Year Books* is another. For it can safely be said, that this is a feat which will never be repeated again by any other man.

Lunn, not for the first time, was reminiscing. In the circumstances, it was hardly surprising. He wrote,

> I began to ski at Chamonix in December, 1898, and for ten seasons I climbed every vertical foot that I skied down and conceived of ski-ing as a branch of mountain adventure. It is, for instance, significant that in the third-class test which I passed in 1905, it was the aggregate time for ascent and descent which was decisive, no separate time being taken for the descent. Here is an extract from my Diary for 10th January, 1905: 'Tobogganed with Miss W. in the morning, and went in for third-class test in the afternoon, up and down 1,500 feet in two hours. Passed easily though ski were coming off whole way up. Came down with ski unfastened.'
>
> On 28th August, 1909, I came away with loose rock on a Welsh climb, an accident which removed two inches from my right leg and left me with an open

wound through which small fragments of bone emerged at intervals during the next eleven years.

I was, of course, advised to take up some other sport, but I am a physical democrat and reject the dictatorship of the body, whose main purpose was to get me to the top of peaks.

The first issue of the *British Ski Year Book* was published in 1920, and was in effect an amalgamation of the *Year Book* of the Ski Club of Great Britain, the *Alpine Ski Club Annual*, the *Scottish Ski Club Magazine*, the *British Ski Association Annual* and the *North of England Ski Club Annual*. As I edited six issues of the *Alpine Ski Club Annual* and both issues of the *British Ski Association Annual*, this the 52nd issue of the *BSYB* is the 60th skiing annual which I have edited.

The Anglo-Swiss [race], in which the odds were against us but which we won from time to time, the last occasion being in 1970, was the kind of event which I enjoyed most. The dinner after the second of these matches in 1926, which we unexpectedly won, remains in my memory as the best of many wonderful parties in my long life, a party which incidentally had a beneficial physical influence on my ski-ing career, for I never again wore the steel splint which transferred much of my weight from the knee of my game leg to my backside. The connection or rather disconnection may not be obvious but it had been a very good party.

The achievements of our racers in the Gothic Age of Alpine racing are recorded in 'The Kandahar Story'. Even in the open international events our best racers sometimes won remarkable successes against the best Alpine racers. Bill Bracken, the best of all British racers, won the first Lauberhorn Cup in 1930 (against a magnificent Swiss, German and Austrian entry) and the Arlberg–Kandahar Slalom in 1931.

In *The Story of Skiing*, Lunn tells the story of how Bracken turned up in Grindelwald for the British Championships in 1949 and won with borrowed skis. 'No other racer has ever won a ski championship at 47,' said Lunn. When Bracken died in 1961, there was a flood of tributes – and memories of the great man. Arnold Lunn wrote,

> In the early days of 1925 I was sitting in Room 4 [at the Palace Hotel] at Mürren when the door burst open and an agitated member of the Kandahar invaded my room and exclaimed: 'Come at once to the Practice Slopes. There's a maniac in a red shirt streaking down from the fence.' Now there was a large notice on the Practice Slopes which I had drafted with care, which was designed to reserve these slopes for beginners and to intimidate speed hogs. I arrived just in time to witness Bill Bracken's third attempt to clear the slopes of beginners. In those days straight running had not reached its present standard, and clusters of awe-struck novices were watching him with amazement.

Evie Pinching, Britain's most successful woman ski racer between the wars, said,

> One of his [Bracken's] special tricks, to give confidence, was to make us sing whilst ski-ing down a difficult slope. This was not particularly easy when numbed with fear and cold! It did the trick – the effort of singing loud enough to be heard was so great that all else was forgotten. This also taught an important lesson in breathing, as racers instinctively hold their breath when tense, which drains away energy.

Konrad Bartelski, the first great downhill racer I ever met – during an early visit to Kaprun, where the British team were training in the mid-70s – has always given me a hard time about my breathing. Or lack of it. Whenever I have begged advice about my skiing technique, it always ends with a scarcely concealed grin spreading across his face and another lecture on breathing properly. Konrad – famous, of course, for his brilliant result at Val Gardena in 1981 when he came within eleven-hundredths of a second of being the fastest downhill racer in the world on the day – has yet, however, to sing a duet with me on the slopes.

Of Bracken, Jimmy Riddell wrote,

> In his prime, Bill was untouchable. He was a pioneer – a 'natural' – and he was brilliant ... We gave him a final send-off which I think will have pleased him. Four of us ... took his ashes to the top of the Shiltgrat ... Carefully, and with many a memory of old times, we sprinkled his ashes from top to bottom of the face of the famous Kandahar course down which he had so often raced with such brilliance.
>
> We did this on the move, and I for one was conscious all the time of performing this solemn, yet curiously happy rite, without slipping or falling; I was equally conscious of a wickedly amusing eye set in a somewhat piratical face, whose owner was constantly muttering ... 'Why don't they ski faster! Damn it all, I taught them how to!'

Peter Lunn, who was Kandahar champion from 1933 to 1937, and only failed to finish once in more than 200 races, used to joke that Bill Bracken would wear rather a lot of badges and recalled one commentator saying that he had won the race by the sheer weight of them. 'With the sort of clothes you wear now you can't wear metal badges,' said Peter, who was fond of skiing steep schusses flat out that no one else had dared to ski. 'In the old days badges meant a lot to people. When I was photographed with Sandy Irvine, who later disappeared on Mount Everest, I was proudly wearing a silver Ski Club of Great Britain badge. In fact, people nearly always wore two badges – the Ski Club and the Kandahar.'

Returning to his theme, Arnold Lunn continues,

> I was very touched by the dismayed reaction of many ski-ing friends to the fact that this is the last issue of *Year Book*, and I welcome Dr Walter Amstutz' letter, not as a funeral tribute, but as a challenge to the Editors of *Ski survey*, and their successors, to maintain a reputation which has taken some earning. *Ski survey*

must continue after I have disappeared from the scene to 'give a good idea of international ski-ing politics'. As my end approaches, it is perhaps slightly disedifying that so much of my thought and time is still devoted to the welfare and status of British ski-ing, but this amiable weakness appears incurable. I look forward to co-operating with my old friend Richard Hennings, Editor of *Ski Notes and Queries*, and to do want we can to ensure that *Ski survey* provides the reader with the best of both the publications of which he and I are the present editors, and continues our tradition of attempting not only to record but also to influence contemporary ski-ing traditions.

The final page of the final *Year Book* closes with this from Lunn:

It is with inevitable sadness that I write this, the last paragraph of the last of 52 *British Ski Year Books*, but the sadness is tempered by gratitude to all those who have conveyed their appreciation for the *Year Book*, and in particular for the moving valedictory tributes by the eminent skiers in the preceding pages.

But the last issue of the *Year Book* was by no means all so solemn. It was particularly enlivened, for example, by a wonderful letter from the MP Sir Charles Taylor, who wrote, from the House of Commons in the late spring of 1971,

Dear Arni,
Many years ago I went on holiday with a very great friend to Zürs, where we had skied with great courage and nonchalance, as you will readily understand because you know me well. We went over the Madloch to Lech, and all the other lovely ski runs. When our holiday was over and we had to leave, my friend Donald and I decided to ski down to Langen, where we were due to catch the train back to Calais and thence to London. There was an awful snowstorm in our wake, and a series of avalanches. Our baggage was coming by

sleigh down the Flexenstrasse which was not, at that time, open to motor cars or petrol vehicles but only to horse-drawn sleighs. Donald and I managed to get down to Langen, but our baggage did not because of the avalanches. Donald's passport and tickets were with his baggage. Mine, I had in my pocket.

There was quite a party of Englishmen going back from Langen to England and so we had to make a plan about how we could get Donald back to England without tickets or passport. It was quite simple. We posted a lookout at each end of our railway coach. When they saw a passport controller or a ticket collector bearing down upon us, Donald and another of our friends went to the lavatory together. When the ticket collector or the passport controller (who, as you know, knock on lavatory doors in trains) knocked on this particular lavatory door, out would come the chap with his tickets and passport but, understandably, neither the passport controller nor the ticket collector thought there would be two men in the lavatory together! By this simple means we managed to get Donald back to England without tickets or passport.

This was tremendous fun, but I hasten to say that we were not cheating either the passport controllers or the ticket collectors – Donald's tickets were paid for and his passport was in order, but they were delayed by the avalanches and they could not get down the Flexenstrasse from Zürs to Langen.

I don't recommend this form of behaviour to the modern generation, should they wish to cheat. No, only if they get into a situation like Donald got into where he temporarily lost his passport and his tickets and where he had to get back to England, would such outrageous behaviour be permissible.

Chapter 27

'ER UPSTAIRS

*He climbed onto my desk and started dictating a race
report for the British Ski Year Book. Without
hesitating, he took the light bulb out, plugged his
razor into the electric light and started shaving.*

The first issue of *Ski survey* was published in 1972. It contained an
impassioned letter concerning the decline of British ski racing
from the Hon. Neil Hogg (president of the Eagle Club and brother
of Quintin, the former Lord Chancellor). A prominent member,
who had often written for the *Year Book*, his letters, for some
reason, had achieved rather less success. If you will excuse the
pun, he had hardly been hogging the correspondence pages. This
time, however, he had finally tasted success. Entitled 'Time for
Change', it started,

> I must hold the record for the number of letters that I
> have written to the Editor of the *BSYB* without getting
> any published. Looking back, I realise that your
> decision may possibly have been right; my strong sense
> of the absurdity of certain developments and

personalities concerned with British skiing has led me in the past to use expressions that might, by the ultra-sensitive, have been considered unfriendly. But now I resolve to do better: I write, as they used to say, in sober sadness.

Hogg appealed for the 'tragic decline of British ski racing' to be halted. 'We are straining our resources to the limit,' he wrote, 'to achieve something patently beyond our powers, and are thereby purchasing ridicule. It must not go on.' He reported overhearing a conversation in which a foreign official had said, 'I really do like to see British competitors. After all, this is showbusiness, like the circus – after the acrobats you bring on the clowns.' This was all just too much for the honourable member. 'Do what you like with this letter,' he wrote. 'Tone it up or down, rehash it or whatever, but do something.'

There was another entertaining missive in the second issue, in October, entitled 'Stopping Ski Tows in Mid-afternoon'. Keith Sayers wrote,

> Given the meagre breakfast which one all too often gets in these Alpine centres, one has to stop for a decent meal at mid-day and as no sensible skier would start again until this has been settled, there may well be then barely two hours left before the patrols are ushering one back to the village. Is it possible to do anything about this? I am serious because I find it a considerable irritation. If, when skiing in Britain, we consider ourselves mature enough to continue to the early evening and then come home by moonlight, why should one not do so in a well-patrolled Alpine centre? Although on reflection perhaps it is because our own skiing weather can be so harsh that we are so mature and that those brought up in sunnier climes need more mollycoddling.

On September 27, at Grindelwald, Arnold Lunn was flown once more to his beloved mountaintops to mark his 85th birthday. This time there would be no walking up to the nearest peak. He wrote,

Phyllis and I reached the top station of the *First* Chairlift shortly before 9am. Suddenly the helicopter appeared circling round the *First* to pick a landing place. We climbed into the helicopter and took off ... we landed on a small ridge, just below the summit, covered with newly fallen snow ... the silence was unbroken and there was nothing to distract my mind from the gratitude evoked by the memory of all that these mountains had meant to me – gratitude far greater than the regret that I could no longer climb. Of my mountain companions only Walter Amstutz still survives – and is still climbing.

By now, perhaps understandably, Lunn was more forgetful than ever, and had developed what he termed a 'senile complex'. He described it like this:

> I am developing a complex – a moment of acute mental blankness when meeting an old friend. At my daughter's wedding I was greeted by a man I realised I not only knew, but knew very well, but the complex clouded my mind. 'Are you thinking,' he said, 'of going over to Ireland again?'
>
> 'I very much want to,' I replied, 'for I'd love to see my cousin again. He's a well-known judge. I dare say you've heard of him. His name is Kingsmill Moore.'
>
> 'Yes, I've heard of him,' replied my cousin, incognito. 'You see, he's my father.'

'Apart from this complex,' said Lunn, 'I hardly feel my age above my neck.' But two years later, Sir Arnold Lunn was dead.

Walter Amstutz, his lifelong Swiss friend and fellow mountaineer, wrote:

> Taking leave of him implies taking leave of an epoch which went with him to the grave. It began with what he called the golden age of skiing, the gilding of which was done by his own hand. It ended in a triumphal finish on a course which he had set himself.

Rosemary Tennant – a key figure at the Ski Club for many years – echoed this sentiment: 'For those of us who worked with him in Hobart Place and Eaton Square,' she wrote, 'it will be the curious feeling of expectation, tempered with the faintly nervous anticipation when we heard the familiar and unmistakable tread on the stairs that we remember best, and the enormous pleasure when we saw his head come round the door.'

Lunn, who had piloted the Ski Club's annals through 50 years, was gone. *Ski survey*, barely into its infancy, would soon be in new hands.

Elisabeth Hussey worked for the club for 28 years – more than a quarter of its existence. 'I can remember going into Eaton Square,' she says, 'and getting inside that rickety lift, and, as I was going up the top, wondering what was going to happen.' At the top she met her new boss. 'And Arnold was rather apt to do strange things,' she recalls. 'On my first day, while I was concentrating on my shorthand, I heard him climbing onto my desk. He started dictating a race report for the *British Ski Year Book*, and, without hesitating, took the light bulb out, plugged his razor into the electric light and started shaving.' It was rather like Churchill dictating to his secretary from his bath.

> You never knew quite what Arnold was going to do next. But I liked it. It was much more interesting than just sitting down and being dictated to. And never boring.
>
> Although he was very determined and could be very abrupt, he was good fun to work for. And he got so involved in things that he wasn't thinking of anything else, and he used to turn my office into a shambles when he came in. He was always worthwhile, but there were strong characters among the Federation, the Scottish and English Ski Councils, the Services and, of course, there was Arnold Lunn. That made an explosive mix, which wasted a great deal of everyone's time.
>
> Arnold worked hard but was careless of accuracy. Fortunately, Phyllis, his wife, small, dynamic and kind, was a huge help. One of her early letters to me

suggests that I should ask the invaluable Mr Hutchings, who published the *Year Book* for 40 years, to return any copy Arnold sent him direct, so that I could correct it before setting. That saved a lot of proof corrections.

The Clubhouse at 118 Eaton Square was a tremendous asset. It had been found by Rosemary Tennant and Jeannette Riddell, an ex-racer and wife of James Riddell. From Hobart Place where the club was lodged in 1952, they saw a 'Lease for Sale' notice on the corner of Eaton Square. They visited, and the lions on the mantelpiece in the hall were so like the British Lion badges awarded to racers that they were persuaded to find out more. Eventually Lord Silsoe issued debentures which paid for the 72-year lease at a rent of only £1,500 a year.

For a four-floor corner house on Eaton Square it was a remarkable bargain with beautiful rooms for receptions, a restaurant, bar, council room and drawing room. Members found it convenient to meet there for lunch or have an early supper before the theatre. In the 1960s even tea was served in the upstairs drawing room. The bar was always busy. Upstairs there were three floors of offices, the top sometimes being converted into a flat for the Secretary or rented off to the Federation. There were some problems: the kitchen in the basement had not changed since Victorian times and the flat was not luxurious for the caretaker

In July 1965, I was asked to drive the Winter Arrangements Secretary, Pauline Bird, on her annual visit to resorts, so that she could meet tourist directors, ask how the previous season had gone and plan the following. Pauline had broken her wrist coming off a chairlift, so could not drive herself. I found it invaluable to visit 14 resorts in France, Italy and Switzerland in as many days, get to know the geography and meet the Tourist Directors. Our 2,335-mile trip cost the club just £65 but, of course, most of the resorts gave us free accommodation.

The only time I repped was in Gstaad when I went

to help Soss with the Schoolgirls' Races she ran there. In the village I wore the reps' armband (our only badge of office at that time) but when we put on skis Soss took over the armband and led the way. The races were the forerunners of excellent Schoolgirl Races still organised each year by the Ladies Ski Club. Conditions were a bit less sophisticated at that time. I remember Soss stopping the car on the way out to cut saplings from the side of the road for future use as slalom poles.

In 1970 grass skis were appearing on the Continent. Ski resorts there used their lifts in summer and provided grass skis – operating on roller belts. The Ski Club organised the first grass ski meeting in Britain on Hampstead Heath. The following year an international meeting was held at Limefitt Park, Cumbria, and from then on grass skiing provided an energetic and exciting occupation for members during summer Sundays. Meetings were held all over the country, wherever smooth, treeless, chalk downs made good tracks.

But there were problems. Our car suspensions suffered from carting heavy skis around. The bathroom on the third floor at Eaton Square never recovered from dozens of skis being washed each Monday morning. It often poured with rain. Operating the rope tow was difficult. I remember an American hurtling down the steep slope at the back of the race course at Goodwood and swearing at what he called the 'gophers' – the moles had dug some interesting hazards down the slope. The Duke of Richmond let us use a slope near the racecourse and the Earl of March came with his children to try it out.

At about the same time, snowboarding was beginning to creep in. Hussey says,

At the beginning we were a bit worried about the snowboarders because they tended to crash into people. This I think was because they started by being skateboarders and they were young and they were energetic. But we always felt it was going to bring about an expansion of the sport and that's good. You have got to have something new for the young to do. The snowboarders eventually took lessons, and once they began to learn about how to skateboard they became much safer. It also had rather a good effect on the ski instructors because most of them had learnt their skiing when they were about 18 months old and had no idea of the difficulties that we had learning to ski. Now they had to learn a new technique. And it made them a lot more sympathetic to us.

By the early 1980s, the club's HQ had become so run down that 'there was a tremendous amount to do in the house in the way of plumbing, wiring, painting and general refurbishment,' says Hussey.

I remember a time when we had no heating. The electricity was doubtful, the lift was still rickety, and the kitchen a disgrace.

The staff were always changing but a delight. The pay was not very good but the chance to ski was a bonus as those in charge of Information, Parties and Reps had to visit resorts. Fortunately many of the girls came from prosperous homes, so money was less important than fun, and efficiency was in the genes.

They worked hard too. Officially hours were from 9.30 to 5.30, but committees could not start until 6.00 p.m. when members left their own work. Occasionally, too, something had to be done at weekends. So it was reasonable to be allowed an afternoon off for Wimbledon or Henley, as well as time to go skiing in the winter.

The assistants I had during my 18 years in the editorial chair were also often quite inexperienced as journalists but they learnt quickly, worked hard and enjoyed the job. They changed all the time, usually to get married. I am still in touch with most of them, who now have grown-up children, so that I feel like a grandmother.

During my time at the club I worked with ten different Secretaries [chief executives]. As each of the later ones arrived they looked at me with grave suspicion. Who was that woman on the third floor who seemed to have been there forever, to know everyone and who must, of course, want to run the club herself?

Fortunately most of them stayed long enough to realise that, far from wanting to interfere, I just wanted to get on with publishing and would make sure that nothing was done without their approval. It was, after all, the best job in the world.

Chapter 28

THE NEXT HUNDRED YEARS

When we heard about you first, me and my cobbers
had it in mind to debag you and throw you down the
mountain. But – hell ... there's hardly a bastard up
here that doesn't bloody nearly love you!

Nothing and nobody lasts for ever, of course, but it is sad to see great athletes grow old and then leave us. The great ski racers who over the years have become my friends – Konrad Bartelski, Martin and Graham Bell, Franz Klammer and Tommy Moe – and those I have also been fortunate enough to ski with now and again, like Hermann Maier, Picabo Street, Ken Read and Steve Podborski, are all still in their prime. Others, like Nancy Greene, and even Stein Eriksen and Toni Sailer, still ski like the wind.

However, of the great names central to Britain's skiing heritage but no longer with us, the man I mourn is Jimmy Riddell, one of Britain's most talented ski racers and writers – the man who skied the Inferno so fast that the timekeepers were still in a local bar when he crossed the finishing line. I hardly knew him, to be honest, but he made a great impact on me with his modesty and charm.

The last time I spoke to the great man was on the telephone

while researching a feature about the history of skiing in Switzerland for the Ski Club of Great Britain's magazine *Ski and Board*. Jimmy, by now 90 and in poor health, told me he was distraught because not only could he no longer ski, but now no longer see to read, either. Cruel old age had finally prevented him from enjoying his passion – even from his armchair. He died not long afterwards. His widow, Alison, was keen to tell *Ski and Board* how he came to be teaching skiing in the Lebanon. She explained,

Jimmy was up a tree in the Congo on a photographic expedition looking for gorillas, when he received news that war had broken out. On his way home to join up, via Cairo and Jerusalem, he was posted to Homs, in Western Syria, as a British Political Officer. He happened to be dining in an Australian mess tent on an 'an almost unbearably hot and sultry evening', with a sandstorm blowing, when a message arrived from HQ, amid much hilarity, asking whether anyone knew anything about extreme cold, mountains, and skiing.

J.R. soon found himself promoted to Major, and attached to the Australian Imperial Forces. As chief instructor, he had the daunting task of transforming a ramshackle, abandoned hotel at the Cedars, at 6,000 feet, into a wartime ski school, equipped to train troops to ski, move safely in the mountains, and survive in extreme cold.

Over the autumn of 1941, he and his fellow Australian officers set about finding almost 500 sets of equipment – no easy task in wartime – clothing, boots, skis, bindings, etc. Using wood from Turkey, local carpenters and army workshops produced skis, sticks and serviceable bindings, while local cobblers made boots, and Lebanese tailors made lightweight white ski suits which could be worn over battledress. Even ski wax was home-made: a concoction of Stockholm tar, beeswax, resin, paraffin – and melted-down gramophone records from the NAAFI!

Out of the first batch of 25 Australian skiers sent to him, only half a dozen proved to be good potential instructors, but with a first intake of 200 troops, the problem was urgent. He went down to Beirut, and managed to locate two useful Czechs serving in the Middle East, and assembled 15 instructors. In time, this grew to 100, capable of training 2,000 troops on the snow at a time.

Riddell himself recalled, 'We had to construct two very large camps of double-skinned Nissen huts, one at each end of a 72-mile stretch of mountains.'

Altogether, more than 15,000 troops would pass through James Riddell's hands at the Cedars – British, Australian, New Zealanders, Greeks, Gurkhas, and many others. As well as learning to ski, they caught the infectious enthusiasm of their chief instructor. Today, his portrait hangs in the Imperial War Museum, commemorating the leading part he played in this unique piece of war history.

One of his greatest successes was the way he charmed his way into the affections of the hard-bitten Australians he taught to ski. Arnold Lunn wrote about this with relish in the 1957 *Year Book*:

> Riddell was a Pommie who was at first regarded with some distrust ... but after a particularly riotous party, the Regimental Sergeant-Major remarked: 'Fancy a stuffy Pommie being able to behave like this as well as ski ... When we heard about you first, me and my cobbers had it in mind to debag you and throw you down the mountain.'
>
> 'You've done practically everything else,' Jimmy pointed out, 'why haven't you done that as well?'
>
> 'Well, hell,' he said, 'there's hardly a bastard up here that doesn't bloody nearly love you!'

In his book, *Dog In The Snow*, Riddell – vice-captain of the British team at the 1936 Winter Olympics – wrote, 'I am most content to know that several thousand men ... came to recognise and learn about mountains and snow, and about the physical and mental joy that a pair of ski can bring to otherwise uninspired feet.'

My favourite story from Jimmy was not about skiing at all, but it just captivated me. It struck me at the time as being charmingly erotic in an unspoken way, all the more so for its innocence. It concerned one of the many adventures he had, just before the last war, with Ruddigore, his faithful Aston Martin. While compiling this book, I contacted his wife Alison, who very kindly searched through his papers and – to my good fortune – managed to locate it. Here it is, slightly shortened, just as he wrote it.

Early one spring morning, somewhere between Freiburg and Brussels, there was a low line of hills we had to cross, and as the road came to the foot of this ridge, the sky was dark with rainclouds, and I hoped I wouldn't have to stop and put the hood up. Just as the road began to climb and Ruddigore was enjoying full throttle, two or three men in brown uniform appeared in the roadway waving flags to stop me. I remember thinking: 'Hell! I've had my fill of ruddy Germans doing road checks ... this time I'm going through ...' And through I went. The soldiers scattered, and I didn't blame them. Ruddigore on the rampage was quite an intimidating sight. Windscreen open, foot flat down, I set the car at the hill. I was enjoying it all enormously when, half a kilometre or so later, there was a loud bang from somewhere, followed by a slight pause, and then suddenly, out of the blue, so to speak, Niagara Falls came down on top of me ...

Never before, nor since (even in tropical rainforest) have I experienced such a devastating downpour. Within half a minute I was drenched through and through, and the open Ruddigore, tonneau cover or no tonneau cover, became a sort of half-filled bath in which I was helplessly sitting. Solid water was flowing down the hill hub-deep like a river. Before I was overwhelmed there was nothing for it but to pull in to the right hand kerb and await developments. The torrential downpour continued unabated.

As I looked around me wondering what the hell I could possibly do about anything, I saw that I had pulled Ruddigore up directly next to a line of small semi-detached houses that must have been on the outskirts of some village. Then, through the rain, I became aware that in the nearest house a net curtain was being waved about in a downstairs window, and a woman was beckoning me through the window urgently to come inside.

I struggled out of the car feeling sodden and heavy – heaved out a suitcase that was equally sodden and heavy – pulled the driving seat part of the tonneau cover over the steering wheel – and staggered up the little path through the downpour to the door.

The woman let me in – she was a pleasant-faced, slim, good-featured person, who must have been about 35 I would think, and I stood there on the mat in front of her with water running off me in rivulets onto her clean floor. Muttering to herself in German, she took my suitcase and put it down at the end of a little entrance passage, then came back, knelt down and took off my shoes and socks.

'Why didn't you stop?' she asked.

'Stop?' I said. 'I have stopped, haven't I?'

'Do you come from Austria?' she asked.

'No, from England.'

'You speak quite well,' she said, 'but I thought there was an Austrian accent.'

'Thanks anyway,' I said, teeth chattering.

'Well, why didn't you stop? At the bottom of the hill, I mean ...'

All the time we were speaking, she was gradually taking my clothes off. First coat, then sweater, next she was tackling my tie ...

'You mean those soldiers with flags?' I asked. I was beginning to shiver uncontrollably.

'Yes. Those soldiers. Why didn't you stop?'

'I thought they were just another bunch of Hitler boys playing silly games.'

'Hush ... you mustn't talk like that ...'

She had a bit of difficulty with my shirt collar

button, but the wet string of my tie joined the other soaked clothing on the floor.

'Why not?'

'If you had stopped, you would have found out what those soldiers were doing, and you wouldn't have been such a nuisance to me.'

By this time all shirt buttons were undone, and this garment quickly joined the others on the floor.

'What were they doing then?' I asked.

'Well ...' she said, dealing very efficiently with my belt and trouser buttons, 'they were carrying out an experiment with artillery and shooting explosive shells into rain clouds to see if they could cause heavy rainfall. Lift your foot up please. Up here, we were all warned about it.'

'Good Lord,' I said, as my trousers were efficiently removed, 'they certainly succeeded ... Hey! Hold on a bit ...' Off came vest and pants, which she wrung out with her hands, and then I was stark naked and speechless ...

'Just wait,' she said, 'I'll be back in a minute,' and, true to her word, she returned in a moment or two with something which looked more like a bedsheet than a towel. She wrapped me up in this and pushed me into a room that was lovely and warm from a tall, tiled stove in the corner.

'Stand over there,' she said, 'wrap up in that, and sit down by the stove.' I sat down with my back to the warm tiles and began to feel better. She fetched all my wet clothes in and did a lot of wringing out over the sink. Then she carefully spread everything out either on top of the stove or on the wires above it.

She brought in my suitcase, opened it up, closed it again, and said: 'Can't do much with that. Would you like some soup? Can't have you catching pneumonia.'

By now the downpour had exhausted itself and the sun was out. 'Yes please,' I said. 'Have you got a coat of any sort? I'd like to see if I can get the car to dry out too.'

Off she went again and returned with a long coat that

obviously belonged to a man and looked as though it was a garment reserved for funerals. Barefooted and with my nakedness covered by the coat, I went out to inspect Ruddigore. There he stood, steaming gently in the sunshine, and with still a sizeable stream flowing down the hill past his tyres. I opened up the tonneau cover and removed it entirely. Nearly all the water inside the car had found its way out through the floorboards. A wash leather took most of the rest off the leather seats. I hung the mats over the hood at the back. All papers, books and maps were a dead loss. I hopefully opened the bonnet on the sunny side and then went back indoors.

'What do you suppose the neighbours are thinking?' I said, as I exchanged the coat for the sheet and sat down again.

'Here's your soup,' she replied. 'Where are you travelling to?'

'Brussels,' I replied. She got on with all sorts of housework, keeping up a conversation pretty well all the time. The soup was delicious; so too was the coffee, and bread and cheese a good deal later. Around midday, after close inspection, she decided my clothes were dry enough to put on again, and she sat and watched me as I dressed. 'Why have you been so kind to me?' I asked.

'Why not?' came the answer. 'Whenever I meet silly young men who disobey authority I like to do my best.'

As Arnold Lunn's son Peter approaches his 90th year, he shows little sign of slowing down. He believes the Inferno is one of the events that keeps him going. Better to ski the Inferno, the race commentator had said after he'd completed the course yet again in the Ski Club's centenary year, than to be in an old people's home. Lunn agrees. 'I'd like to go on skis until I die,' he says.

Peter's father Sir Arnold had similar sentiments. He wrote,

Do what you can in order to remain *young* as long as possible. Don't give up until you are forced to do so. Don't strive too much after comfort – it is *the* foe of old age. Advancing years may compel you to curtail your ambition. But if your heart is still young, you will be able to make tours to the High Alps even after sixty. The sternest efforts of your youth are no longer possible, but thirty-metre jumps are not absolutely necessary for happiness.

Content yourself, then, to ski up, say, to the Steiger Hut on the Lötschenlücke and thence, on a fine afternoon, to climb the Ebnefluh for the sunset. You will behold a spectacle never to be forgotten, and will feel that life has lost little of all that makes it worth living when first you heard the call of the hills.

As we have already seen, when the Ski Club of Great Britain started in May, 1903, women were considered lightweights and of secondary importance. These days the club is very much women orientated. In fact, its Wimbledon HQ, where it moved in 1996 after 44 years in Eaton Square, is positively teeming with them!

Its Chairman is Sally Cartwright, OBE, the publisher of *Hello! Magazine*, and its chief executive is Caroline Stuart-Taylor, who could comfortably see off most of the club's male members on the slopes. In fact most of the staff at the appropriately named White House are young, female and strong skiers. *Ski survey*, the club's magazine launched in 1972 as a replacement for the *Year Book* and *Ski Notes and Queries*, was renamed *Ski and Board* in the late 1990s, and attempts to keep up to date with the latest trends in 'new school' skiing and snowboarding without alienating 'old school' members. It's an essential but slightly uneasy mix. The old guard – members who include more than a handful of the survivors of the old military culture – don't always see eye to eye with the snowboarding brigade, and find some of their vernacular (littered with words and phrases like 'wicked', 'mute grab', 'sick', 'misty flips' and 'gnarly ride') confusing and even slightly irritating. As editor of the magazine, I am aware that we have to move with the times without upsetting our traditional readership. My deputy, Nick Hutchings, is an irrepressible 25-year-old skateboarder and snowboarder who is passionate about the snowboard 'quotient' in the magazine. He is a breath of fresh air, but I have to ensure that he doesn't become a hurricane who blows away the colonels of Tunbridge Wells.

Like the *British Ski Year Book*, its venerable ancestor, the magazine attempts to provide entertaining articles and useful information on the latest developments in the winter-sports world, but the sombre-looking tomes have been replaced by a rather glossier, more exciting image, sustained by its talented designer, Andrew Reeves, of Tenalps RMA, a company owned by Bob Geldof.

The club's information department, incorporating a state-of-the-art website is, along with the magazine, the shop window of the club's operation. Membership is now at an all-time high of 27,500. As the club passes a major milestone, all seems well in the land of British skiing.

When Caroline Stuart-Taylor took over at the helm seven years ago, she was keen to set the record straight about the club's long-ago elitist image: 'We're not exclusive,' she said, 'and we're not hooray-Henries. We're not old-fashioned fuddy-duddies, or cliquey, or stuffy, or elitist. We're just normal people who like skiing. Absolutely anyone can join.'

There are, of course – as ever – great characters around from the current crop of veteran skiers whose memories stretch back to what now seems long ago. One of the Ski Club's members, Laura Hett, recently celebrated her 100th birthday. My own childhood, back in the 1940s, now seems prehistoric. My first and only time 'on ski' at Andermatt, as a youngster of 16, before I took it up on a regular basis in the 1970s, was on skis that towered above my head, with cable bindings and lace-up leather boots.

And skiing in England, quaint notion though that now seems, continues happily. There are ski clubs to this day in Cumbria, Northumberland and County Durham. One Ski Club member, Peter Malpas, recalls skiing like the Richardsons 'et al.' while working in Cheshire. He says,

> I used to load my skis into my ancient old Morris, and drive round Snowdonia, the Lake District and the Derbyshire Peaks in search of snow, much to the amazement of the local farmers when I asked if I could borrow their hill.

On Kinder Scout, Edale, *we used to slalom round the dead sheep* in the snow-filled gullies. All such fun, with a sense of adventure in those days. All very different now – adventure there still is, and I have had some wonderful powder skiing in the Alps over the years, but you have to push out the frontier further and further to get that exhilaration of being in deep and steep powder, with sometimes fear clutching at your throat, sometimes forgetting to breathe, but always being on a high.

So when exactly were 'those days' that Malpas recalls so evocatively? They sound as though they have been taken from the Golden Age of skiing. In fact, he is referring to the 1950s.

Chapter 29

RECOLLECTIONS – SELIGMAN'S LAMENT

Those were days when the sound of ski on a frozen road brought the dogs flying at our heels ... and kept a whole village from church. We had never seen an expert ski-runner, and our running position was that of a long-legged man who had ridden a very small pony into a bog and had not changed his attitude when the pony sank from under him.

So, dear readers, there you have it. A hundred years of wonderfully evocative, stirring and, for the most part (apart from the odd bout of internecine warfare), extraordinarily good-natured banter, bravado, bathos and more than a touch of bravery. It's all a far cry from that inspirational dinner in London on that May evening in 1903. And yet ... there are still many echoes.

Before we leave the Golden Age, the Silver Age, the Gothic Age (when Downhill racing was finally recognised by the FIS) and even the future ages of this wonderful pastime that gives us such an exhilarating connection with the mountains, let us look back one more time at those idyllic early days – this time through the eyes of Richard Seligman, probably the first person to cross the St

Gotthard on ski, and one of those 12 or more young men who sat
down to dinner at the Café Royal a century ago. In 1925, he wrote
a delightfully evocative and poignant feature for the *British Ski
Year Book*: 'Recollections'. Much has changed, but the passion he
had for skiing is very much the same as the passion the Ski Club of
Great Britain embodies today – and the reasons for doing it. He
speaks of the 'joy unspeakable of escaping from the slush and
gloom of the city ... or overcrowded office ... to the lure of Alpine
skies and the diamond powdered snows' – sentiments that apply
even more today, perhaps, than in his day. Here we reprint the best
of Richard Seligman's enchanting daydream of yesteryear.

As I turned over the leaves of the *Year Book* ... lo! – the
floodgates opened wide, and I was borne back on a
mighty wave of memory ... to snowfields glittering in
the brilliant spring sunlight, to a wide tumble of jagged
mountains, seen across a deep valley, stretching peak
beyond peak ...

I am moved to make you share my daydreams and to
burden you with some of those far-off 'great days in the
distance enchanted, days of fresh air in the snows and
the sun.' Those were days when a ski track in the Alps
was as startling as a footprint in the sands of Robinson
Crusoe's island; when the sound of ski on a frozen road
brought the dogs flying at our heels; when the news
that ski-runners were about kept a whole village from
church, and set the villagers trooping to the nearest
slopes to see, and jeer at our clumsy gambols. We had
never seen an expert ski-runner, and our running
position was that of a long-legged man who had ridden
a very small pony into a bog and had not changed his
attitude when the pony sank from under him ...

I have wandered from my path (how hard we
greybeards find it to avoid doddering away into side
tracks!) What I really wanted to do was to tell you of a
short week-end I spent on the St Gotthard when the
20th century was new-born. For thenadays we stole
our skiing between our labours either at week-ends or

in the moonlight or before sunrise brought the day's work, and sweet were those stolen hours as 'stolen water is sweet and bread eaten in silence.'

Loading myself with food for the week-end, I joined a St Gotthard train and travelled with my friends to Göschenen. There was no railway then up the Reuss Valley ... but we found the road open and an *einspänner* [one-horse carriage] to take us up to Andermatt; not, mark you, to the Andermatt of today with its great modern hotels and its fields alive with youths and maidens, but to a little village deep in winter snow and sleeping, save for the soldiers who then, as now, mounted guard over Helvetia's rockbound citadel ... (At that time the Swiss Army was beginning to use ski; experimentally, I believe..)

Seligman recalls a run which pleased him greatly:

In my truant memory, that run stands out as one of the recollections to be treasured through a lifetime. No doubt it would not count as much of a run today, and I am certain it would not provide a thrill to the expert as we now know him, but to us who knew no turns nor tricks it savoured of paradise.

The next day my friends spent on the east side of the St Gotthard, but my time was up. And so I left them, running down alone in the early morning through the eerie, avalanche-festooned gorge of the Tremola to Airolo, which I reached without other incident than a misunderstanding with an avalanche shute which all but cost me my life and completely lost me an excellent pair of trousers.

One other word before the gates of memory swing to again ...

Our little piece was played on a much smaller stage ... but now that I am 'feeble of foot and rheumatic of shoulder' I like to believe that we bore our part in making possible the wondrous development of ski-ing which recent years have brought.

Seligman pays tribute to the 'youth of today' ... his day, of course.

We had none of his skill, and little of his knowledge,
but we knew, as he knows, the pain, half-joy, of forcing
our way through the ice-laden wind and the night to
our objectives, humble though they were compared
with his. And we carried the lamp to the remote
villages, and always and everywhere we were winning
fresh recruits for the army which has grown now past
our wildest dreams.

And richly were we rewarded, even in the doing!
The joy unspeakable of escaping from the slush and
gloom of the city, from overheated classroom or
overcrowded office to the brilliance of the Alpine
noontide, to the lure of Alpine skies and the diamond-
powdered snows.

But this I count above all. We were pioneers. We
had a new world before us, and wherever we turned in
the mountains, we went where, in winter, no man had
been before us.